MW00425220

Immanuel Kant

# PHILOSOPHICAL WRITINGS

# The German Library: Volume 13
Volkmar Sander, General Editor

# Immanuel Kant

# PHILOSOPHICAL WRITINGS

Edited by Ernst Behler
Foreword by René Wellek

CONTINUUM · NEW YORK

1993

The Continuum Publishing Company
370 Lexington Avenue, New York, NY 10017

The German Library
is published in cooperation with Deutsches Haus,
New York University.
This volume has been supported with a grant
from The Marie Baier Foundation, Inc.

Printed in the United States of America

*Library of Congress Cataloging in Publication Data*

Kant, Immanuel, 1724–1804.
Philosophical writings.

(The German library ; v. 13)
Contents: Critique of pure reason—Foundations of
the metaphysics of morals—Critique of judgement—
[etc.]
1. Philosophy—Addresses, essays, lectures.
2. Ethics—Addresses, essays, lectures.   3. History—
Philosophy—Addresses, essays, lectures.   I. Behler,
Ernst, 1928–   .  II. Title.   III. Series.
B2758   1986        193        85-29915
ISBN 0-8264-0298-4
ISBN 0-8264-0299-2 (pbk.)

Acknowledgments will be found on page 312,
which constitutes an extension of the copyright page.

# Contents

## ON HISTORY

*Translated by Lewis White Beck*

# Foreword

If we should examine almost anyone in the English-speaking world—not a student of philosophy—on what he knows about Kant, we would probably hear, assuming that he is reasonably well read and has some interest in things German, that Kant was a philosopher who lived in the eighteenth century in Königsberg, Prussia (since 1945 called Kaliningrad, Russia) as a professor at the university. He was a bachelor who never left his hometown and was a local legend for the regularity of his daily habits. Supposedly, the citizens of Königsberg could set their watches by Professor Kant's timing of his daily walk. Our imaginary educated man might even have read that Kant once missed it when he got absorbed in reading Rousseau. Kant appears as the quintessential German—"dry-as-dust." But all this is only biographical and merely anecdotal.

If asked about Kant's philosophy and doctrines, our average reader will probably answer that Kant was an "idealist," the originator of the German movement that culminated in Hegel, that he propounded a "transcendental" philosophy similar to American transcendentalism, that he thought time and space unreal and the whole world of things appearance or illusion, under which there is a mysterious "thing-in-itself." He also will have heard of the rigorism of Kant's ethics, of the "categorical imperative," the absolute obedience to duty that seems a peculiarly Prussian defense of discipline and even of authoritarianism, implying blind obedience to the state. If he has interest in art and literature, our imaginary reader will know that Kant was a "formalist." Some American critics, the so-called New Critics, were supposedly Kantian formalists. Kant preached art for art's sake, "disinterested satisfaction," divorcing art from any purpose in society. Finally, he will have heard something of Kant's project for eternal peace, of a league of nations, and perhaps of his "religion within the bounds of mere reason."

This will be about all. An expert will find in this list of answers confirmation of the gloomy recognition that even the greatest thinkers survive only in slogans and catch-phrases: Descartes starting with *cogito ergo sum,* Spinoza equating God and nature, Leibniz stating "the world is the best of all possible worlds," Hume denying the self and causality, Schopenhauer praising the denial of the will, Nietzsche exalting the superman, the will to power, the blond beast, and so on and on.

The following anthology of excerpts should correct, modify, amplify, and deepen these superficial bits of information by confronting the reader with the actual text of some of Kant's writings chosen to illustrate the main branches of his philosophy: theory of knowledge first fully exploded in the *Critique of Pure Reason* (1781), ethics represented by *Foundations of the Metaphysics of Morals* (1785), a treatise that preceded the fuller exposition in the *Critique of Practical Reason* (1788), aesthetics expounded in the *Critique of Judgement* (1790), and political and historical thought represented by three short treatises on the Enlightenment (1784), on the idea of a universal history, and finally the project for perpetual peace (1793). Only the philosophy of nature, the cosmology and anthropology are not represented here, as they are inevitably dated by the advances of the natural and social sciences since his day. Actually, even before he discovered "critical" philosophy, Kant contributed importantly to speculations about the origin of the universe. In 1755 he proposed in a *General History and Theory of Heavens* a nebular hypothesis of the origin of our solar system, which anticipated the later conjectures of the French astronomer and mathematician Pierre Simon de Laplace in his *System of the World* (1798).

Our selection can do nothing, however, to correct the misconceptions about Kant's personality. We would have to quote the testimony of many witnesses and his first biographers that Kant was a very sociable man who assembled his friends once a week at his table. He cared for the Roman poets and the German writers of his youth: an old-fashioned taste at the time of the height of his fame, in the 1790s, when Goethe and Schiller dominated the literary scene. He was a human and polite man, totally absorbed in his work, which required long meditation and much painstaking writing and rewriting.

Kant's style shows his struggle. The qualifications, the sometimes tortuous definitions, the many new terms invented by Kant make for slow reading. We should realize that the tradition of German style was at that time and long afterward determined by Latin, mainly Ciceronian syntax. In English, we have to go back to Sir Thomas Browne in the seventeenth century or to Dr. Johnson's early writings in the *Rambler* to find analogues to the ponderosity and even crabbedness of Kant's writings. Still, there is truth in Goethe's saying that one feels like entering a lighted room while reading Kant. Kant illuminates everything he ever pondered.

In his time, Kant was often called the "all-crushing" *(der All-zermahler)*, the destroyer of religion. In the *Critique of Pure Reason*, he tried to show that all the traditional proofs for the existence of God are invalid: the so-called ontological argument, which assumes that God is perfect, and as existence is perfection, so God exists; the cosmological argument, which postulates the necessity of a first cause; and the physico-theological argument, or the argument from design, which argues that a systematic, complex world order points to a purposeful, intelligent creator. Kant shows that all these arguments have no validity: that existence is no predicate, that first cause leads to insoluble contradictions of an infinite regress, and that the order of the world does not require a creator, though it may require an architect. But Kant's destruction of traditional metaphysics is only the preparation for what he thought his central task: "abolishing knowledge in order to make room for faith" (B, XXXX). Faith to him does not, however, mean the dogmas of any particular religion, but faith in an intelligible world, distinct from the world of appearance, a world of moral freedom that guarantees the existence of God and the immortality of the soul. In a famous passage in the conclusion of the *Critique of Practical Reason*, Kant states this basic dualism: "Two things fill the mind with ever new and increasing admiration and awe, the oftener and more steadily they are reflected on: the starry heaven above me and the moral law within me" (V, 167).

The *Critique of Pure Reason*, while trying to demonstrate the limits of our knowledge, supports firmly the science of the day: the system of the universe as conceived by Newton. Kant has a strong empiricist strain. The very first sentence of the *Critique* declares: "all our knowledge begins with experience." The method of his philosophy, which he calls "transcendental," is an examination of our experience. It denies that there is anything "transcendent" to our experience. But our experience is not only sense experience, but is founded on rules of understanding, on pure concepts not innate in any temporal sense, but logically prior, *a priori*. Kant tries to demonstrate the principles of mathematics from the ideas of space and time and the principles of physics from the concept of causality. A whole table of categories is deduced on the analogy of Aristotelian logic. Today much of the detail of the *Critique of Pure Reason* seems obsolete in view of modern physics, the new Einsteinian ideas about space and time, and much seems scholastic, hair-splitting, tortuous, and even contradictory in Kant's argumentation. The Kantian view of the world as appearance runs into insoluble difficulties, as he has to postulate a thing-in-itself, which remains totally unknowable. But Kant should not be called an "idealist," if we mean that he would deny the existence of an external world as Berkeley did (a whole section of the *Critique* is devoted to a refutation of idealism). Still, in Kant's phenomenalism are the germs of a new idealism. His immediate pupil, Fichte, discarded the thing-in-itself and "construed" the world from the ego, while Schelling proclaimed the identity of mind and nature. Paradoxically, just that theory of knowledge to which Kant ascribed a "Copernican revolution" in philosophy seems today the most controversial part of his philosophy and the part that has least withstood the assault of criticism from both his idealist successors and the whole later developments in positivism, realism, pragmatism, and many other modern trends in philosophy and logic.

Kant's ethics revolves around the concept of the "categorical imperative." "Categorical" means unconditional, completely separate from any aim. Kant defines it as commanding us "to act according to the maxim through which you can at the same time will that it should become a universal law" (IV, 421). It is an ethics that is opposed to any "eudaemonism," later in Utilitarian theory formulated as the "greatest happiness of the greatest number," to any Epicureanism, which advocates pleasure, and even to Stoicism, which sees morality in personal inner perfection. Nor of course does Kant approve a morality imposed by religion or state. According to Kant, man is free, autonomous, although subject to an inner command, to an "ought," a self-imposed law that is not just the voice of conscience, but a rational demand for a realm of ends. In practice, Kant envisions a free humanity living in a republic, by which he means a government with a division of executive, legislative, and judicial powers like the United States, though the executive could be a king. The free and equal states would cooperate in a "league of nations," which would bring about "perpetual peace." A general will, a good will, is assumed to carry out the social contract (which is not thought of as an historical event). Kant recognizes, however, that there is "radical evil" in human nature, but is still an optimist about the future of humanity, which is thought of as a slow education toward the state of freedom that for Kant is the same as reason, rationality. Kant advocates enlightenment, man's "emergence from his self-incurred immaturity"—immaturity meaning man's "inability to use one's own understanding without the guidance of another" (VIII, 35). Kant sympathized with the French Revolution, but rejected rebellion. When the new king of Prussia, Friedrich Wilhelm II, forbade him to publish anything new on religion, Kant submitted. It was the year of the Terror (1793) in France, when all the monarchs in Europe had the fright of their lives.

Much of this is of great, if mainly historical interest, while Kant's aesthetics and reflections on the theory of criticism seem today as true and relevant as in 1790. Kant, though he had some predecessors, most clearly defined the beautiful in distinction from the good, the useful, the true, the pleasurable, and the moving. Kant spoke of "disinterested satisfaction," a phrase that is often misunderstood. It means that in looking at a picture, for instance, we do not experience it aesthetically if we think of its price, or feel our mouth water at a still life, or are aroused by an erotic subject, or think of the effect of a religious scene on a pious audience. Kant's formula means the lack of interference from desire, from any immediate end. The aesthetic realm is defended against sensualism, which reduces art to pleasure, against emotionalism, which makes art a stimulus of feelings, against didacticism, and against intellectualism, which sees in art an inferior form of philosophy. Art in Kant is a realm of imagination, represented, distanced, contemplated. But it

would be a total misunderstanding to think of Kant as an advocate
of art for art's sake, or anything resembling late nineteenth-century
aestheticism. On the contrary, he thinks of art in the most exalted
terms: as the mediator between necessity and freedom, between the
world of nature and the world of moral action. Art bridges the gulf
between the two realms, heals the dualism, and thus guarantees the
existence of the "supersensuous." Kant speaks of the aesthetic "idea"
as reconciling the general and the particular, intuition and thought,
imagination and reason. "Idea" is similar to what today would be
called symbol. Kant finds another way out of any purely formal
concept of art by contrasting the beautiful and the sublime and
seeing the sublime as another road to the supersensuous glimpsed
by imagination. Today we may feel that these claims for art are
excessive: we do not believe in the reconciliation of art and nature.

Kant has also much to say on the theory of criticism. He discusses
it largely under the term of "taste," inherited from the eighteenth
century. Kant sides with those who argue that judgements of taste
are subjective, can neither be refuted nor enforced. Kant rejects any
criticism appealing to fixed rules or laws. Still, judgements of aesthetic taste differ from judgements about garlic or snails by claiming
universality. The aesthetic judgement is subjective, but it appeals
to a general judgement; otherwise, it would be senseless to discuss
works of art. Criticism is personal, but it assumes some standard
of correctness in the judgement. Kant tries to avoid both the anarchy
of subjectivity and any absolutism of rules. Paradoxically, he sees
something like an aesthetic imperative. Nobody need like olives or
oysters but we *should* respond to great art and be able to distinguish
between the good and the bad in art. The aesthetic "ought" is not
the same as the ethical "ought": it is only subjective and contemplative. Criticism is always judging by examples, concrete and historical. The comparative method is thus *the* method of criticism.
The capacity of choosing with universal validity, which is another
definition of taste, is nothing but the capacity of comparing oneself
with others.

All this is being debated today. Relativism versus dogmatism is
as much an issue as in Kant's time. Kant has other pertinent things
to say about genius as "the talent by which nature prescribes rules
of art" and on the interaction of nature and art. Kant picked up
the old idea derived from Plato and Aristotle of a work of art as

analogous to an organism. The work of art is parallel to a living organism because art and organic nature share in what Kant rather oddly calls "purposeless purposiveness." Purpose means harmony of parts, unity, totality, every member having its function in a system, while "purposeless" harks back to the view that art is disinterested *(inter-esse)*, undisturbed by immediate, useful ends. We may today have doubts about pressing the parallel hard, but Kant instigated a motif that until recently was very much alive, particularly in American criticism.

There cannot be any question of Kant's enormous importance in any history of thought. In epistemology, in ethics, in aesthetics, and even in political thought, Kant was crucial and often decisive. But his thought is not merely of historical importance. Kant is still the focus not only of an enormous specialized debate and literature. He is often the starting point for new theories. Space and time, the categories, the antimonies, the proofs for the existence of God, the foundations of morality, the nature of aesthetic experience and the principles of criticism, and even the organization of society and the future of humanity are still being discussed in his terms. He presents a challenge here and now and should be read in the original context, undiluted by paraphrase, commentary, and criticism as in this selection, in translations that are as accurate as they can possibly be.

RENÉ WELLEK

# Introduction

The following anthology attempts to present a comprehensive survey of the main domains of Kant's thought and collects in its first section texts from the *Critique of Pure Reason*. The aim in this first section is not to reproduce the structure of the colossal work with its manifold ramifications in abbreviated fashion. Any selection would fall short of this task, and whoever wishes to acquaint himself with the various parts of this *Critique* must study the entire work. Instead the anthology concentrates on those sections of Kant's work which thematize the central topic of the critique of reason by reason itself, as in the "Preface to the Second Edition" and the "Introduction" to the entire work, or pursue this theme in historical fashion as in the sections included from the "Transcendental Doctrine of Method."

The first edition appeared in 1781. Kant considerably modified and augmented his work when he published the second edition of 1787. J. M. D. Meiklejohn produced the first complete English translation in 1855, followed by Max Müller's translation of 1881. Norman Kemp Smith accomplished in 1929 what has been considered the standard translation in the English speaking world. As the license for reproducing parts from this translation was not made available by the Macmillan publishing house, the sections selected from the *Critique of Pure Reason* in this volume follow J. M. D. Meiklejohn's translation. This appeared justified because the texts selected from this *Critique* present the broader issues of a critique of pure reason and not the execution of this task in its particular technical terminology.

Kant's establishment of the supreme and *a priori* principle of morality has not been presented on the basis of his comprehensive *Critique of Practical Reason* of 1788, but on the earlier and more concise *Foundations of the Metaphysics of Morals* of 1785. The main reason for this decision was the desire to produce, whenever possible in this edition, texts in their entirety. This work is by all means fully representative of the second main topic of Kant's thought, that is, morals. There are several English translations available. Our anthology presents the text in Lewis White Beck's version.

The "third" critique, Kant's *Critique of Judgement,* constitutes the basis for the third section of this volume. Because of the importance of Kant's aesthetics and its impact upon the history of criticism and contemporary thought, this volume focuses on the first great part of this *Critique,* the "Critique of Aesthetic Judgement," and foregoes the second, the "Critique of Teleological Judgement." The "Introduction" demonstrates, however, how these two parts interrelate and how this work in its entirety mediates between the first and the second critiques and, as Henry Crabb Robinson put it as early as 1803, "fills up the critical arch, binding and uniting the distinct systems of theoretical and practical philosophy, unfolded in his former works." The *Critique of Judgement* did not appear until 1790. The best known complete translations of it are the one by J. H. Bernard of 1892 and the one by J. C. Meredith of 1928. The selections of this volume are in J. C. Meredith's translation.

The fourth section presents three famous essays by Kant which deal with history or rather with his philosophy of history. The first, "Idea for a Universal History from a Cosmopolitan Point of View," appeared in the *Berlinische Monatsschrift* of 1784, where Kant published a good number of articles at that time. Kant approaches the teleological principle in history from the point of view of a complete development of all of man's potentialities and pursues this idea into questions concerning human society and international relationships among states. The following two essays continue and expand what he had said in his "Idea for a Universal History." His answer to the question "What Is Enlightenment?" appeared in the same year and depicts the dominion of moral freedom as the principle of law and the state. "Perpetual Peace" is presented in the form of a peace treaty and appeared in 1795. The text relates to the principles of his moral philosophy, first formulated in his *Foun-*

*dations of the Metaphysics of Morals,* as well as to the p
realization of these principles outlined in the two previous
In the appendix Kant discusses the relationship between m
and politics. Because of the nature of the topic, but also b
of the more popular manner of presentation, "Perpetual Pea
been widely read and related to the crucial issue of peace f
the twentieth century and in our own time. Several English
lations of these essays are available. As in the case of the
*dations of the Metaphysics of Morals,* the present volume pu
Lewis White Beck's translation.

I should like to thank my colleague Professor Friedrich Ka
at the University of Münster who was so kind as to advise
I selected the texts for this volume.

E. F

# CRITIQUE OF PURE REASON

# Preface to
# the Second Edition

Whether the treatment of that portion of our knowledge which lies within the province of pure reason, advances with that undeviating certainty which characterises the progress of *science,* we shall be at no loss to determine. If we find those who are engaged in metaphysical pursuits, unable to come to an understanding as to the method which they ought to follow; if we find them, after the most elaborate preparations, invariably brought to a stand before the goal is reached, and compelled to retrace their steps and strike into fresh paths, we may then feel quite sure that they are far from having attained to the certainty of scientific progress, and may rather be said to be merely groping about in the dark. In these circumstances we shall render an important service to reason if we succeed in simply indicating the path along which it must travel, in order to arrive at any results,—even if it should be found necessary to abandon many of those aims which, without reflection, have been proposed for its attainment.

That *Logic* has advanced in this sure course, even from the earliest times, is apparent from the fact that, since Aristotle, it has been unable to advance a step, and thus to all appearance has reached its completion. For, if some of the moderns have thought to enlarge its domain by introducing *psychological* discussions on the mental faculties, such as imagination and wit, *metaphysical* discussions on the origin of knowledge and the different kinds of certitude, according to the difference of the objects (Idealism, Scepticism, and so on), or *anthropological* discussions on prejudices, their causes and remedies: this attempt, on the part of these authors, only shows their ignorance of the peculiar nature of logical science. We do not enlarge, but disfigure the sciences when we lose sight of their respective limits, and allow them to run into one another. Now logic is enclosed within limits which admit of perfectly clear definition; it is a science which has for its object nothing but the exposition and proof of the *formal* laws of all thought, whether it be *a priori* or empirical, whatever be its origin or its object, and whatever the difficulties—natural or accidental—which it encounters in the human mind.

The early success of logic must be attributed exclusively to the narrowness of its field, in which abstraction may, or rather must, be made of all the objects of cognition with their characteristic distinctions, and in which the understanding has only to deal with itself and with its own forms. It is, obviously, a much more difficult task for reason to strike into the sure path of science, where it has to deal not simply with itself, but with objects external to itself. Hence, logic is properly only a *propaedeutic*—forms, as it were, the vestibule of the sciences; and while it is necessary to enable us to form a correct judgment with regard to the various branches of knowledge, still the acquisition of real, substantive knowledge is to be sought only in the sciences properly so called, that is, in the objective sciences.

Now these sciences, if they can be termed rational at all, must contain elements of *a priori* cognition, and this cognition may stand in a two-fold relation to its object. Either it may have to *determine* the conception of the object—which must be supplied extraneously, or it may have to *establish its reality.* The former is *theoretical,* the latter *practical,* rational cognition. In both, the *pure* or *a priori* element must be treated first, and must be carefully distinguished from that which is supplied from other sources. Any other method can only lead to irremediable confusion.

*Mathematics* and *Physics* are the two theoretical sciences which have to determine their objects *a priori.* The former is purely *a priori,* the latter is partially so, but is also dependent on other sources of cognition.

When Galilei experimented with balls of a definite weight on the inclined plane, when Torricelli caused the air to sustain a weight which he had calculated beforehand to be equal to that of a definite column of water, or when Stahl, at a later period, converted metals into lime, and reconverted lime into metal, by the addition and subtraction of certain elements;[1] a light broke upon all natural philosophers. They learned that reason only perceives that which it produces after its own design; that it must not be content to follow, as it were, in the leading-strings of nature, but must proceed in advance with principles of judgment according to unvarying laws, and compel nature to reply to its questions. For accidental observations, made according to no preconceived plan, cannot be united under a necessary law. But it is this that reason seeks for and requires. It is only the principles of reason which can give to concordant phenomena the validity of laws, and it is only when experiment is directed by these rational principles, that it can have any real utility. Reason must approach nature with the view, indeed, of receiving information from it, not, however, in the character of a pupil, who listens to all that his master chooses to tell him, but in that of a judge, who compels the witnesses to reply to those questions which he himself thinks fit to propose. To this single idea must the revolution be ascribed, by which, after groping in the dark for so many centuries, natural science was at length conducted into the path of certain progress.

We come now to *metaphysics,* a purely speculative science, which occupies a completely isolated position, and is entirely independent of the teachings of experience. It deals with mere conceptions—not, like mathematics, with conceptions applied to intuition—and in it, reason is the pupil of itself alone. It is the oldest of the sciences, and would still survive, even if all the rest were swallowed up in the abyss of an all-destroying barbarism. But it has not yet had the good fortune to attain to the sure scientific method. This will be apparent, if we apply the tests which we proposed at the outset. We find that reason perpetually comes to a stand, when it attempts to gain *a priori* the perception even of those laws which the most common experience confirms. We find it compelled to retrace its steps in innumerable instances, and to abandon the path on which it had entered, because this does not lead to the desired result. We

---

1. I do not here follow with exactness the history of the experimental method, of which, indeed, the first steps are involved in some obscurity.

ıt those who are engaged in metaphysical pursuits are
ng able to agree among themselves, but that, on the
s science appears to furnish an arena specially adapted
ıor tıı .. ᵖ ay of skill or the exercise of strength in mock-contests—
a field in which no combatant ever yet succeeded in gaining an inch
of ground, in which, at least, no victory was ever yet crowned with
permanent possession.

This leads us to enquire why it is that, in metaphysics, the sure
path of science has not hitherto been found. Shall we suppose that
it is impossible to discover it? Why then should nature have visited
our reason with restless aspirations after it, as if it were one of our
weightiest concerns? Nay, more, how little cause should we have
to place confidence in our reason, if it abandons us in a matter
about which, most of all, we desire to know the truth—and not
only so, but even allures us to the pursuit of vain phantoms, only
to betray us in the end? Or, if the path has only hitherto been
missed, what indications do we possess to guide us in a renewed
investigation, and to enable us to hope for greater success than has
fallen to the lot of our predecessors?

It appears to me that the examples of mathematics and natural
philosophy, which, as we have seen, were brought into their present
condition by a sudden revolution, are sufficiently remarkable to fix
our attention on the essential circumstances of the change which
has proved so advantageous to them, and to induce us to make the
experiment of imitating them, so far as the analogy which, as rational sciences, they bear to metaphysics may permit. It has hitherto
been assumed that our cognition must conform to the objects; but
all attempts to ascertain anything about these objects *a priori,* by
means of conceptions, and thus to extend the range of our knowledge, have been rendered abortive by this assumption. Let us then
make the experiment whether we may not be more successful in
metaphysics, if we assume that the objects must conform to our
cognition. This appears, at all events, to accord better with the
*possibility* of our gaining the end we have in view, that is to say,
of arriving at the cognition of objects *a priori,* of determining something with respect to these objects, before they are given to us. We
here propose to do just what Copernicus did in attempting to explain the celestial movements. When he found that he could make
no progress by assuming that all the heavenly bodies revolved round
the spectator, he reversed the process, and tried the experiment of

assuming that the spectator revolved, while the stars remained at rest. We may make the same experiment with regard to the intuition of objects. If the intuition must conform to the nature of the objects, I do not see how we can know anything of them *a priori*. If, on the other hand, the object conforms to the nature of our faculty of intuition, I can then easily conceive the possibility of such an *a priori* knowledge. Now as I cannot rest in the mere intuitions, but—if they are to become cognitions—must refer them, as *representations,* to something, as *object,* and must determine the latter by means of the former, here again there are two courses open to me. *Either,* first, I may assume that the conceptions, by which I effect this determination, conform to the object—and in this case I am reduced to the same perplexity as before; *or* secondly, I may assume that the objects, or, which is the same thing, that *experience,* in which alone as given objects, they are cognized, conform to my conceptions—and then I am at no loss how to proceed. For experience itself is a mode of cognition which requires understanding. Before objects are given to me, that is, *a priori,* I must presuppose in myself laws of the understanding which are expressed in conceptions *a priori*. To these conceptions, then, all the objects, of experience must necessarily conform. Now there are objects which reason *thinks,* and that necessarily, but which cannot be given in experience, or, at least, cannot be given *so* as reason thinks them. The attempt to think these objects will hereafter furnish an excellent test of the new method of thought which we have adopted, and which is based on the principle that we only cognize in things *a priori* that which we ourselves place in them.[2]

This attempt succeeds as well as we could desire, and promises

2. This method, accordingly, which we have borrowed from the natural philosopher, consists in seeking for the elements of pure reason in that *which admits of confirmation or refutation by experiment*. Now the propositions of pure reason, especially when they transcend the limits of possible experience, do not admit of our making any experiment with their *objects,* as in natural science. Hence, with regard to those *conceptions* and *principles* which we assume *a priori,* our only course will be to view them from two different sides. We must regard one and the same conception, *on the one hand,* in relation to experience as an object of the senses and of the understanding, *on the other hand,* in relation to reason, isolated and transcending the limits of experience, as an object of mere thought. Now if we find that, when we regard things from this double point of view, the result is in harmony with the principle of pure reason, but that, when we regard them from a single point of view, reason is involved in self-contradiction, then the experiment will establish the correctness of this distinction.

to metaphysics, in its first part—that is, where it is occupied with conceptions *a priori,* of which the corresponding objects may be given in experience—the certain course of science. For by this new method we are enabled perfectly to explain the possibility of *a priori* cognition, and, what is more, to demonstrate satisfactorily the laws which lie *a priori* at the foundation of nature, as the sum of the objects of experience—neither of which was possible according to the procedure hitherto followed. But from this deduction of the faculty of *a priori* cognition in the first part of Metaphysics, we derive a surprising result, and one which, to all appearance, militates against the great end of Metaphysics, as treated in the second part. For we come to the conclusion that our faculty of cognition is unable to transcend the limits of possible experience; and yet this is precisely the most essential object of this science. The estimate of our rational cognition *a priori* at which we arrive is that it has only to do with phaenomena, and that things in themselves, while possessing a real existence, lie beyond its sphere. Here we are enabled to put the justice of this estimate to the test. For that which of necessity impels us to transcend the limits of experience and of all phaenomena, is the *unconditioned,* which reason absolutely requires in things as they are in themselves, in order to complete the series of conditions. Now, if it appears that when, on the one hand, we assume that our cognition conforms to its objects as things in themselves, *the unconditioned cannot be thought without contradiction,* and that when, on the other hand, we assume that our representation of things as they are given to us, does not conform to these things as they are in themselves, but that these objects, as phaenomena, conform to our mode of representation, *the contradiction disappears:* we shall then be convinced of the truth of that which we began by assuming for the sake of experiment; we may look upon it as established that the unconditioned does not lie in things as we know them, or as they are given to us, but in things as they are in themselves, beyond the range of our cognition.[3]

3. This experiment of pure reason has a great similarity to that of the *Chemists,* which they term the experiment of *reduction,* or, more usually, the *synthetic* process. The *analysis* of the metaphysician separates pure cognition *a priori* into two heterogeneous elements, viz., the cognition of things as phaenomena, and of things in themselves. *Dialectic* combines these again into harmony with the necessary rational idea of the unconditioned, and finds that this harmony never results except through the above distinction, which is, therefore, concluded to be just.

*using only logic —or experience as basis of thinking*
*limits possibilities—*

But, after we have thus denied the power of speculative reason to make any progress in the sphere of the supersensible, it still remains for our consideration whether data do not exist in *practical* cognition, which may enable us to determine the transcendent conception of the unconditioned, to rise beyond the limits of all possible experience from a *practical* point of view, and thus to satisfy the great ends of metaphysics. Speculative reason has thus, at least, made room for such an extension of our knowledge; and, if it must leave this space vacant, still it does not rob us of the liberty to fill it up, if we can, by means of practical data—nay, it even challenges us to make the attempt.[4]

This attempt to introduce a complete revolution in the procedure of metaphysics, after the *example* of the Geometricians and Natural Philosophers, constitutes the aim of the Critique of Pure Speculative Reason. It is a treatise on the method to be followed, not a system of the science itself. But, at the same time, it marks out and defines both the external boundaries and the internal structure of this Science. For pure speculative reason has this peculiarity, that, in choosing the various objects of thought, it is able to define the limits of its own faculties, and even to give a complete enumeration of the possible modes of proposing problems to itself, and thus to sketch out the entire system of metaphysics. For, on the one hand, in cognition *a priori*, nothing must be attributed to the objects but what the thinking subject derives from itself; and, on the other hand, reason is, in regard to the principles of cognition, a perfectly distinct, independent unity, in which, as in an organised body, every member exists for the sake of the others, and all for the sake of each, so that no principle can be viewed, with safety, in one relationship, unless it is, at the same time, viewed in relation to the total use of pure reason. Hence, too, metaphysics has this singular

4. So the central laws of the movements of the heavenly bodies established the truth of that which Copernicus, at first, assumed only as a hypothesis, and, at the same time, brought to light that invisible force (Newtonian attraction) which holds the universe together. The latter would have remained for ever undiscovered, if Copernicus had not ventured on the experiment—contrary to the senses, but still just—of looking for the observed movements not in the heavenly bodies, but in the spectator. In this Preface I treat the new metaphysical method as a hypothesis with the view of rendering apparent the first attempts at such a change of method, which are always hypothetical. But in the Critique itself it will be demonstrated, not hypothetically, but apodeictically, from the nature of our representations of space and time, and from the elementary conceptions of the understanding.

advantage—an advantage which falls to the lot of no other science which has to do with *objects*—that, if once it is conducted into the sure path of science, by means of this criticism, it can then take in the whole sphere of its cognitions, and can thus complete its work, and leave it for the use of posterity, as a capital which can never receive fresh accessions. For metaphysics has to deal only with principles and with the limitations of its own employment as determined by these principles. To this perfection it is, therefore, bound, as the fundamental science, to attain, and to it the maxim may justly be applied:—

Nil actum reputans, si quid superesset agendum.

But, it will be asked, what kind of a treasure is this that we propose to bequeath to posterity? What is the real value of this system of metaphysics, purified by criticism, and thereby reduced to a permanent condition? A cursory view of the present work will lead to the supposition that its use is merely *negative,* that it only serves to warn us against venturing, with speculative reason, beyond the limits of experience. This is, in fact, its primary use. But this, at once, assumes a *positive* value, when we observe that the principles with which speculative reason endeavours to transcend its limits, lead inevitably, not to the *extension,* but to the *contraction* of the use of reason, inasmuch as they threaten to extend the limits of sensibility, which is their proper sphere, over the entire realm of thought, and thus to supplant the pure (practical) use of reason. So far, then, as this criticism is occupied in confining speculative reason within its proper bounds, it is only negative; but, inasmuch as it thereby, at the same time, removes an obstacle which impedes and even threatens to destroy the use of practical reason, it possesses a positive and very important value. In order to admit this, we have only to be convinced that there is an absolutely necessary use of pure reason—the moral use—in which it inevitably transcends the limits of sensibility, without the aid of speculation, requiring only to be insured against the effects of a speculation which would involve it in contradiction with itself. To deny the positive advantage of the service which this criticism renders us, would be as absurd as to maintain that the system of police is productive of no positive benefit, since its main business is to prevent the violence which citizen has to apprehend from citizen, that so each may pursue his vocation in peace and security. That space and time are only forms of sensible intuition, and hence are only conditions of the existence of things as phaenomena; that, moreover, we have no conceptions of the understanding, and, consequently, no elements for the cognition of things, except in so far as a corresponding intuition can be given to these conceptions; that, accordingly, we can have no cognition of an object, as a thing in itself, but only as an object of sensible intuition, that is, as a phaenomenon,—all this is proved in the Analytical part of the Critique; and from this the limitation of all possible speculative cognition to the mere objects of *experience,* follows as a necessary result. At the same time, it must be carefully borne in mind that, while we surrender the power of *cognizing,* we still reserve the power of *thinking* objects, as things in themselves.[5] For, otherwise, we should require to affirm the existence of an appearance, without something that appears—which would be absurd. Now let us suppose, for a moment, that we had not undertaken this criticism, and, accordingly, had not drawn the necessary distinction between things, as objects of experience, and things, as they are in themselves. The principle of causality, and, by consequence, the mechanism of nature as determined by causality, would then have absolute validity in relation to all things as efficient causes. I should then be unable to assert, with regard to one and the same being, *e.g.,* the human soul, that its will is *free,* and yet, at the same time, subject to natural necessity, that is, *not free,* without falling into a palpable contradiction, for in both propositions I should take the soul in *the same signification,* as a thing in general, as a thing in itself—as, without previous criticism, I could not but take it. Suppose now, on the other hand, that we *have* undertaken this criticism, and have learnt that an object may be taken in *two senses,* first, as a phaenomenon, secondly, as a thing in itself; and that,

---

5. In order to *cognize* an object, I must be able to prove its possibility, either from its reality as attested by experience, or *a priori,* by means of reason. But I can *think* what I please, provided only I do not contradict myself; that is, provided my conception is a possible thought, though I may be unable to answer for the existence of a corresponding object in the sum of possibilities. But something more is required before I can attribute to such a conception objective validity, that is real possibility— the other possibility being merely logical. We are not, however, confined to theoretical sources of cognition for the means of satisfying this additional requirement, but may derive them from practical sources.

according to the deduction of the conceptions of the understanding, the principle of causality has reference only to things in the first sense. We then see how it does not involve any contradiction to assert, on the one hand, that the will, in the phaenomenal sphere— in visible action, is necessarily obedient to the law of nature, and, in so far *not free;* and, on the other hand, that, as belonging to a thing in itself, it is not subject to that law, and, accordingly, is *free.* Now, it is true that I cannot, by means of speculative reason, and still less by empirical observation, *cognize* my soul as a thing in itself, and consequently, cannot cognize liberty as the property of a being to which I ascribe effects in the world of sense. For, to do so, I must cognize this being as existing, and yet not in time, which— since I cannot support my conception by any intuition—is impossible. At the same time, while I cannot *cognize,* I can quite well *think* freedom, that is to say, my representation of it involves at least no contradiction, if we bear in mind the critical distinction of the two modes of representation (the sensible and the intellectual) and the consequent limitation of the conceptions of the pure understanding, and of the principles which flow from them. Suppose now that morality necessarily presupposed liberty, in the strictest sense, as a property of our will; suppose that reason contained certain practical, original principles *a priori,* which were absolutely impossible without this presupposition; and suppose, at the same time, that speculative reason had proved that liberty was incapable of being thought at all. It would then follow that the moral presupposition must give way to the speculative affirmation, the opposite of which involves an obvious contradiction, and that *liberty* and, with it, morality must yield to the *mechanism of nature;* for the negation of morality involves no contradiction, except on the presupposition of liberty. Now morality does not require the speculative cognition of liberty; it is enough that I can think it, that its conception involves no contradition, that it does not interfere with the mechanism of nature. But even this requirement we could not satisfy, if we had not learnt the two-fold sense in which things may be taken; and it is only in this way that the doctrine of morality and the doctrine of nature are confined within their proper limits. For this result, then, we are indebted to a criticism which warns us of our unavoidable ignorance with regard to things in themselves, and establishes the necessary limitation of our theoretical *cognition* to mere phaenomena.

The positive value of the critical principles of pure reason in relation to the conception of *God* and of the *simple nature* of the *soul,* admits of a similar exemplification; but on this point I shall not dwell. I cannot even make the assumption—as the practical interests of morality require—of God, Freedom, and Immortality, if I do not deprive speculative reason of its pretensions to transcendent insight. For to arrive at these, it must make use of principles which, in fact, extend only to the objects of possible experience, and which cannot be applied to objects beyond this sphere without converting them into phaenomena, and thus rendering the *practical extension* of pure reason impossible. I must, therefore, abolish *knowledge,* to make room for *belief.* The dogmatism of metaphysics, that is, the presumption that it is possible to advance in metaphysics without previous criticism, is the true source of the unbelief (always dogmatic) which militates against morality.

Thus, while it may be no very difficult task to bequeath a legacy to posterity, in the shape of a system of metaphysics constructed in accordance with the Critique of Pure Reason, still the value of such a bequest is not to be depreciated. It will render an important service to reason, by substituting the certainty of scientific method for that random groping after results without the guidance of principles, which has hitherto characterised the pursuit of metaphysical studies. It will render an important service to the inquiring mind of youth, by leading the student to apply his powers to the cultivation of genuine science, instead of wasting them, as at present, on speculations which can never lead to any result, or on the idle attempt to invent new ideas and opinions. But, above all, it will confer an inestimable benefit on morality and religion, by showing that all the objections urged against them may be silenced for ever by the *Socratic* method, that is to say, by proving the ignorance of the objector. For, as the world has never been, and, no doubt, never will be, without a system of metaphysics of one kind or another, it is the highest and weightiest concern of philosophy to render it powerless for harm, by closing up the sources of error.

This important change in the field of the sciences, this loss of its fancied possessions, to which speculative reason must submit, does not prove in any way detrimental to the general interests of humanity. The advantages which the world has derived from the teachings of pure reason, are not at all impaired. The loss falls, in its whole extent, on the *monopoly of the schools,* but does not in the slightest degree touch the *interests of mankind*. I appeal to the most obstinate dogmatist, whether the proof of the continued existence of the soul after death, derived from the simplicity of its substance; of the freedom of the will in opposition to the general mechanism of nature, drawn from the subtle but impotent distinction of subjective and objective practical necessity; or of the existence of God, deduced from the conception of an *ens realissimum*,—the contingency of the changeable, and the necessity of a prime mover, has ever been able to pass beyond the limits of the schools, to penetrate the public mind, or to exercise the slightest influence on its convictions. It must be admitted that this has not been the case, and that, owing to the unfitness of the common understanding for such subtle speculations, it can never be expected to take place. On the contrary, it is plain that *the hope of a future life* arises from the feeling, which exists in the breast of every man, that the temporal is inadequate to meet and satisfy the demands of his nature. In like manner, it cannot be doubted that the clear exhibition of duties in opposition to all the claims of inclination, gives rise to the consciousness of *freedom,* and that the glorious order, beauty, and providential care, everywhere displayed in nature, give rise to the belief in a wise and great Author of the Universe. Such is the genesis of these general convictions of mankind, so far as they depend on rational grounds; and this public property not only remains undisturbed, but is even raised to greater importance, by the doctrine that the schools have no right to arrogate to themselves a more profound insight into a matter of general human concernment, than that to which the great mass of men, ever held by us in the highest estimation, can without difficulty attain, and that the schools should therefore confine themselves to the elaboration of these universally comprehensible, and, from a moral point of view, amply satisfactory proofs. The change, therefore, affects only the arrogant pretensions of the schools, which would gladly retain, in their own exclusive possession, the key to the truths which they impart to the public.

Quod mecum nescit, solus vult scire videri.

At the same time it does not deprive the speculative philosopher of his just title to be the sole depositor of a science which benefits the public without its knowledge—I mean, the Critique of Pure Reason.

This can never become popular, and, indeed, has no o[
be so; for fine-spun arguments in favour of useful truths[
as little impression on the public mind as the equally subtle objections brought against these truths. On the other hand, since both
inevitably force themselves on every man who rises to the height
of speculation, it becomes the manifest duty of the schools to enter
upon a thorough investigation of the rights of speculative reason,
and thus to prevent the scandal which metaphysical controversies
are sure, sooner or later, to cause even to the masses. It is only by
criticism that metaphysicians (and, as such, theologians too) can
be saved from these controversies and from the consequent per-
version of their doctrines. Criticism alone can strike a blow at the
root of Materialism, Fatalism, Atheism, Free-thinking, Fanaticism,
and Superstition, which are universally injurious—as well as of
Idealism and Scepticism, which are dangerous to the schools, but
can scarcely pass over to the public. If governments think proper
to interfere with the affairs of the learned, it would be more consistent with a wise regard for the interests of science, as well as for
those of society, to favour a criticism of this kind, by which alone
the labours of reason can be established on a firm basis, than to
support the ridiculous despotism of the schools, which raise a loud
cry of danger to the public over the destruction of cobwebs, of
which the public has never taken any notice, and the loss of which,
therefore, it can never feel.

This critical science is not opposed to the *dogmatic procedure*
of reason in pure cognition; for pure cognition must always be
dogmatic, that is, must rest on strict demonstration from sure principles *a priori*— but to *dogmatism,* that is, to the presumption that
it is possible to make any progress with a pure cognition, derived
from (philosophical) conceptions, according to the principles which
reason has long been in the habit of employing—without first inquiring in what way and by what right reason has come into the
possession of these principles. Dogmatism is thus the dogmatic
procedure of pure reason *without previous criticism of its own
powers,* and in opposing this procedure, we must not be supposed
to lend any countenance to that loquacious shallowness which ar-
rogates to itself the name of popularity, nor yet to scepticism, which
makes short work with the whole science of metaphysics. On the
contrary, our criticism is the necessary preparation for a thoroughly

scientific system of metaphysics, which must perform its task entirely *a priori,* to the complete satisfaction of speculative reason, and must, therefore, be treated, not popularly, but scholastically. In carrying out the plan which the Critique prescribes, that is, in the future system of metaphysics, we must have recourse to the strict method of the celebrated Wolf, the greatest of all dogmatic philosophers. He was the first to point out the necessity of establishing fixed principles, of clearly defining our conceptions, and of subjecting our demonstrations to the most severe scrutiny, instead of rashly jumping at conclusions. The example which he set, served to awaken that spirit of profound and thorough investigation which is not yet extinct in Germany. He would have been peculiarly well fitted to give a truly scientific character to metaphysical studies, had it occurred to him to prepare the field by a criticism of the *organum,* that is, of pure reason itself. That he failed to perceive the necessity of such a procedure, must be ascribed to the dogmatic mode of thought which characterized his age, and on this point the philosophers of his time, as well as of all previous times, have nothing to reproach each other with. Those who reject at once the method of Wolf, and of the Critique of Pure Reason, can have no other aim but to shake off the fetters of *science,* to change labour into sport, certainty into opinion, and philosophy into philodoxy.

In this *second edition,* I have endeavoured, as far as possible, to remove the difficulties and obscurity, which, without fault of mine perhaps, have given rise to many misconceptions even among acute thinkers. In the propositions themselves, and in the demonstrations by which they are supported, as well as in the form and the entire plan of the work, I have found nothing to alter; which must be attributed partly to the long examination to which I had subjected the whole before offering it to the public, and partly to the nature of the case. For pure speculative reason is an organic structure in which there is nothing isolated or independent, but every single part is essential to all the rest; and hence, the slightest imperfection, whether defect or positive error, could not fail to betray itself in use. I venture, further to hope, that this system will maintain the same unalterable character for the future. I am led to entertain this confidence, not by vanity, but by the evidence which the equality of the result affords, when we proceed, first, from the simplest elements up to the complete whole of pure reason, and then, backwards from the whole to each individual part. We find that the attempt to make the slightest alteration, in any part, leads inevitably to contradictions, not merely in this system, but in human reason itself At the same time, there is still much room for improvement in the *exposition* of the doctrines contained in this work. In the present edition, I have endeavoured to remove misapprehensions of the aesthetical part, especially with regard to the conception of Time; to clear away the obscurity which has been found in the deduction of the conceptions of the understanding; to supply the supposed want of sufficient evidence in the demonstration of the principles of the pure understanding; and, lastly, to obviate the misunderstanding of the paralogisms which immediately precede the Rational Psychology. Beyond this point—the end of the second Main division of the Transcendental Dialectic—I have not extended my alterations,[6] partly from want of time, and partly

6. The only addition, properly so called—and that only in the method of proof— which I have made in the present edition, consists of a new refutation of psychological *Idealism* and a strict demonstration—the only one possible, as I believe—of the objective reality of external intuition. However harmless Idealism may be considered—although in reality it is not so—in regard to the essential ends of metaphysics, it must still remain a scandal to philosophy and to the general human reason to be obliged to assume, as an article of mere belief, the existence of things external to ourselves (from which, yet, we derive the whole material of cognition even for the internal sense), and not to be able to oppose a satisfactory proof to any one who may call it in question. As there is some obscurity of expression in the demonstration as it stands in the text, I propose to alter the passage in question as follows: "But this permanent cannot be an intuition in me. For all the determining grounds of my existence which can be found in me, are representations, and, as such, do themselves require a permanent, distinct from them, which may determine my existence in relation to their changes, that is, my existence in time, wherein they change." It may, probably, be urged in opposition to this proof, that, after all, I am only conscious immediately of that which is in me, that is, of my *representation* of external things, and that, consequently, it must always remain uncertain whether anything corresponding to this representation, does or does not exist externally to me. But I am conscious, through internal *experience,* of my *existence in time,* (consequently, also, of the determinability of the former in the latter), and that is more than the simple consciousness of my representation. It is, in fact, the same as the *empirical consciousness of my existence,* which can only be determined in relation to something, which, while connected with my existence, is *external to me.* This consciousness of my existence in time is, therefore, identical with the consciousness of a relation to something external to me, and it is, therefore, experience, not fiction, sense, not imagination, which inseparably connects the external with my internal sense. For the external sense is, in itself, the relation of intuition to something real, external to me; and the reality of this something, as opposed to the mere imagination of it, rests solely on its inseparable connection with internal experience as the condition of its possibility. If with the *intellectual consciousness* of my existence, in the

because I am not aware that any portion of the remainder has given rise to misconceptions among intelligent and impartial critics, whom I do not here mention with that praise which is their due, but who will find that their suggestions have been attended to in the work itself.

In attempting to render the exposition of my views as intelligible as possible, I have been compelled to leave out or abridge various passages which were not essential to the completeness of the work, but which many readers might consider useful in other respects, and might be unwilling to miss. This trifling loss, which could not be avoided without swelling the book beyond due limits, may be supplied, at the pleasure of the reader, by a comparison with the first edition, and will, I hope, be more than compensated for by the greater clearness of the exposition as it now stands.

I have observed, with pleasure and thankfulness, in the pages of various reviews and treatises, that the spirit of profound and thorough investigation is not extinct in Germany, though it may have

---

representation: *I am,* which accompanies all my judgments, and all the operations of my understanding, I could, at the same time, connect a determination of my existence by *intellectual intuition,* then the consciousness of a relation to something external to me would not be necessary. But the internal intuition in which alone my existence can be determined, though preceded by that purely intellectual consciousness, is itself sensible and attached to the condition of time. Hence this determination of my existence, and consequently my internal experience itself, must depend on something permanent which is not in me, which can be, therefore, only in something external to me, to which I must look upon myself as being related. Thus the reality of the external sense is necessarily connected with that of the internal, in order to the possibility of experience in general; that is, I am just as certainly conscious that there are things external to me related to my sense, as I am that I myself exist, as determined in time. But in order to ascertain to what given intuitions objects, external to me, really correspond, in other words, what intuitions belong to the external sense and not to imagination, I must have recourse, in every particular case, to those rules according to which experience in general (even internal experience) is distinguishd from imagination, and which are always based on the proposition that there is an external experience.—We may add the remark, that the representation of something *permanent* in existence, is not the same thing as the *permanent representation;* for a representation may be very variable and changing— as all our representations, even that of matter, are—and yet refer to something permanent, which must, therefore, be distinct from all my representations and external to me, the existence of which is necessarily included in the determination of my own existence, and with it constitutes *one* experience—an experience which would not even be possible internally, if it were not also at the same time, in part, external. To the question *How?* we are no more able to reply, than we are, in general, to think the stationary in time, the co-existence of which with the variable, produces the conception of change.

been overborne and silenced for a time by the fashionable tone of a license in thinking, which gives itself the airs of genius—and that the difficulties which beset the paths of Criticism have not prevented energetic and acute thinkers from making themselves masters of the science of pure reason to which these paths conduct—a science which is not popular, but scholastic in its character, and which alone can hope for a lasting existence or possess an abiding value. To these deserving men, who so happily combine profundity of view with a talent for lucid exposition—a talent which I myself am not conscious of possessing—I leave the task of removing any obscurity which may still adhere to the statement of my doctrines. For, in this case, the danger is not that of being refuted, but of being misunderstood. For my own part, I must henceforward abstain from controversy, although I shall carefully attend to all suggestions, whether from friends or adversaries, which may be of use in the future elaboration of the system of this Propaedeutic. As, during these labours, I have advanced pretty far in years—this month I reach my sixty-fourth year—it will be necessary for me to economize time, if I am to carry out my plan of elaborating the Metaphysics of Nature as well as of Morals, in confirmation of the correctness of the principles established in this Critique of Pure Reason, both Speculative and Practical; and I must, therefore, leave the task of clearing up the obscurities of the present work— inevitable, perhaps, at the outset—as well as the defence of the whole, to those deserving men who have made my system their own. A philosophical system cannot come forward armed at all points like a mathematical treatise, and hence it may be quite possible to take objection to particular passages, while the organic structure of the system, considered as a unity, has no danger to apprehend. But few possess the ability, and still fewer the inclination, to take a comprehensive view of a new system. By confining the view to particular passages, taking these out of their connection and comparing them with one another, it is easy to pick out apparent contradictions, especially in a work written with any freedom of style. These contradictions place the work in an unfavourable light in eyes of those who rely on the judgment of others, but are easily reconciled by those who have mastered the idea of the whole. If a theory possesses stability in itself, the action and reaction which seemed at first to threaten its existence, serve only, in the course of

time, to smooth down any superficial roughness or inequality, and—
if men of insight, impartiality, and truly popular gifts, turn their
attention to it—to secure to it, in a short time, the requisite elegance
also.

Königsberg, April 1787

# Introduction

## I

## OF THE DIFFERENCE BETWEEN PURE
## AND EMPIRICAL KNOWLEDGE

That all our knowledge begins with experience there can be no doubt. For how is it possible that the faculty of cognition should be awakened into exercise otherwise than by means of objects which affect our senses, and partly of themselves produce representations, partly rouse our powers of understanding into activity, to compare, to connect, or to separate these, and so to convert the raw material of our sensuous impressions into a knowledge of objects, which is called experience? In respect of time, therefore, no knowledge of ours is antecedent to experience, but begins with it.

But, though all our knowledge begins with experience, it by no means follows, that all arises out of experience. For, on the contrary, it is quite possible that our empirical knowledge is a compound of that which we receive through impressions, and that which the faculty of cognition supplies from itself (sensuous impressions giving merely the *occasion*), an addition which we cannot distinguish from the original element given by sense, till long practice has made us attentive to, and skilful in separating it. It is, therefore, a question which requires close investigation, and it is not to be answered at first sight,—whether there exists a knowledge altogether independent of experience, and even of all sensuous impressions? Knowledge of this kind is called *a priori*, in contradistinction to empirical knowledge, which has its sources *a posteriori*, that is, in experience.

But the expression, *"a priori,"* is not as yet definite enough, adequately to indicate the whole meaning of the question above started. For, in speaking of knowledge which has its sources in experience, we are wont to say, that this or that may be known *a priori,* because we do not derive this knowledge immediately from experience, but from a general rule, which, however, we have itself borrowed from experience. Thus, if a man undermined his house, we say, "he might know *a priori* that it would have fallen;" that is, he needed not to have waited for the experience that it did actually fall. But still, *a priori,* he could not know even this much. For, that bodies are heavy, and, consequently, that they fall when their supports are taken away, must have been known to him previously, by means of experience.

By the term "knowledge a priori," therefore, we shall in the sequel understand, not such as is independent of this or that kind of experience, but such as is absolutely so of *all* experience. Opposed to this is empirical knowledge, or that which is possible only *a posteriori,* that is, through experience. Knowledge *a priori* is either pure or impure. Pure knowledge *a priori* is that with which no empirical element is mixed up. For example, the proposition, "Every change has a cause," is a proposition *a priori,* but impure, because change is a conception which can only be derived from experience.

## II

### THE HUMAN INTELLECT, EVEN IN AN UNPHILOSOPHICAL STATE, IS IN POSSESSION OF CERTAIN COGNITIONS *A PRIORI*

The question now is as to a *criterion,* by which we may securely distinguish a pure from an empirical cognition. Experience no doubt teaches us that this or that object is constituted in such and such a manner, but not that it could not possibly exist otherwise. Now, in the first place, if we have a proposition which contains the idea of necessity in its very conception, it is a judgment *a priori;* if, moreover, it is not derived from any other proposition, unless from one equally involving the idea of necessity, it is absolutely *a priori.* Secondly, an empirical judgment never exhibits strict and absolute, but only assumed and comparative universality (by induction); therefore, the most we can say is,—so far as we have hitherto observed, there is no exception to this or that rule. If, on the other hand, a judgment carries with it strict and absolute universality, that is, admits of no possible exception, it is not derived from experience, but is valid absolutely *a priori*.

Empirical universality is, therefore, only an arbitrary extension of validity, from that which may be predicated of a proposition valid in most cases, to that which is asserted of a proposition which holds good in all; as, for example, in the affirmation, "all bodies are heavy." When, on the contrary, strict universality characterizes a judgment, it necessarily indicates another peculiar source of knowledge, namely, a faculty of cognition *a priori*. Necessity and strict universality, therefore, are infallible tests for distinguishing pure from empirical knowledge, and are inseparably connected with each other. But as in the use of these criteria the empirical limitation is sometimes more easily detected than the contingency of the judgment, or the unlimited universality which we attach to a judgment is often a more convincing proof than its necessity, it may be advisable to use the criteria separately, each being by itself infallible.

Now, that in the sphere of human cognition, we have judgments which are necessary, and in the strictest sense universal, consequently pure *a priori,* it will be an easy matter to show. If we desire an example from the sciences, we need only take any proposition in mathematics. If we cast our eyes upon the commonest operations of the understanding, the proposition, "every change must have a cause," will amply serve our purpose. In the latter case, indeed, the conception of a cause so plainly involves the conception of a necessity of connexion with an effect, and of a strict universality of the law, that the very notion of a cause would entirely disappear, were we to derive it, like Hume, from a frequent association of what happens with that which precedes, and the habit thence originating of connecting representations—the necessity inherent in the judgment being therefore merely subjective. Besides, without seeking for such examples of principles existing *a priori* in cognition, we might easily show that such principles are the indispensable basis of the possibility of experience itself, and consequently prove their existence *a priori*. For whence could our experience itself acquire certainty, if all the rules on which it depends were themselves empirical, and consequently fortuitous? No one, therefore, can admit the validity of the use of such rules as first principles.

But, for the present, we may content ourselves with having established the fact, that we do possess and exercise a faculty of pure *a priori* cognition; and, secondly, with having pointed out the proper tests of such cognition, namely, universality and necessity.

Not only in judgments, however, but even in conceptions, is an *a priori* origin manifest. For example, if we take away by degrees from our conceptions of a body all that can be referred to mere sensuous experience—colour, hardness or softness, weight, even impenetrability—the body will then vanish; but the space which it occupied still remains, and this it is utterly impossible to annihilate in thought. Again, if we take away, in like manner, from our empirical conception of any object, corporeal or incorporeal, all properties which mere experience has taught us to connect with it, still we cannot think away those through which we cogitate it as substance, or adhering to substance, although our conception of substance is more determined than that of an object. Compelled, therefore, by that necessity with which the conception of substance forces itself upon us, we must confess that it has its seat in our faculty of cognition *a priori*.

## III

### PHILOSOPHY STANDS IN NEED OF A SCIENCE WHICH SHALL DETERMINE THE POSSIBILITY, PRINCIPLES, AND EXTENT OF HUMAN KNOWLEDGE *A PRIORI*

Of far more importance than all that has been above said, is the consideration that certain of our cognitions rise completely above the sphere of all possible experience, and by means of conceptions, to which there exists in the whole extent of experience no corresponding object, seem to extend the range of our judgments beyond its bounds. And just in this transcendental or supersensible sphere, where experience affords us neither instruction nor guidance, lie the investigations of *Reason,* which, on account of their importance, we consider far preferable to, and as having a far more elevated aim than, all that the understanding can achieve within the sphere of sensuous phaenomena. So high a value do we set upon these investigations, that even at the risk of error, we persist in following them out, and permit neither doubt nor disregard nor indifference to restrain us from the pursuit. These unavoidable problems of mere pure reason are *God, Freedom* (of will) and *Immortality.* The science which, with all its preliminaries, has for its especial object the solution of these problems is named metaphysics,—a science which is at the very outset dogmatical, that is, it confidently takes upon itself the execution of this task without any previous investigation of the ability or inability of reason for such an undertaking.

Now the safe ground of experience being thus abandoned, it seems nevertheless natural that we should hesitate to erect a building with the cognitions we possess, without knowing whence they come, and on the strength of principles, the origin of which is undiscovered. Instead of thus trying to build without a foundation, it is rather to be expected that we should long ago have put the question, how the understanding can arrive at these *a priori* cognitions, and what is the extent, validity, and worth which they may possess? We say, this is natural enough, meaning by the word natural, that which is consistent with a just and reasonable way of thinking; but if we understand by the term, that which usually happens, nothing indeed could be more natural and more comprehensible than that this investigation should be left long unattempted. For one part of our pure knowledge, the science of mathematics, has been long firmly established, and thus leads us to form flattering expectations with regard to others, though these may be of quite a different nature. Besides, when we get beyond the bounds of experience, we are of course safe from opposition in that quarter; and the charm of widening the range of our knowledge is so great, that unless we are brought to a stand-still by some evident contradiction, we hurry on undoubtingly in our course. This, however, may be avoided, if we are sufficiently cautious in the construction of our fictions, which are not the less fictions on that account.

Mathematical science affords us a brilliant example, how far, independently of all experience, we may carry our *a priori* knowledge. It is true that the mathematician occupies himself with objects and cognitions only in so far as they can be represented by means of intuition. But this circumstance is easily overlooked, because the said intuition can itself be given *a priori,* and therefore is hardly to be distinguished from a mere pure conception. Deceived by such a proof of the power of reason, we can perceive no limits to the extension of our knowledge. The light dove cleaving in free flight the thin air, whose resistance it feels might imagine that her movements would be far more free and rapid in airless space. Just in the same way did Plato, abandoning the world of sense because of the narrow limits it sets to the understanding, venture upon the wings of ideas beyond it, into the void space of pure intellect. He did not reflect that he made no real progress by all his efforts; for he met with no resistance which might serve him for a support, as it were, whereon to rest, and on which he might apply his powers, in order to let the intellect acquire momentum for its progress. It is, indeed, the common fate of human reason in speculation, to finish the imposing edifice of thought as rapidly as possible, and then for the first time to begin to examine whether the foundation is a solid one or no. Arrived at this point, all sorts of excuses are sought after, in order to console us for its want of stability, or rather indeed, to enable us to dispense altogether with so late and dangerous an investigation. But what frees us during the process of building from all apprehension or suspicion, and flatters us into the belief of its solidity, is this. A great part, perhaps the greatest part, of the business of our reason consists in the analysation of the conceptions which we already possess of objects. By this means we gain a multitude of cognitions, which although really nothing more than elucidations or explanations of that which (though in a confused manner) was already thought in our conceptions, are, at least in respect of their form, prized as new introspections; whilst, so far as regards their matter or content, we have really made no addition to our conceptions, but only disinvolved them. But as this process does furnish real *a priori* knowledge, which has a sure progress and useful results, reason, deceived by this, slips in, without being itself aware of it, assertions of a quite different kind; in which, to given conceptions it adds others, *a priori* indeed, but entirely foreign to them, without our knowing how it arrives at these, and, indeed, without such a question ever suggesting itself. I shall therefore at once proceed to examine the difference between these two modes of knowledge.

## IV

### OF THE DIFFERENCE BETWEEN ANALYTICAL
### AND SYNTHETICAL JUDGMENTS

In all judgments wherein the relation of a subject to the predicate is cogitated, (I mention affirmative judgments only here; the application to negative will be very easy,) this relation is possible in two different ways. Either the predicate B belongs to the subject A, as somewhat which is contained (though covertly) in the conception A; or the predicate B lies completely out of the conception A, although it stands in connexion with it. In the first instance, I term the judgment analytical, in the second, synthetical. Analytical judgments (affirmative) are therefore those in which the connection of the predicate with the subject is cogitated through identity; those in which this connexion is cogitated without identity, are called synthetical judgments. The former may be called *explicative,* the latter *augmentative* judgments; because the former add in the predicate nothing to the conception of the subject, but only analyse it into its constituent conceptions, which were thought already in the subject, although in a confused manner; the latter add to our conceptions of the subject a predicate which was not contained in it, and which no analysis could ever have discovered therein. For example, when I say, "all bodies are extended," this is an analytical judgment. For I need not go beyond the conception of *body* in order to find extension connected with it, but merely analyse the conception, that is, become conscious of the manifold properties which I think in that conception, in order to discover this predicate in it: it is therefore an analytical judgment. On the other hand, when I say, "all bodies are heavy," the predicate is something totally different from that which I think in the mere conception of a body. By the addition of such a predicate therefore, it becomes a synthetical judgment.

Judgments of experience, as such, are always synthetical. For it would be absurd to think of grounding an analytical judgment on experience, because in forming such a judgment, I need not go out of the sphere of my conceptions, and therefore recourse to the testimony of experience is quite unnecessary. That "bodies are extended" is not an empirical judgment, but a proposition which stands firm *a priori.* For before addressing myself to experience, I already have in my conception all the requisite conditions for the judgment, and I have only to extract the predicate from the conception, according to the principle of contradiction, and thereby at the same time become conscious of the necessity of the judgment, a necessity which I could never learn from experience. On the other hand, though at first I do not at all include the predicate of weight in my conception of body in general, that conception still indicates an object of experience, a part of the totality of experience, to which

I can still add other parts; and this I do when I recognize by observation that bodies are heavy. I can cognize beforehand by analysis
the conception of body through the characteristics of extension,
impenetrability, shape, etc., all which are cogitated in this conception. But now I extend my knowledge, and looking back on experience from which I had derived this conception of body, I find
weight at all times connected with the above characteristics, and
therefore I synthetically add to my conceptions this as a predicate,
and say, "all bodies are heavy." This it is experience upon which
rests the possibility of the synthesis of the predicate of weight with
the conception of body, because both conceptions, although the
one is not contained in the other, still belong to one another (only
contingently, however), as parts of a whole, namely, of experience,
which is itself a synthesis of intuitions.

But to synthetical judgments *a priori,* such aid is entirely wanting.
If I go out of and beyond the conception A, in order to recognize
another B as connected with it, what foundation have I to rest on,
whereby to render the synthesis possible? I have here no longer the
advantage of looking out in the sphere of experience for what I
want. Let us take, for example, the proposition, "everything that
happens has a cause." In the conception of *something that happens,*
I indeed think an existence which a certain time antecedes, and
from this I can derive analytical judgments. But the conception of
a cause lies quite out of the above conception, and indicates something entirely different from "that which happens," and is consequently not contained in that conception. How then am I able to
assert concerning the general conception—"that which happens"—
something entirely different from that conception, and to recognize
the conception of cause although not contained in it, yet as belonging to it, and even necessarily? what is here the unknown =
X, upon which the understanding rests when it believes it has found,
out of the conception A a foreign predicate B, which it nevertheless
considers to be connected with it? It cannot be experience, because
the principle adduced annexes the two representations, cause and
effect, to the representation existence, not only with universality,
which experience cannot give, but also with the expression of necessity, therefore completely *a priori* and from pure conceptions.
Upon such synthetical, that is augmentative propositions, depends
the whole aim of our speculative knowledge *a priori;* for although
analytical judgments are indeed highly important and necessary,

they are so, only to arrive at that clearness of conceptions which is requisite for a sure and extended synthesis, and this alone is a real acquisition.

V

1. Mathematical judgments are always synthetical. Hitherto this fact, though incontestibly true and very important in its consequences, seems to have escaped the analysts of the human mind, nay, to be in complete opposition to all their conjectures. For as it was found that mathematical conclusions all proceed according to the principle of contradiction (which the nature of every apodeictic certainty requires), people became persuaded that the fundamental principles of the science also were recognised and admitted in the same way. But the notion is fallacious; for although a synthetical proposition can certainly be discerned by means of the principle of contradiction, this is possible only when another synthetical proposition precedes, from which the latter is deducted, but never of itself.

Before all, be it observed, that proper mathematical propositions are always judgments *a priori,* and not empirical, because they carry along with them the conception of necessity, which cannot be given by experience. If this be demurred to, it matters not; I will then limit my assertion to *pure* mathematics, the very conception of which implies, that it consists of knowledge altogether nonempirical and *a priori.*

We might, indeed, at first suppose that the proposition $7 + 5 = 12$, is a merely analytical proposition, following (according to the principle of contradiction), from the conception of a sum of seven and five. But if we regard it more narrowly, we find that our conception of the sum of seven and five contains nothing more than the uniting of both sums into one, whereby it cannot at all be cogitated what this single number is which embraces both. The conception of twelve is by no means obtained by merely cogitating the union of seven and five; and we may analyze our conception of such a possible sum as long as we will, still we shall never discover in it the notion of twelve. We must go beyond these conceptions, and have recourse to an intuition which corresponds to one of the two—our five fingers, for example, or like Segner in his "Arithmetic," five points, and so by degrees, add the units contained in the five given in the intuition, to the conception of seven. For I first take the number 7, and, for the conception of 5 calling in the aid of the fingers of my hand as objects of intuition, I add the units, which I before took together to make up the number 5, gradually now by means of the material image my hand, to the number 7, and by this process, I at length see the number 12 arise. That 7 should be added to 5, I have certainly cogitated in my conception of a sum $= 7 + 5$, but not that this sum was equal to 12. Arithmetical propositions are therefore always synthetical, of which we may become more clearly convinced by trying large numbers. For it will thus become quite evident, that turn and twist our conceptions as we may, it is impossible, without having recourse to intuition, to arrive at the sum total or product by means of the mere analysis of our conceptions. Just as little is any principle of pure geometry analytical. "A straight line between two points is the shortest," is a synthetical proposition. For my conception of *straight*, contains no notion of *quantity*, but is merely *qualitative*. The conception of the *shortest* is therefore wholly an addition, and by no analysis can it be extracted from our conception of a straight line. Intuition must therefore here lend its aid, by means of which and thus only, our synthesis is possible.

Some few principles preposited by geometricians are, indeed, really analytical, and depend on the principle of contradiction. They serve, however, like identical propositions, as links in the chain of method, not as principles—for example, $a = a$, the whole is equal to itself, or $(a + b) > a$, the whole is greater than its part. And yet even these principles themselves, though they derive their validity from pure conceptions, are only admitted in mathematics because they can be presented in intuition. What causes us here commonly to believe that the predicate of such apodeictic judgments is already contained in our conception, and that the judgment is therefore analytical, is merely the equivocal nature of the expression. We must join in thought a certain predicate to a given conception, and this necessity cleaves already to the conception. But the question is, not what we must join in thought to the given conception, but what we really think therein, though only obscurely, and then it becomes manifest, that the predicate pertains to these conceptions, necessarily indeed, yet not as thought in the conception itself, but by virtue of an intuition, which must be added to the conception.

2. The science of Natural Philosophy (Physics) contains in itself synthetical judgments *a priori,* as principles. I shall adduce two propositions. For instance, the proposition, "in all changes of the material world, the quantity of matter remains unchanged;" or, that, "in all communication of motion, action and re-action must always be equal." In both of these, not only is the necessity, and therefore their origin *a priori* clear, but also that they are synthetical propositions. For in the conception of matter, I do not cogitate its permanency, but merely its presence in space, which it fills. I therefore really go out of and beyond the conception of matter, in order to think on to it something *a priori,* which I did not think in it. The proposition is therefore not analytical, but synthetical, and nevertheless conceived *a priori;* and so it is with regard to the other propositions of the pure part of natural philosophy.

3. As to Metaphysics, even if we look upon it merely as an attempted science, yet, from the nature of human reason, an indispensable one, we find that it must contain synthetical propositions *a priori.* It is not merely the duty of metaphysics to dissect, and thereby analytically to illustrate the conceptions which we form *a priori* of things; but we seek to widen the range of our *a priori* knowledge. For this purpose, we must avail ourselves of such principles as add something to the original conception—something not identical with, nor contained in it, and by means of synthetical judgments *à priori,* leave far behind us the limits of experience; for example, in the proposition, "the world must have a beginning," and such like. Thus metaphysics, according to the proper aim of the science, consists merely of synthetical propositions *à priori.*

## VI

### THE UNIVERSAL PROBLEM OF PURE REASON

It is extremely advantageous to be able to bring a number of investigations under the formula of a single problem. For in this manner, we not only facilitate our own labour, inasmuch as we define it clearly to ourselves, but also render it more easy for others to decide whether we have done justice to our undertaking. The proper problem of pure reason, then, is contained in the question, "How are synthetical judgments *a priori* possible?"

That metaphysical science has hitherto remained in so vacillating a state of uncertainty and contradiction, is only to be attributed to the fact, that this great problem, and perhaps even the difference between analytical and synthetical judgments, did not sooner suggest itself to philosophers. Upon the solution of this problem, or upon sufficient proof of the impossibility of synthetical knowledge *a priori,* depends the existence or downfall of the science of metaphysics. Among philosophers, David Hume came the nearest of all to this problem; yet it never acquired in his mind sufficent precision, nor did he regard the question in its universality. On the contrary, he stopped short at the synthetical proposition of the connection of an effect with its cause, *(principium causalitatis),* insisting that such proposition *a priori* was impossible. According to his conclusions, then, all that we term metaphysical science is a mere delusion, arising from the fancied insight of reason into that which is in truth borrowed from experience, and to which habit has given the appearance of necessity. Against this assertion, destructive to all pure philosophy, he would have been guarded, had he had our problem before his eyes in its universality. For he would then have perceived that, according to his own argument, there likewise could not be any pure mathematical science, which assuredly cannot exist without synthetical propositions *a priori,*—an absurdity from which his good understanding must have saved him.

In the solution of the above problem is at the same time comprehended the possibility of the use of pure reason in the foundation and construction of all sciences which contain theoretical knowledge *a priori* of objects, that is to say, the answer to the following questions:

How is pure mathematical science possible?

How is pure natural science possible?

Respecting these sciences, as they do certainly exist, it may with propriety be asked, *how* they are possible?—for that they must be possible, is shown by the fact of their really existing.[1] But as to

1. As to the existence of pure natural science, or physics, perhaps many may still express doubts. But we have only to look at the different propositions which are commonly treated of at the commencement of proper (empirical) physical science— those, for example, relating to the permanence of the same quantity of matter, the *vis inertiae,* the equality of action and reaction, etc.—to be soon convinced that they form a science of pure physics (*physica pura,* or *rationalis*), which well deserves to be separately exposed as a special science, in its whole extent, whether that be great or confined.

metaphysics, the miserable progress it has hitherto made, and the fact that of no one system yet brought forward, as far as regards its true aim, can it be said that this science really exists, leaves any one at liberty to doubt with reason the very possibility of its existence.

Yet, in a certain sense, this kind of knowledge must unquestionably be looked upon as *given;* in other words, metaphysics must be considered as really existing, if not as a science, nevertheless as a natural disposition of the human mind *(metaphysica naturalis).* For human reason, without any instigations imputable to the mere vanity of great knowledge, unceasingly progresses, urged on by its own feeling of need, towards such questions as cannot be answered by any empirical application of reason, or principles derived therefrom; and so there has ever really existed in every man some system of metaphysics. It will always exist, so soon as reason awakes to the exercise of its power of speculation. And now the question arises—How is metaphysics, as a natural disposition, possible? In other words, how, from the nature of universal human reason, do those questions arise which pure reason proposes to itself, and which it is impelled by its own feeling of need to answer as well as it can?

But as in all the attempts hitherto made to answer the questions which reason is prompted by its very nature to propose to itself, for example, whether the world had a beginning, or has existed from eternity, it has always met with unavoidable contradictions, we must not rest satisfied with the mere natural disposition of the mind to metaphysics, that is, with the existence of the faculty of pure reason, whence, indeed, some sort of metaphysical system always arises; but it must be possible to arrive at certainty in regard to the question whether we know or do not know the things of which metaphysics treats. We must be able to arrive at a decision on the subjects of its questions, or on the ability or inability of reason to form any judgment respecting them; and therefore either to extend with confidence the bounds of our pure reason, or to set strictly defined and safe limits to its action. This last question, which arises out of the above universal problem, would properly run thus: How is metaphysics possible as a science?

Thus, the critique of reason leads at last, naturally and necessarily, to science; and, on the other hand, the dogmatical use of reason without criticism leads to groundless assertions, against which others equally specious can always be set, thus ending unavoidably in scepticism.

Besides, this science cannot be of great and formidable prolixity, because it has not to do with objects of reason, the variety of which is inexhaustible, but merely with reason herself and her problems; problems which arise out of her own bosom, and are not proposed to her by the nature of outward things, but by her own nature. And when once reason has previously become able completely to understand her own power in regard to objects which she meets with in experience, it will be easy to determine securely the extent and limits of her attempted application to objects beyond the confines of experience.

We may and must, therefore, regard the attempts hitherto made to establish metaphysical science dogmatically as nonexistent. For what of analysis, that is, mere dissection of conceptions, is contained in one or other, is not the aim of, but only a preparation for metaphysics proper, which has for its object the extension, by means of synthesis, of our *a priori* knowledge. And for this purpose, mere analysis is of course useless, because it only shows what is contained in these conceptions, but not how we arrive, *a priori*, at them; and this it is her duty to show, in order to be able afterwards to determine their valid use in regard to all objects of experience, to all knowledge in general. But little self-denial, indeed, is needed to give up these pretensions, seeing the undeniable, and in the dogmatic mode of procedure, inevitable contradictions of Reason with herself, have long since ruined the reputation of every system of metaphysics that has appeared up to this time. It will require more firmness to remain undeterred by difficulty from within, and opposition from without, from endeavouring, by a method quite opposed to all those hitherto followed, to further the growth and fruitfulness of a science indispensable to human reason—a science from which every branch it has borne may be cut away, but whose roots remain indestructible.

# VII
### IDEA AND DIVISION OF A PARTICULAR SCIENCE,
### UNDER THE NAME OF A CRITIQUE OF PURE REASON

From all that has been said, there results the idea of a particular science, which may be called the *Critique of Pure Reason*. For reason is the faculty which furnishes us with the principles of knowledge *a priori*. Hence, pure reason is the faculty which contains the principles of cognizing any thing absolutely *a priori*. An Organon of pure reason would be a compendium of those principles according to which alone all pure cognitions *a priori* can be obtained. The completely extended application of such an organon would afford us a system of pure reason. As this, however, is demanding a great deal, and it is yet doubtful whether any extension of our knowledge be here possible, or if so, in what cases; we can regard a science of the mere criticism of pure reason, its sources and limits, as the *propaedeutic* to a system of pure reason. Such a science must not be called a Doctrine, but only a Critique of pure Reason; and its use, in regard to speculation, would be only negative, not to enlarge the bounds of, but to purify our reason, and to shield it against error,—which alone is no little gain. I apply the term *transcendental* to all knowledge which is not so much occupied with objects as with the mode of our cognition of these objects, so far as this mode of cognition is possible *a priori*. A system of such conceptions would be called *Transcendental Philosophy*. But this, again, is still beyond the bounds of our present essay. For as such a science must contain a complete exposition not only of our synthetical *a priori*, but of our analytical *a priori* knowledge, it is of too wide a range for our present purpose, because we do not require to carry our analysis any farther than is necessary to understand, in their full extent, the principles of synthesis *a priori*, with which alone we have to do. This investigation, which we cannot properly call a doctrine, but only a transcendental critique, because it aims not at the enlargement, but at the correction and guidance of our knowledge, and is to serve as a touchstone of the worth or worthlessness of all knowledge *a priori*, is the sole object of our present essay. Such a critique is consequently, as far as possible, a preparation for an organon; and if this new organon should be found to fail, at least for a canon of pure reason, according to which the complete system of the philosophy of pure reason, whether it extend or limit the bounds of that reason, might one day be set forth both analytically and synthetically. For that this is possible, nay, that such a system is not of so great extent as to preclude the hope of its ever being completed, is evident. For we have not here to do with the nature of outward objects, which is infinite, but solely with the mind, which judges of the nature of objects, and, again, with the mind only in respect of its cognition *a priori*. And the object of our investigations, as it is not to be sought without, but altogether within ourselves, cannot remain concealed, and in all probability is limited enough to be completely surveyed and fairly estimated, according to its worth or worthlessness. Still less let the reader here expect a critique of books and systems of pure reason; our present object is exclusively a critique of the faculty of pure reason itself. Only when we make this critique our foundation, do we possess a pure touchstone for estimating the philosophical value of ancient and modern writings on this subject; and without this criterion, the incompetent historian or judge decides upon and corrects the groundless assertions of others with his own, which have themselves just as little foundation.

Transcendental philosophy is the idea of a science, for which the Critique of Pure Reason must sketch the whole plan architectonically, that is, from principles, with a full guarantee for the validity and stability of all the parts which enter into the building. It is the system of all the principles of pure reason. If this Critique itself does not assume the title of transcendental philosophy, it is only because, to be a complete system, it ought to contain a full analysis of all human knowledge *a priori*. Our critique must, indeed, lay before us a complete enumeration of all the radical conceptions which constitute the said pure knowledge. But from the complete analysis of these conceptions themselves, as also from a complete investigation of those derived from them, it abstains with reason; partly because it would be deviating from the end in view to occupy itself with this analysis, since this process is not attended with the difficulty and insecurity to be found in the synthesis, to which our critique is entirely devoted, and partly because it would be inconsistent with the unity of our plan to burden this essay with the vindication of the completeness of such an analysis and deduction, with which, after all, we have at present nothing to do. This completeness of the analysis of these radical conceptions, as well as of the deduction from the conceptions *a priori* which may be given by the analysis, we can, however, easily attain, provided only that we are in possession of all these radical conceptions, which are to serve as principles of the synthesis, and that in respect of this main purpose nothing is wanting.

To the Critique of Pure Reason, therefore, belongs all that constitutes transcendental philosophy; and it is the complete idea of transcendental philosophy, but still not the science itself; because it only proceeds so far with the analysis as is necessary to the power of judging completely of our synthetical knowledge *a priori.*

The principal thing we must attend to, in the division of the parts of a science like this, is: that no conceptions must enter it which contain aught empirical; in other words, that the knowledge *a priori* must be completely pure. Hence, although the highest principles and fundamental conceptions of morality are certainly cognitions *a priori,* yet they do not belong to transcendental philosophy; because, though they certainly do not lay the conceptions of pain, pleasure, desires, inclinations, etc., (which are all of empirical origin) at the foundation of its precepts, yet still into the conception of duty,—as an obstacle to be overcome, or as an incitement which should not be made into a motive,—these empirical conceptions must necessarily enter, in the construction of a system of pure morality. Transcendental philosophy is consequently a philosophy of the pure and merely speculative reason. For all that is practical, so far as it contains motives, relates to feelings, and these belong to empirical sources of cognition.

If we wish to divide this science from the universal point of view of a science in general, it ought to comprehend, first, a *Doctrine of the Elements,* and, secondly, a *Doctrine of the Method* of pure reason. Each of these main divisions will have its subdivisions, the separate reasons for which we cannot here particularise. Only so much seems necessary by way of introduction or premonition, that there are two sources of human knowledge (which probably spring from a common, but to us unknown root), namely, sense and understanding. By the former, objects are *given* to us; by the latter, *thought.* So far as the faculty of sense may contain representations *a priori,* which form the conditions under which objects are given, in so far it belongs to transcendental philosophy. The transcendental doctrine of sense must form the first part of our science of elements, because the conditions under which alone the objects of human knowledge are given, must precede those under which they are thought.

# Transcendental
# Doctrine of Method

## Third Chapter
## The Architectonic of Pure Reason

By the term *Architectonic* I mean the art of constructing a system. Without systematic unity, our knowledge cannot become science; it will be an aggregate, and not a system. Thus Architectonic is the doctrine of the scientific in cognition, and therefore necessarily forms part of our Methodology.

Reason cannot permit our knowledge to remain in an unconnected and rhapsodistic state, but requires that the sum of our cognitions should constitute a system. It is thus alone that they can advance the ends of reason. By a system I mean the unity of various cognitions under one idea. This idea is the conception—given by reason—of the form of a whole, in so far as the conception determines *a priori* not only the limits of its content, but the place which each of its parts is to occupy. The scientific idea contains, therefore, the end, and the form of the whole which is in accordance with that end. The unity of the end, to which all the parts of the system relate, and through which all have a relation to each other, communicates unity to the whole system, so that the absence of any part can be immediately detected from our knowledge of the rest; and it determines *a priori* the limits of the system, thus excluding all contingent or arbitrary additions. The whole is thus an organism (*articulatio*), and not an aggregate (*coacervatio*); it may grow from within *(per intussusceptionem)*, but it cannot increase by external additions *(per appositionem)*. It is thus like an animal body, the growth of which does not add any limb, but, without changing their proportions, makes each in its sphere stronger and more active.

We require, for the execution of the idea of a system, a *schema*, that is, a content and an arrangement of parts determined *a priori* by the principle which the aim of the system prescribes. A schema which is not projected in accordance with an idea, that is, from the stand-point of the highest aim of reason, but merely empirically, in accordance with accidental aims and purposes (the number of which cannot be predetermined), can give us nothing more than *technical* unity. But the schema which is originated from an idea (in which case reason presents us with aims *a priori,* and does not look for them to experience), forms the basis of *architectonical* unity. A science, in the proper acceptation of that term, cannot be formed *technically,* that is, from observation of the similarity existing between different objects, and the purely contingent use we make of our knowledge *in concreto* with reference to all kinds of arbitrary external aims; its constitution must be framed on architectonical principles, that is, its parts must be shown to possess an essential affinity, and be capable of being deduced from one supreme and internal aim or end, which forms the condition of the possibility of the scientific whole. The schema of a science must give *a priori* the plan of it *(monogramma),* and the division of the whole into parts, in conformity with the idea of the science; and it must also distinguish this whole from all others, according to certain understood principles.

No one will attempt to construct a science, unless he have some idea to rest on as a proper basis. But, in the elaboration of the science he finds that the schema, nay, even the definition which he at first gave of the science, rarely corresponds with his idea; for this idea lies, like a germ, in our reason, its parts undeveloped and hid even from miscroscopical observation. For this reason, we ought to explain and define sciences, not according to the description which the originator gives of them, but according to the idea which we find based in reason itself, and which is suggested by the natural unity of the parts of the science already accumulated. For it will often be found, that the originator of a science, and even his latest successors, remain attached to an erroneous idea, which they cannot render clear to themselves, and that they thus fail in determining the true content, the articulation or systematic unity, and the limits of their science.

It is unfortunate that, only after having occupied ourselves for a long time in the collection of materials, under the guidance of an idea which lies undeveloped in the mind, but not according to any definite plan of arrangement,—nay, only after we have spent much time and labour in the technical disposition of our materials, does it become possible to view the idea of a science in a clear light, and to project, according to architectonical principles, a plan of the whole, in accordance with the aims of reason. Systems seem, like certain worms, to be formed by a kind of *generatio aequivoca*— by the mere confluence of conceptions, and to gain completeness only with the program of time. But the schema or germ of all lies in reason; and thus is not only every system organized according to its own idea, but all are united into one grand system of human knowledge, of which they form members. For this reason, it is possible to frame an architectonic of all human cognition, the formation of which, at the present time, considering the immense materials collected or to be found in the ruins of old systems, would not indeed be very difficult. Our purpose at present is merely to sketch the plan of the *Architectonic* of all cognition given by *pure reason;* and we begin from the point where the main root of human knowledge divides into two, one of which is *reason.* By reason I understand here the whole higher faculty of cognition, the *rational* being placed in contradistinction to the *empirical.*

If I make complete abstraction of the content of cognition, objectively considered, all cognition is, from a subjective point of view, either historical or rational. Historical cognition is *cognitio ex datis,* rational, *cognitio ex principiis.* Whatever may be the original source of a cognition, it is, in relation to the person who possesses it, merely historical, if he knows only what has been given him from another quarter, whether that knowledge was communicated by direct experience or by instruction. Thus the person who has *learned* a system of philosophy,—say the Wolfian,—although he has a perfect knowledge of all the principles, definitions and arguments in that philosophy, as well as of the divisions that have been made of the system, he possesses really no more than a *historical* knowledge of the Wolfian system; he knows only what has been told him, his judgments are only those which he has received from his teachers.

Dispute the validity of a definition, and he is at completely a loss to find another. He has formed his mind on another's; but the imitative faculty is not the productive. His knowledge has not been drawn from reason; and, although, objectively considered, it is rational knowledge, subjectively, it is merely historical. He has learned this or that philosophy, and is merely a plaster-cast of a living man. Rational cognitions which are objective, that is, which have their source in reason, can be so termed from a subjective point of view, only when they have been drawn by the individual himself from the sources of reason, that is, from principles; and it is in this way alone that criticism, or even the rejection of what has been already learned, can spring up in the mind.

All rational cognition is, again, based either on conceptions, or on the construction of conceptions. The former is termed philosophical, the latter mathematical. I have already shown the essential difference of these two methods of cognition in the first chapter. A cognition may be objectively philosophical and subjectively historical,—as is the case with the majority of scholars and those who cannot look beyond the limits of their system, and who remain in a state of pupillage all their lives. But it is remarkable that mathematical knowledge, when committed to memory, is valid, from the subjective point of view, as rational knowledge also, and that the same distinction cannot be drawn here as in the case of philosophical cognition. The reason is, that the only way of arriving at this knowledge is through the essential principles of reason, and thus it is always certain and indisputable; because reason is employed *in concreto*—but at the same time *a priori*— that is, in pure, and therefore, infallible intuition; and thus all causes of illusion and error are excluded. Of all the *a priori* sciences of reason, therefore, mathematics alone can be learned. Philosophy—unless it be in an historical manner—cannot be learned; we can at most learn to *philosophize*.

*Philosophy* is the system of all philosophical cognition. We must use this term in an objective sense, if we understand by it the archetype of all attempts at philosophizing, and the standard by which all subjective philosophies are to be judged. In this sense, philosophy is merely the idea of a possible science, which does not exist *in concreto,* but to which we endeavour in various ways to approximate, until we have discovered the right path to pursue— a path overgrown by the errors and illusions of sense,—and the image we have hitherto tried to shape in vain, has become a perfect copy of the great prototype. Until that time, we cannot learn philosophy—it does not exist; if it does, where is it, who possesses it, and how shall we know it? We can only learn to philosophize; in other words, we can only exercise our powers of reasoning in accordance with general principles, retaining at the same time, the right of investigating the sources of these principles, of testing, and even of rejecting them.

Until then, our conception of philosophy is only a *scholastic conception*—a conception, that is, of a system of cognition which we are trying to elaborate into a science; all that we at present know, being the systematic unity of this cognition and consequently the *logical* completeness of the cognition for the desired end. But there is also a *cosmical conception (conceptus cosmicus)* of philosophy, which has always formed the true basis of this term, especially when philosophy was personified and presented to us in the ideal of a *philosopher*. In this view, philosophy is the science of the relation of all cognition to the ultimate and essential aims of human reason *(teleologia rationis humanae),* and the philosopher is not merely an artist—who occupies himself with conceptions, but a law-giver—legislating for human reason. In this sense of the word, it would be in the highest degree arrogant to assume the title of philosopher, and to pretend that we had reached the perfection of the prototype which lies in the idea alone.

The mathematician, the natural philosopher, and the logician,—how far soever the first may have advanced in rational, and the two latter in philosophical knowledge,—are merely artists, engaged in the arrangement and formation of conceptions; they cannot be termed philosophers. Above them all, there is the ideal teacher, who employs them as instruments for the advancement of the essential aims of human reason. Him alone can we call philosopher; but he nowhere exists. But the idea of his legislative power resides in the mind of every man, and it alone teaches us what kind of systematic unity philosophy demands in view of the ultimate aims of reason. This idea is, therefore, a cosmical conception.[1]

In view of the complete systematic unity of reason, there can

1. By a *cosmical conception,* I mean one in which all men necessarily take an interest; the *aim* of a science must accordingly be determined according to *scholastic* [or partial] *conceptions,* if it is regarded merely as a means to certain arbitrarily proposed ends.

only be one ultimate end of all the operations of the mind. To this all other aims are subordinate, and nothing more than means for its attainment. This ultimate end is the destination of man, and the philosophy which relates to it is termed Moral Philosophy. The superior position occupied by moral philosophy, above all other spheres for the operations of reason, sufficiently indicates the reason why the ancients always included the idea—and in an especial manner—of Moralist in that of Philosopher. Even at the present day, we call a man who appears to have the power of self-government, even although his knowledge may be very limited, by the name of philosopher.

The legislation of human reason, or philosophy, has two objects—Nature and Freedom, and thus contains not only the laws of nature, but also those of ethics, at first in two separate systems, which, finally, merge into one grand philosophical system of cognition. The philosophy of Nature relates to that *which is,* that of Ethics to that which *ought to be.*

But all philosophy is either cognition on the basis of pure reason, or the cognition of reason on the basis of empirical principles. The former is termed pure, the latter empirical philosophy.

The philosophy of pure reason is either *propaedeutic,* that is, an inquiry into the powers of reason in regard to pure *a priori* cognition, and is termed Critical Philosophy; or it is, secondly, the system of pure reason—a science containing the systematic presentation of the whole body of philosophical knowledge, true as well as illusory, given by pure reason, and is called Metaphysics. This name may, however, be also given to the whole system of pure philosophy, critical philosophy included, and may designate the investigation into the sources or possibility of *a priori* cognition, as well as the presentation of the *a priori* cognitions which form a system of pure philosophy—excluding, at the same time, all empirical and mathematical elements.

Metaphysics is divided into that of the *speculative* and that of the *practical* use of pure reason, and is, accordingly, either the *Metaphysics of Nature,* or the *Metaphysics of Ethics.* The former contains all the pure rational principles—based upon conceptions alone (and thus excluding mathematics)—of all *theoretical* cognition; the latter, the principles which determine and necessitate *a priori* all *action.* Now moral philosophy alone contains a code of laws—for the regulation of our actions—which are deduced from principles entirely *a priori*. Hence the Metaphysics of Ethics is the only pure moral philosophy, as it is not based upon anthropological or other empirical considerations. The metaphysics of speculative reason is what is commonly called Metaphysics in the more limited sense. But as pure Moral Philosophy properly forms a part of this system of cognition, we must allow it to retain the name of Metaphysics, although it is not requisite that we should insist on so terming it in our present discussion.

It is of the highest importance to separate those cognitions which differ from others both in kind and in origin, and to take great care that they are not confounded with those, with which they are generally found connected. What the chemist does in the analysis of substances, what the mathematician in pure mathematics, is, in a still higher degree, the duty of the philosopher, that the value of each different kind of cognition, and the part it takes in the operations of the mind, may be clearly defined. Human reason has never wanted a Metaphysics of some kind, since it attained the power of thought, or rather of reflection; but it has never been able to keep this sphere of thought and cognition pure from all admixture of foreign elements. The idea of a science of this kind is as old as speculation itself; and what mind does not speculate—either in the scholastic or in the popular fashion? At the same time, it must be admitted that even thinkers by profession have been unable clearly to explain the distinction between the two elements of our cognition—the one completely *a priori*, the other *a posteriori*; and hence the proper definition of a peculiar kind of cognition, and with it the just idea of a science which has so long and so deeply engaged the attention of the human mind, has never been established. When it was said—Metaphysics is the science of the first principles of human cognition, this definition did not signalise a peculiarity in kind, but only a difference in degree; these first principles were thus declared to be more general than others, but no criterion of distinction from empirical principles was given. Of these some are more general, and therefore higher, than others; and—as we cannot distinguish what is completely *a priori*, from that which is known to be *a posteriori*—where shall we draw the line which is to separate the higher and so-called first principles, from the lower and subordinate principles of cognition? What would be said if we were asked to be satisfied with a division of the epochs of the world into the earlier centuries and those following them? Does the fifth, or the tenth century belong to the earlier centuries? it would be asked. In the same way I ask: Does the conception of extension belong to metaphysics? You answer, yes. Well, that of body too? Yes. And that of a fluid body? You stop, you are unprepared to admit this; for if you do, everything will belong to metaphysics. From this it is evident that the mere degree of subordination—of the particular to the general—cannot determine the limits of a science; and that, in the present case, we must expect to find a difference in the conceptions of metaphysics both in kind and in origin. The fundamental idea of metaphysics was obscured on another side, by the fact that this kind of *à priori* cognition showed a certain similarity in character with the science of mathematics. Both have the property in common of possessing an *a priori* origin; but, in the one, our knowledge is based upon conceptions, in the other, on the construction of conceptions. Thus a decided dissimilarity between philosophical and mathematical cognition comes out—a dissimilarity which was always felt, but which could not be made distinct for want of an insight into the criteria of the difference. And thus it happened that, as philosophers themselves failed in the proper development of the idea of their science, the elaboration of the science could not proceed with a definite aim, or under trustworthy guidance. Thus, too, philosophers, ignorant of the path they ought to pursue, and always disputing with each other regarding the discoveries which each asserted he had made, brought their science into disrepute with the rest of the world, and finally, even among themselves.

All pure *a priori* cognition forms, therefore, in view of the peculiar faculty which originates it, a peculiar and distinct unity; and metaphysic is the term applied to the philosophy which attempts to represent that cognition in this systematic unity. The speculative part of metaphysics, which has especially appropriated this appellation,—that, which we have called the *Metaphysics* of *Nature*,— and which considers everything, as it is (not as it ought to be), by means of *a priori* conceptions, is divided in the following manner.

Metaphysics, in the more limited acceptation of the term, consists of two parts—*Transcendental Philosophy* and the *Physiology* of pure reason. The former presents the system of all the conceptions and principles belonging to the understanding and the reason, and which relate to objects in general, but not to any particular given objects *(Ontologia);* the latter has *nature* for its subject-matter, that is, the sum of given objects—whether given to the senses, or, if we will, to some other kind of intuition,—and is accordingly *Physiology*, although only *rationalis*. But the use of the faculty of reason in this rational mode of regarding nature is either physical or hyperphysical, or, more properly speaking, *immanent* or *transcendent*. The former relates to nature, in so far as our knowledge regarding it may be applied in experience *(in concreto);* the latter to that connection of the objects of experience, which transcends all experience. *Transcendent Physiology* has, again, an *internal* and an *external* connection with its object, both, however, transcending possible experience; the former is the Physiology of nature as a whole, or *transcendental cognition of the world,* the latter of the connection of the whole of nature with a being above nature, or transcendental *cognition of God.*

Immanent physiology, on the contrary, considers nature as the sum of all sensuous objects, consequently, as it is presented to us—but still according to *a priori* conditions, for it is under these alone that nature can be presented to our minds at all. The objects of immanent physiology are of two kinds: 1. those of the external senses, or *corporeal nature;* 2. the object of the internal sense, the soul, or, in accordance with our fundamental conceptions of it, *thinking nature.* The metaphysics of corporeal nature is called *Physics,* but, as it must contain only the principles of an *a priori* cognition of nature, we must term it *rational physics.* The metaphysics of thinking nature is called *Psychology,* and for the same reason is to be regarded as merely the *rational cognition* of the soul.

Thus the whole system of metaphysics consists of four principal parts: 1. *Ontology;* 2. *Rational Physiology;* 3. *Rational Cosmology;* and 4. *Rational Theology.* The second part—that of the rational doctrine of nature—may be subdivided into two, *physica rationalis*[2] and *psychologia rationalis.*

2. It must not be supposed that I mean by this appellation what is generally called *physica generalis,* and which is rather mathematics, than a philosophy of nature. For the metaphysic of nature is completely different from mathematics, nor is it so rich in results, although it is of great importance as a critical test of the application of pure understanding-cognition to nature. For want of its guidance, even mathematicians, adopting certain common notions—which are, in fact, metaphysical—have unconsciously crowded their theories of nature with hypotheses, the fallacy of which becomes evident upon the application of the principles of this metaphysic, without detriment, however, to the employment of mathematics in this sphere of cognition.

The fundamental idea of a philosophy of pure reason of necessity dictates this division; it is, therefore, *architectonical*—in accordance with the highest aims of reason, and not merely *technical,* or according to certain accidentally-observed similarities existing between the different parts of the whole science. For this reason, also, is the division immutable and of legislative authority. But the reader may observe in it a few points to which he ought to demur, and which may weaken his conviction of its truth and legitimacy.

In the first place, how can I desire an *a priori* cognition or metaphysics of objects, in so far as they are given *a posteriori?* and how is it possible to cognize the nature of things according to *a priori* principles, and to attain to a *rational* physiology? The answer is this. We take from experience nothing more than is requisite to present us with an object (in general) of the external, or of the internal sense; in the former case, by the mere conception of matter (impenetrable and inanimate extension), in the latter, by the conception of a thinking being—given in the internal empirical representation, *I think.* As to the rest, we must not employ in our metaphysics of these objects any empirical principles, (which add to the content of our conceptions by means of experience), for the purpose of forming by their help any judgments respecting these objects.

Secondly, what place shall we assign to *empirical psychology,* which has always been considered a part of Metaphysics, and from which in our time such important philosophical results have been expected, after the hope of constructing an *a priori* system of knowledge had been abandoned? I answer: It must be placed by the side of empirical physics or physics proper; that is, must be regarded as forming a part of *applied* philosophy, the *a priori* principles of which are contained in pure philosophy, which is therefore connected, although it must not be confounded, with psychology. Empirical psychology must therefore be banished from the sphere of Metaphysics, and is indeed excluded by the very idea of that science. In conformity, however, with scholastic usage, we must permit it to occupy a place in metaphysics—but only as an appendix to it. We adopt this course from motives of economy; as psychology is not as yet full enough to occupy our attention as an independent study, while it is, at the same time, of too great importance, to be entirely excluded or placed where it has still less affinity than it has with the subject of metaphysics. It is a stranger who has been long a guest; and we make it welcome to stay, until it can take up a more suitable abode in a complete system of Anthropology—the pendant to empirical physics.

The above is the general idea of Metaphysics, which, as more was expected from it than could be looked for with justice, and as these pleasant expectations were unfortunately never realised, fell into general disrepute. Our Critique must have fully convinced the reader, that, although metaphysics cannot form the foundation of religion, it must always be one of its most important bulwarks, and that human reason, which naturally pursues a dialectical course, cannot do without this science, which checks its tendencies towards dialectic, and, by elevating reason to a scientific and clear self-knowledge, prevents the ravages which a lawless speculative reason would infallibly commit in the sphere of morals as well as in that of religion. We may be sure, therefore, whatever contempt may be thrown upon metaphysics by those who judge a science not by its own nature, but according to the accidental effects it may have produced, that it can never be completely abandoned, that we must always return to it as to a beloved one who has been for a time estranged, because the questions with which it is engaged relate to the highest aims of humanity, and reason must always labour either to attain to settled views in regard to these, or to destroy those which others have already established.

Metaphysics, therefore—that of nature, as well as that of ethics, but in an especial manner the criticism which forms the propae-deutic to all the operations of reason—forms properly that department of knowledge which may be termed, in the truest sense of the word, philosophy. The path which it pursues is that of science, which, when it has once been discovered, is never lost, and never misleads. Mathematics, natural science, the common experience of men, have a high value as means, for the most part, to accidental ends,—but at last also, to those which are necessary and essential to the existence of humanity. But to guide them to this high goal, they require the aid of rational cognition on the basis of pure conceptions, which, be it termed as it may, is properly nothing but metaphysics.

For the same reason, metaphysics forms likewise the completion of the *culture* of human reason. In this respect, it is indispensable, setting aside altogether the influence which it exerts as a science.

For its subject-matter is the elements and highest maxims of reason, which form the basis of the *possibility* of some sciences and of the *use* of all. That, as a purely speculative science, it is more useful in preventing error, than in the extension of knowledge, does not detract from its value; on the contrary, the supreme office of censor which it occupies, assures to it the highest authority and importance. This office it administers for the purpose of securing order, harmony, and well-being to science, and of directing its noble and fruitful labours to the highest possible aim—the happiness of all mankind.

# Fourth Chapter
# The History of Pure Reason

This title is placed here merely for the purpose of designating a division of the system of pure reason, of which I do not intend to treat at present. I shall content myself with casting a cursory glance, from a purely transcendental point of view—that of the nature of pure reason, on the labours of philosophers up to the present time. They have aimed at erecting an edifice of philosophy; but to my eye this edifice appears to be in a very ruinous condition.

It is very remarkable, although naturally it could not have been otherwise, that, in the infancy of philosophy, the study of the nature of God, and the constitution of a future world, formed the commencement, rather than the conclusion, as we should have it, of the speculative efforts of the the human mind. However rude the religious conceptions generated by the remains of the old manners and customs of a less cultivated time, the intelligent classes were not thereby prevented from devoting themselves to free inquiry into the existence and nature of God; and they easily saw that there could be no surer way of pleasing the invisible ruler of the world, and of attaining to happiness in another world at least, than a good and honest course of life in this. Thus theology and morals formed the two chief motives, or rather the points of attraction in all abstract inquiries. But it was the former that especially occupied the attention of speculative reason, and which afterwards became so celebrated under the name of metaphysics.

I shall not at present indicate the periods of time at which the greatest changes in metaphysics took place, but shall merely give a hasty sketch of the different ideas which occasioned the most important revolutions in this sphere of thought. There are three different ends, in relation to which these revolutions have taken place.

1. *In relation to the object* of the cognition of reason, philosophers may be divided into *Sensualists* and *Intellectualists. Epicurus* may be regarded as the head of the former, *Plato* of the latter. The distinction here signalised, subtle as it is, dates from the earliest times, and was long maintained. The former asserted, that reality resides in sensuous objects alone, and that everything else is merely imaginary; the latter, that the senses are the parents of illusion, and that truth is to be found in the understanding alone. The former did not deny to the conceptions of the understanding a certain kind of reality; but with them it was merely *logical,* with the others it was *mystical.* The former admitted *intellectual* conceptions, but declared that sensuous objects alone possessed real existence. The latter maintained that all real objects were *intelligible,* and believed that the pure understanding possessed a faculty of *intuition* apart from sense, which, in their opinion, served only to confuse the ideas of the understanding.

2. *In relation to the origin* of the pure cognitions of reason, we find one school maintaining that they are derived entirely from experience, and another, that they have their origin in reason alone. *Aristotle* may be regarded as the head of the *Empiricists,* and *Plato,* of the *Noologists. Locke,* the follower of Aristotle in modern times, and *Leibnitz* of Plato (although he cannot be said to have imitated him in his mysticism), have not been able to bring this question to a settled conclusion. The procedure of Epicurus in his sensual system, in which he always restricted his conclusions to the sphere of experience, was much more consequent than that of Aristotle and Locke. The latter especially, after having derived all the conceptions and principles of the mind from experience, goes so far, in the employment of these conceptions and principles, as to maintain that we can prove the existence of God and the immortality of the soul—both of them objects lying beyond the limits of possible experience—with the same force of demonstration, as any mathematical proposition.

3. *In relation to method.* Method is procedure *according to principles.* We may divide the methods at present employed in the field

of inquiry into the *naturalistic* and the *scientific*. The *naturalist* of pure reason lays it down as his principle, that common reason, without the aid of science—which he calls sound reason, or common sense—can give a more satisfactory answer to the most important questions of metaphysics than speculation is able to do. He must maintain, therefore, that we can determine the content and circumference of the moon more certainly by the naked eye, than by the aid of mathematical reasoning. But this system is mere misology reduced to principles; and, what is the most absurd thing in this doctrine, the neglect of all scientific means is paraded as a *peculiar method* of extending our cognition. As regards those who are *naturalists* because they know no better, they are certainly not to be blamed. They follow common sense, without parading their ignorance as a method which is to teach us the wonderful secret, how we are to find the truth which lies at the bottom of the well of Democritus.

> Quod sapio satis est mihi, non ego curo
> Esse quod Arcesilas aerumnosique Solones,—Pers.

is their motto, under which they may lead a pleasant and praiseworthy life, without troubling themselves with science, or troubling science with them.

As regards those who wish to pursue a scientific method, they have now the choice of following either the *dogmatical* or the *sceptical,* while they are bound never to desert the *systematic* mode of procedure. When I mention, in relation to the former, the celebrated *Wolf,* and as regards the latter, *David Hume,* I may leave, in accordance with my present intention, all others unnamed. The *critical* path alone is still open. If my reader has been kind and patient enough to accompany me on this hitherto untravelled route, he can now judge whether, if he and others will contribute their exertions towards making this narrow foot-path a high-road of thought, that, which many centuries have failed to accomplish, may not be executed before the close of the present—namely, to bring Reason to perfect contentment in regard to that which has always, but without permanent results, occupied her powers and engaged her ardent desire for knowledge.

# FOUNDATIONS
# OF THE METAPHYSICS
# OF MORALS

# Preface

Ancient Greek philosophy was divided into three sciences: physics, ethics, and logic. This division conforms perfectly to the nature of the subject, and one can improve on it perhaps only by supplying its principle in order both to insure its exhaustiveness and to define correctly the necessary subdivisions.

All rational knowledge is either material, and concerns some object, or formal, and is occupied merely with the form of understanding and reason itself and with the universal roles of thinking without regard to distinctions between objects. Formal philosophy is called logic. Material philosophy, however, which has to do with definite objects and the laws to which they are subject, is itself divided into two parts. This is because these laws are either laws of nature or laws of freedom. The science of the former is called physics and that of the latter ethics. The former is also called theory of nature and the latter theory of morals.

Logic can have no empirical part—a part in which universal and necessary laws of thinking would rest upon grounds taken from experience. For in that case it would not be logic, i.e., a canon for understanding or reason which is valid for all thinking and which must be demonstrated. But, on the other hand, natural and moral philosophy can each have its empirical part. The former must do so, for it must determine the laws of nature as an object of experience, and the latter because it must determine the human will so far as it is affected by nature. The laws of the former are laws according to which everything happens; those of the latter are laws according to which everything should happen, but allow for conditions under which what should happen often does not.

All philosophy, so far as it is based on experience, may be called empirical; but, so far as it presents its doctrines solely on the basis of a priori principles, it may be called pure philosophy. The latter, when merely formal, is logic; when limited to define objects of understanding, it is metaphysics.

In this way there arises the idea of a twofold metaphysics—a metaphysics of nature and a metaphysics of morals. Physics, therefore, will have an empirical and also a rational part, and ethics likewise. In ethics, however, the empirical part may be called more specifically practical anthropology; the rational part, morals proper.

All crafts, handiworks, and arts have gained by the division of labor, for when one person does not do everything, but each limits himself to a particular job which is distinguished from all the others by the treatment it requires, he can do it with greater perfection and with more facility. Where work is not thus differentiated and divided, where everyone is a jack-of-all-trades, the crafts remain at a barbaric level. It might be worth considering whether pure philosophy in each of its parts does not require a man particularly devoted to it, and whether it would not be better for the learned profession as a whole to warn those who are in the habit of catering to the taste of the public by mixing up the empirical with the rational in all sorts of proportions which they do not themselves know and who call themselves independent thinkers (giving the name of speculator to those who apply themselves to the merely rational part). This warning would be that they should not at one and the same time carry on two employments which differ widely in the treatment they require, and for each of which perhaps a special talent is needed since the combination of these talents in one person produces only bunglers. I ask only whether the nature of the science does not require that a careful separation of the empirical from the rational part be made, with a metaphysics of nature put before real (empirical) physics and a metaphysics of morals before practical anthropology. These prior sciences must be carefully purified of everything empirical so that we can know how much pure reason can accomplish in each case and from what sources it creates its a priori teaching, whether the latter inquiry be conducted by all moralists (whose name is legion) or only by some who feel a calling to it.

Since my purpose here is directed to moral philosophy, I narrow the proposed question to this: Is it not of the utmost necessity to construct a pure moral philosophy which is completely freed from everything which may be only empirical and thus belong to anthropology? That there must be such a philosophy is self-evident from the common idea of duty and moral laws. Everyone must admit that a law, if it is to hold morally, i.e., as a ground of obligation, must imply absolute necessity; he must admit that the command, "Thou shalt not lie," does not apply to men only, as if other rational beings had no need to observe it. The same is true for all other moral laws properly so called. He must concede that the ground of obligation here must not be sought in the nature of man or in the circumstances in which he is placed, but sought a priori solely in the concepts of pure reason, and that every other precept which rests on principles of mere experience, even a precept which is in certain respects universal, so far as it leans in the least on empirical grounds (perhaps only in regard to the motive involved), may be called a practical rule but never a moral law.

Thus not only are moral laws together with their principles essentially different from all practical knowledge in which there is anything empirical, but all moral philosophy rests solely on its pure part. Applied to man, it borrows nothing from knowledge of him (anthropology) but gives him, as a rational being, a priori laws. No doubt these laws require a power of judgment sharpened by experience, partly in order to decide in what cases they apply and partly to procure for them an access to man's will and an impetus to their practice. For man is affected by so many inclinations that, though he is capable of the idea of practical pure reason, he is not so easily able to make it concretely effective in the conduct of his life.

A metaphysics of morals is therefore indispensable, not merely because of motives to speculate on the source of the a priori practical principles which lie in our reason, but also because morals themselves remain subject to all kinds of corruption so long as the guide and supreme norm for their correct estimation is lacking. For it is not sufficient to that which should be morally good that it conform to the law; it must be done for the sake of the law. Otherwise the conformity is merely contingent and spurious, because, though the unmoral ground may indeed now and then produce lawful actions, more often it brings forth unlawful ones. But the moral law can be found in its purity and genuineness (which is the central concern in the practical) nowhere else than in a pure philosophy; therefore, this (i.e., metaphysics) must lead the way, and without it there can be no moral philosophy. Philosophy which mixes pure principles with empirical ones does not deserve the name, for what distinguishes philosophy from common rational knowledge is its treatment in separate sciences of what is confusedly comprehended in such knowledge. Much less does it deserve the name of moral philosophy, since by this confusion it spoils the purity of morals themselves and works contrary to its own end.

It should not be thought that what is here required is already present in the celebrated Wolff's propaedeutic to his moral philosophy, i.e., in what he calls universal practical philosophy, and that it is not an entirely new field that is to be opened. Precisely because his work was to be universal practical philosophy, it deduced no will of any particular kind, such as one determined without any empirical motives but completely by a priori principles; in a word, it had nothing which could be called a pure will, since it considered only volition in general with all the actions and conditions which pertain to it in this general sense. Thus his propaedeutic differs from a metaphysics of morals in the same way that general logic is distinguished from transcendental philosophy, the former expounding the actions and rules of thinking in general, and the latter presenting the particular actions and rules of pure thinking, i.e., of thinking by which objects are known completely a priori. For the metaphysics of morals is meant to investigate the idea and principles of a possible pure will and not the actions and conditions of the human volition as such, which are for the most part drawn from psychology.

That in general practical philosophy laws and duty are discussed (though improperly) is no objection to my assertion. For the authors of this science remain even here true to their idea of it. They do not distinguish the motives which are presented completely a priori by reason alone, and which are thus moral in the proper sense of the word, from the empirical motives which the understanding, by comparing experiences, elevates to universal concepts. Rather, they consider motives without regard to the difference in their source but only with reference to their greater or smaller number (as they are considered to be all of the same kind); they thus formulate their concept of obligation, which is anything but moral, but which is all that can be desired in a philosophy that does not decide whether the origin of all possible practical concepts is a priori or only a posteriori.

As a preliminary to a metaphysics of morals which I intend some day to publish, I issue these *Foundations*. There is, to be sure, no other foundation for such a metaphysics than a critical examination of a pure practical reason, just as there is no other foundation for metaphysics than the already published critical examination of the pure speculative reason. But, in the first place, a critical examination of pure practical reason is not of such extreme importance as that of speculative reason, because human reason, even in the commonest mind, can easily be brought to a high degree of correctness and completeness in moral matters, while, on the other hand, in its theoretical but pure use it is entirely dialectical. In the second place, I require of a critical examination of a pure practical reason, if it is to be complete, that its unity with the speculative be subject to presentation under a common principle, because in the final analysis there can be but one and the same reason which must be differentiated only in application. But I could not bring this to such a completeness without bringing in observations of an altogether different kind and without thereby confusing the reader. For these reasons I have employed the title, *Foundation of the Metaphysics of Morals*, instead of *Critique of Pure Practical Reason*.

Because, in the third place, a metaphysics of morals, in spite of its forbidding title, is capable of a high degree of popularity and adaptation to common understanding, I find it useful to separate this preliminary work of laying the foundation in order not to have to introduce unavoidable subtleties into the later, more comprehensive work.

The present foundations, however, are nothing more than the search for and establishment of the supreme principle of morality. This constitutes a task altogether complete in its intention and one which should be kept separate from all other moral inquiry.

My conclusions concerning this important question, which has not yet been discussed nearly enough, would, of course, be clarified by application of the principle to the whole system of morality, and it would receive much confirmation by the adequacy which it would everywhere show. But I must forego this advantage, which would in the final analysis be more privately gratifying than commonly useful, because ease of use and apparent adequacy of a principle are not any sure proof of its correctness, but rather awaken a certain partiality which prevents a rigorous investigation and evaluation of it for itself without regard to consequences.

I have adopted in this writing the method which is, I think, most suitable if one wishes to proceed analytically from common knowledge to the determination of its supreme principle, and then synthetically from the examination of this principle and its sources back to common knowledge where it finds its application. The division is therefore as follows:

1. First Section. Transition from the Common Rational Knowledge of Morals to the Philosophical
2. Second Section. Transition from the Popular Moral Philosophy to the Metaphysics of Morals
3. Third Section. Final Step from the Metaphysics of Morals to the Critical Examination of Pure Practical Reason.

# First Section

*Transition from the Common
Rational Knowledge of Morals
to the Philosophical*

Nothing in the world—indeed nothing even beyond the world—
can possibly be conceived which could be called good without
qualification except a *good will*. Intelligence, wit, judgment, and
the other talents of the mind, however they may be named, or
courage, resoluteness, and perseverance as qualities of temperament, are doubtless in many respects good and desirable. But they
can become extremely bad and harmful if the will, which is to make
use of these gifts of nature and which in its special constitution is
called character, is not good. It is the same with the gifts of fortune.
Power, riches, honor, even health, general well-being, and the contentment with one's condition which is called happiness, make for
pride and even arrogance if there is not a good will to correct their
influence on the mind and on its principles of action so as to make
it universally conformable to its end. It need hardly be mentioned
that the sight of a being adorned with no feature of a pure and
good will, yet enjoying uninterrupted prosperity, can never give
pleasure to a rational impartial observer. Thus the good will seems
to constitute the indispensable condition even of worthiness to be
happy.

Some qualities seem to be conducive to this good will and can
facilitate its action, but, in spite of that, they have no intrinsic
unconditional worth. They rather presuppose a good will, which
limits the high esteem which one otherwise rightly has for them

and prevents their being held to be absolutely good. Moderation in emotions and passions, self-control, and calm deliberation not only are good in many respects but even seem to constitute a part of the inner worth of the person. But however unconditionally they were esteemed by the ancients, they are far from being good without qualification. For without the principle of a good will they can become extremely bad, and the coolness of a villain makes him not only far more dangerous but also more directly abominable in our eyes than he would have seemed without it.

The good will is not good because of what it effects or accomplishes or because of its adequacy to achieve some proposed end; it is good only because of its willing, i.e., it is good of itself. And, regarded for itself, it is to be esteemed incomparably higher than anything which could be brought about by it in favor of any inclination or even of the sum total of all inclinations. Even if it should happen that, by a particularly unfortunate fate or by the niggardly provision of a stepmotherly nature, this will should be wholly lacking in power to accomplish its purpose, and if even the greatest effort should not avail it to achieve anything of its end, and if there remained only the good will (not as a mere wish but as the summoning of all the means in our power), it would sparkle like a jewel in its own right, as something that had its full worth in itself. Usefulness or fruitfulness can neither diminish nor augment this worth. Its usefulness would be only its setting, as it were, so as to enable us to handle it more conveniently in commerce or to attract the attention of those who are not yet connoisseurs, but not to recommend it to those who are experts or to determine its worth.

But there is something so strange in this idea of the absolute worth of the will alone, in which no account is taken of any use, that, notwithstanding, the agreement even of common sense, the suspicion must arise that perhaps only high-flown fancy is its hidden basis, and that we may have misunderstood the purpose of nature in its appointment of reason as the ruler of our will. We shall therefore examine this idea from this point of view.

In the natural constitution of an organized being, i.e., one suitably adapted to life, we assume as an axiom that no organ will be found for any purpose which is not the fittest and best adapted to that purpose. Now if its preservation, its welfare—in a word, its happiness—were the real end of nature in a being having reason and will, then nature would have hit upon a very poor arrangement in appointing the reason of the creature to be the executor of this purpose. For all the actions which the creature has to perform with this intention, and the entire rule of its conduct, would be dictated much more exactly by instinct, and that end would be far more certainly attained by instinct than it ever could be by reason. And if, over and above this, reason should have been granted to the favored creature, it would have served only to let it contemplate the happy constitution of its nature, to admire it, to rejoice in it, and to be grateful for it to its beneficent cause. But reason would not have been given in order that the being should subject its faculty of desire to that weak and delusive guidance and to meddle with the purpose of nature. In a word, nature would have taken care that reason did not break forth into practical use nor have the presumption, with its weak insight, to think out for itself the plan of happiness and the means of attaining it. Nature would have taken over not only the choice of ends but also that of the means, and with wise foresight she would have entrusted both to instinct alone.

And, in fact, we find that the more of a cultivated reason deliberately devotes itself to the enjoyment of life and happiness, the more the man falls short of true contentment. From this fact there arises in many persons, if only they are candid enough to admit it, a certain degree of misology, hatred of reason. This is particularly the case with those who are most experienced in its use. After counting all the advantages which they draw—I will not say from the invention of the arts of common luxury—from the sciences (which in the end seem to them to be also a luxury of the understanding), they nevertheless find that they have actually brought more trouble on their shoulders instead of gaining in happiness; they finally envy, rather than despise, the common run of men who are better guided by mere natural instinct and who do not permit their reason much influence on their conduct. And we must at least admit that a morose attitude or ingratitude to the goodness with which the world is governed is by no means found always among those who temper or refute the boasting eulogies which are given of the advantages of happiness and contentment with which reason is supposed to supply us. Rather their judgment is based on the idea of another and far more worthy purpose of their existence for which, instead of happiness, their reason is properly intended, this purpose, therefore, being the supreme condition to which the private purposes of men must for the most part defer.

Reason is not, however, competent to guide the will safely with regard to its objects and the satisfaction of all our needs (which it in part multiplies), and to this end an innate instinct would have led with far more certainty. But reason is given to us as a practical faculty, i.e., one which is meant to have an influence on the will. As nature has elsewhere distributed capacities suitable to the functions they are to perform, reason's proper function must be to produce a will good in itself and not one good merely as a means, for to the former reason is absolutely essential. This will must indeed not be the sole and complete good but the highest good and the condition of all others, even of the desire for happiness. In this case it is entirely compatible with the wisdom of nature that the cultivation of reason, which is required for the former unconditional purpose, at least in this life restricts in many ways—indeed can reduce to less than nothing—the achievement of the latter conditional purpose, happiness. For one perceives that nature here does not proceed unsuitably to its purpose, because reason, which recognizes its highest practical vocation in the establishment of a good will, is capable only of a contentment of its own kind, i.e., one that springs from the attainment of a purpose which is determined by reason, even though this injures the ends of inclination.

We have, then, to develop the concept of a will which is to be esteemed as good of itself without regard to anything else. It dwells already in the natural sound understanding and does not need so much to be taught as only to be brought to light. In the estimation of the total worth of our actions it always takes first place and is the condition of everything else. In order to show this, we shall take the concept of duty. It contains that of a good will, though with certain subjective restrictions and hindrances; but these are far from concealing it and making it unrecognizable, for they rather bring it out by contrast and make it shine forth all the brighter.

I here omit all actions which are recognized as opposed to duty, even though they may be useful in one respect or another, for with these the question does not arise at all as to whether they may be carried out *from* duty, since they conflict with it. I also pass over the actions which are really in accordance with duty and to which one has no direct inclination, rather executing them because impelled to do so by another inclination. For it is easily decided whether an action in accord with duty is performed from duty or from some selfish purpose. It is far more difficult to note this difference when the action is in accordance with duty and, in addition, the subject has a direct inclination to do it. For example, it is in fact in accordance with duty that a dealer should not overcharge an inexperienced customer, and wherever there is much business the prudent merchant does not do so, having a fixed price for everyone, so that a child may buy of him as cheaply as any other. Thus the customer is honestly served. But this is far from sufficient to justify the belief that the merchant has behaved in this way from duty and principles of honesty. His own advantage required this behavior; but it cannot be assumed that over and above that he had a direct inclination to the purchaser and that, out of love, he gave none an advantage in price over another. Therefore the action was done neither from duty nor from direct inclination but only for a selfish purpose.

On the other hand, it is a duty to preserve one's life, and moreover everyone has a direct inclination to do so. But for that reason the often anxious care which most men take of it has no intrinsic worth, and the maxim of doing so has no moral import. They preserve their lives according to duty, but not from duty. But if adversities and hopeless sorrow completely take away the relish for life, if an unfortunate man, strong in soul, is indignant rather than despondent or dejected over his fate and wishes for death, and yet preserves his life without loving it and from neither inclination nor fear but from duty—then his maxim has a moral import.

To be kind where one can is duty, and there are, moreover, many persons so sympathetically constituted that without any motive of vanity or selfishness they find an inner satisfaction in spreading joy, and rejoice in the contentment of others which they have made possible. But I say that, however dutiful and amiable it may be, that kind of action has no true moral worth. It is on a level with [actions arising from] other inclinations, such as the inclination to honor, which, if fortunately directed to what in fact accords with duty and is generally useful and thus honorable, deserve praise and encouragement but no esteem. For the maxim lacks the moral import of an action done not from inclination but from duty. But assume that the mind of that friend to mankind was clouded by a sorrow of his own which extinguished all sympathy with the lot of others and that he still had the power to benefit others in distress, but that their need left him untouched because he was preoccupied with his own need. And now suppose him to tear himself, unsolicited by inclination, out of this dead insensibility and to perform this action only from duty and without any inclination—then for the first time his action has genuine moral worth. Furthermore, if nature has put little sympathy in the heart of a man, and if he, though an honest man, is by temperament cold and indifferent to the sufferings of others, perhaps because he is provided with special gifts of patience and fortitude and expects or even requires that others should have the same—and such a man would certainly not be the meanest product of nature—would not he find in himself a source from which to give himself a far higher worth than he could have got by having a good-natured temperament? This is unquestionably true even though nature did not make him a philanthropic, for it is just here that the worth of the character is brought out, which is morally and incomparably the highest of all: he is beneficent not from inclination but from duty.

To secure one's own happiness is at least indirectly a duty, for discontent with one's condition under pressure from many cares and amid unsatisfied wants could easily become a great temptation to transgress duties. But without any view to duty all men have the strongest and deepest inclination to happiness, because in this idea all inclinations are summed up. But the precept of happiness is often so formulated that it definitely thwarts some inclinations, and men can make no definite and certain concept of the sum of satisfaction of all inclinations which goes under the name of happiness. It is not to be wondered at, therefore, that a single inclination, definite as to what it promises and as to the time at which it can be satisfied, can outweigh a fluctuating idea, and that, for example, a man with the gout can choose to enjoy what he likes and to suffer what he may, because according to his calculations at least on this occasion he has not sacrificed the enjoyment of the present moment to a perhaps groundless expectation of a happiness supposed to lie in health. But even in this case, if the universal inclination to happiness did not determine his will, and if health were not at least for him a necessary factor in these calculations, there yet would remain, as in all other cases, a law that he ought to promote his happiness, not from inclination but from duty. Only from this law would his conduct have true moral worth.

It is in this way, undoubtedly, that we should understand those passages of Scripture which command us to love our neighbor and even our enemy, for love as an inclination cannot be commanded. But beneficence from duty, when no inclination impels it and even when it is opposed by a natural and unconquerable aversion, is practical love, not pathological love; it resides in the will and not in the propensities of feeling, in principles of action and not in tender sympathy; and it alone can be commanded.

[Thus the first proposition of morality is that to have moral worth an action must be done from duty.] The second proposition is: An action performed from duty does not have its moral worth in the purpose by which is to be achieved through it but in the maxim by which it is determined. Its moral value, therefore, does not depend on the realization of the object of the action but merely on the principle of volition by which the action is done, without any regard to the objects of the faculty of desire. From the preceding discussion it is clear that the purposes we may have for our actions and their effects as ends and incentives of the will cannot give the actions any unconditional and moral worth. Wherein, then, can this worth lie, if it is not in the will in relation to its hoped-for effect? It can lie nowhere else than in the principle of the will, irrespective of the ends which can be realized by such action. For the will stands, as it were, at the crossroads halfway between its a priori principle which is formal and its a posteriori incentive which is material. Since it must be determined by something, if it is done from duty it must be determined by the formal principle of volition as such since every material principle has been withdrawn from it.

The third principle, as a consequence of the two preceding, I would express as follows: Duty is the necessity of an action executed from respect for law. I can certainly have an inclination to the object as an effect of the proposed action, but I can never have respect for it precisely because it is a mere effect and not an activity of a will. Similarly, I can have no respect for any inclination whatsoever, whether my own or that of another; in the former case I can at most approve of it and in the latter I can even love it, i.e., see it as favorable to my own advantage. But that which is connected with my will merely as ground and not as consequence, that which does not serve my inclination but overpowers it or at least excludes it from being considered in making a choice—in a word, law itself—can be an object of respect and thus a command. Now as an act from duty wholly excludes the influence of inclination and therewith every object of the will, nothing remains which can determine the will objectively except the law, and nothing subjectively except pure respect for this practical law. This subjective element is the maxim[1] that I ought to follow such a law even if it thwarts all my inclinations.

Thus the moral worth of an action does not lie in the effect which is expected from it or in any principle of action which has to borrow its motive from this expected effect. For all these effects (agreeableness of my own condition, indeed even the promotion of the happiness of others) could be brought about through other causes and would not require the will of a rational being, while the highest and unconditional good can be found only in such a will. Therefore, the pre-eminent good can consist only in the conception of the law in itself (which can be present only in a rational being) so far as this conception and not the hoped-for effect is the determining ground of the will. This pre-eminent good, which we call moral, is already present in the person who acts according to this conception, and we do not have to look for it first in the result.[2]

But what kind of a law can that be, the conception of which must determine the will without reference to the expected result?

1. A maxim is the subjective principle of volition. The objective principle (i.e., that which would serve all rational beings also subjectively as a practical principle if reason had full power over the faculty of desire) is the practical law.

2. It might be objected that I seek to take refuge in an obscure feeling behind the word "respect," instead of clearly resolving the question with a concept of reason. But though respect is a feeling, it is not one received through any [outer] influence but is self-wrought by a rational concept: thus it differs specifically from all feelings of the former kind which may be referred to inclination or fear. What I recognize directly as a law for myself I recognize with respect, which means merely the consciousness of the submission of my will to a law without the intervention of other influences on my mind. The direct determination of the will by the law and the consciousness of this determination is respect: this respect can be regarded as the effect of the law on the subject and not as the cause of the law. Respect is properly the conception of a worth which thwarts my self-love. Thus it is regarded as an object neither of inclination nor of fear, though it has something analogous to both. The only object of respect is the law, and indeed only the law which we impose on ourselves and yet recognize as necessary in itself. As a law, we are subject to it without consulting self-love; as imposed on us by ourselves, it is a consequence of our will. In the former respect it is analogous to fear and in the latter to inclination. All respect for a person is only respect for the law (of righteousness, etc.) of which the person provides an example. Because we see the improvement of our talents as a duty, we think of a person of talents as the example of a law, as it were (the law that we should by practice become like him in his talents), and that constitutes our respect. All so-called moral interest consists solely in respect for the law.

Under this condition alone the will can be called absolutely good without qualification. Since I have robbed the will of all impulses which could come to it from obedience to any law, nothing remains to serve as a principle of the will except universal conformity of its action to law as such. That is, I should never act in such a way that I could not also will that my maxim should be a universal law. Mere conformity to law as such (without assuming any particular law applicable to certain actions) serves as the principle of the will, and it must serve as such a principle if duty is not to be a vain delusion and chimerical concept. The common reason of mankind in its practical judgments is in perfect agreement with this and has this principle constantly in view.

Let the question, for example, be: May I, when in distress, make a promise with the intention not to keep it? I easily distinguish the two meanings which the question can have, viz., whether it is prudent to make a false promise, or whether it conforms to my duty. Undoubtedly the former can often be the case, though I do see clearly that it is not sufficient merely to escape from the present difficulty by this expedient, but that I must consider whether inconveniences much greater than the present one may not later spring from this lie. Even with all my supposed cunning, the consequences cannot be so easily foreseen. Loss of credit might be far more disadvantageous than the misfortune I now seek to avoid, and it is hard to tell whether it might not be more prudent to act according to a universal maxim and to make it a habit not to promise anything without intending to fulfill it. But it is soon clear to me that such a maxim is based only on an apprehensive concern with consequences.

To be truthful from duty, however, is an entirely different thing from being truthful out of fear of disadvantageous consequences, for in the former case the concept of the action itself contains a law for me, while in the latter I must first look about to see what results for me may be connected with it. For to deviate from the principle of duty is certainly bad, but to be unfaithful to my maxim of prudence can sometimes be very advantageous to me, though it is certainly safer to abide by it. The shortest but most infallible way to find the answer to the question as to whether a deceitful promise is consistent with duty is to ask myself: Would I be content that my maxim (of extricating myself from difficulty by a false promise) should hold as a universal law for myself as well as for others? And could I say to myself that everyone may make a false promise when he is in a difficulty from which he otherwise cannot escape? I immediately see that I could will the lie but not a universal law to lie. For with such a law there would be no promises at all, inasmuch as it would be futile to make a pretense of my intention in regard to future actions to those who would not believe this pretense or— if they overhastily did so—who would pay me back in my own coin. Thus my maxim would necessarily destroy itself as soon as it was made a universal law.

I do not, therefore, need any penetrating acuteness in order to discern what I have to do in order that my volition may be morally good. Inexperienced in the course of the world, incapable of being prepared for all its contingencies, I ask myself only: Can I will that my maxim become a universal law? If not, it must be rejected, not because of any disadvantage accruing to myself or even to others, but because it cannot enter as a principle into a possible universal legislation, and reason extorts from me an immediate respect for such legislation. I do not as yet discern on what it is grounded (a question the philosopher may investigate), but I at least understand that it is an estimation of the worth which far outweighs all the worth of whatever is recommended by the inclinations, and that the necessity of my actions from pure respect for the practical law constitutes duty. To duty every other motive must give place, because duty is the condition of a will good in itself, whose worth transcends everything.

Thus within the moral knowledge of common human reason we have attained its principle. To be sure, common human reason does not think of it abstractly in such a universal form, but it always has it in view and uses it as the standard of its judgments. It would be easy to show how common human reason, with this compass, knows well how to distinguish what is good, what is bad, and what is consistent or inconsistent with duty. Without in the least teaching common reason anything new, we need only to draw its attention to its own principle, in the manner of Socrates, thus showing that neither science nor philosophy is needed in order to know what one has to do in order to be honest and good, and even wise and virtuous. We might have conjectured beforehand that the knowledge of what everyone is obliged to do and thus also to know would be within the reach of everyone, even the most ordinary man. Here we cannot but admire the great advantages which the practical faculty of judgment has over the theoretical in ordinary human understanding. In the theoretical, if ordinary reason ventures to go beyond the laws of experience and perceptions of the senses, it falls into sheer inconceivabilities and self-contradictions, or at least into a chaos of uncertainty, obscurity, and instability. In the practical, on the other hand, the power of judgment first shows itself to advantage when common understanding excludes all sensuous incentives from practical laws. It then becomes even subtle, quibbling with its own conscience or with other claims to what should be called right, or wishing to determine correctly for its own instruction the worth of certain actions. But the most remarkable thing about ordinary reason in its practical concern is that it may have as much hope as any philosopher of hitting the mark. In fact, it is almost more certain to do so than the philosopher, because he has no principle which the common understanding lacks, while his judgment is easily confused by a mass of irrelevant considerations, so that it easily turns aside from the correct way. Would it not, therefore, be wiser in moral matters to acquiesce in the common rational judgment, or at most to call in philosophy in order to make the system of morals more complete and comprehensible and its rules more convenient for use (especially in disputation) than to steer the common understanding from its happy simplicity in practical matters and to lead it through philosophy into a new path of inquiry and instruction?

Innocence is indeed a glorious thing, but, on the other hand, it is very sad that it cannot well maintain itself, being easily led astray. For this reason, even wisdom—which consists more in acting than in knowing—needs science, not to learn from it but to secure admission and permanence to its precepts. Man feels in himself a powerful counterpoise against all commands of duty which reason presents to him as so deserving of respect; this counterpoise is his needs and inclinations, the complete satisfaction of which he sums up under the name of happiness. Now reason issues inexorable commands without promising anything to the inclinations. It disregards, as it were, and holds in contempt those claims which are so impetuous and yet so plausible, and which will not allow themselves to be abolished by any command. From this a natural dialectic arises, i.e., a propensity to argue against the stern laws of duty and their validity, or at least to place their purity and strictness in doubt and, where possible, to make them more accordant with our wishes and inclinations. This is equivalent to corrupting them in their very foundations and destroying their dignity—a thing which even common practical reason cannot ultimately call good.

In this way common human reason is impelled to go outside its sphere and to take a step into the field of practical philosophy. But it is forced to do so not by any speculative need, which never occurs to it so long as it is satisfied to remain merely healthy reason; rather, it is so impelled on practical grounds in order to obtain information and clear instruction respecting the source of its principle and the correct determination of this principle in its opposition to the maxims which are based on need and inclination. It seeks this information in order to escape from the perplexity of opposing claims and to avoid the danger of losing all genuine moral principles through the equivocation in which it is easily involved. Thus, when practical common reason cultivates itself, a dialectic surreptitiously ensues which forces it to seek aid in philosophy, just as the same thing happens in the theoretical use of reason. In this case, as in the theoretical, it will find rest only in a thorough critical examination of our reason.

# Second Section
## Transition from the Popular Moral Philosophy to the Metaphysics of Morals

If we have derived our earlier concept of duty from the common use of our practical reason, it is by no means to be inferred that we have treated it as an empirical concept. On the contrary, if we attend to our experience of the way men act, we meet frequent and, as we ourselves confess, justified complaints that we cannot cite a single sure example of the disposition to act from pure duty. There are also justified complaints that, though much may be done that accords with what duty commands, it is nevertheless always doubtful whether it is done from duty, and thus whether it has moral worth. There have always been philosophers who for this reason have absolutely denied the reality of this disposition in human actions, attributing everything to more or less refined self-love. They have done so without questioning the correctness of the concept of morality. Rather they have spoken with sincere regret of the frailty and corruption of human nature, which is noble enough to take as its precept an idea so worthy of respect but which at the same time is too weak to follow it, employing reason, which should legislate for human nature, only to provide for the interest of the inclinations either singly or, at best, in their greatest possible harmony with one another.

It is in fact absolutely impossible by experience to discern with complete certainty a single case in which the maxim of an action, however much it may conform to duty, rested solely on moral grounds and on the conception of one's duty. It sometimes happens that in the most searching self-examination we can find nothing except the moral ground of duty which could have been powerful enough to move us to this or that good action and to such great sacrifice. But from this we cannot by any means conclude with certainty that a secret impulse of self-love, falsely appearing as the idea of duty, was not actually the true determining cause of the will. For we like to flatter ourselves with a pretended nobler motive, while in fact even the strictest examination can never lead us entirely behind the secret incentives, for, when moral worth is in question, it is not a matter of actions which one sees but of their inner principles which one does not see.

Moreover, one cannot better serve the wishes of those who ridicule all morality as a mere phantom of human imagination overreaching itself through self-conceit than by conceding to them that the concepts of duty must be derived only from experience (for they are ready to believe from indolence that this is true of all other concepts too). For, by this concession, a sure triumph is prepared for them. Out of love for humanity I am willing to admit that most of our actions are in accordance with duty; but, if we look more closely at our thoughts and aspirations, we everywhere come upon the dear self, which is always there, and it is this instead of the stern command of duty (which would often require self-denial), which supports our plans. One need not be an enemy of virtue, but only a cool observer who does not confuse even the liveliest aspiration for the good with its reality, to be doubtful sometimes whether true virtue can really be found anywhere in the world. This is especially true as one's years increase and one's power of judgment is made wiser by experience and more acute in observation. This being so, nothing can secure us against the complete abandonment of our ideas of duty and preserve in us a well-founded respect for its law except the clear conviction that, even if there never were actions springing from such pure sources, our concern is not whether this or that was done but that reason of itself and independently of all appearances commands what ought to be done. Our concern is with actions of which perhaps the world has never had an example, with actions whose feasibility might be seriously doubted by those who base everything on experience, and yet with actions inexorably commanded by reason. For example, pure sincerity in friendship can be demanded of every man, and this demand is not in the least diminished if a sincere friend has never existed, because this duty, as duty in general, prior to all experience, lies in the idea of a reason which determines the will by a priori grounds.

It is clear that no experience can give occasion for inferring the possibility of such apodictic laws. This is especially clear when we add that, unless we wish to deny all truth to the concept of morality and renounce its application to any possible object, we cannot refuse to admit that the law of this concept is of such broad significance that it holds not merely for men but for all rational beings as such; we must grant that it must be valid with absolute necessity and not merely under contingent conditions and with exceptions. For with what right could we bring into unlimited respect something that might be valid only under contingent human conditions? And how could laws of the determination of our will be held to be laws of the determination of the will of a rational being in general and of ourselves in so far as we are rational beings, if they were merely empirical and did not have their origin completely a priori in pure, but practical, reason?

Nor could one give poorer counsel to morality than to attempt to derive it from examples. For each example of morality which is exhibited to me must itself have been previously judged according to principles of morality to see whether it is worthy to serve as an original example, i.e., as a model. By no means could it authoritatively furnish the concept of morality. Even the Holy One of the Gospel must be compared with our ideal of moral perfection before He is recognized as such; even He says of Himself, "Why call ye Me (whom you see) good? None is good (the archetype of the good) except God only (whom you do not see)." But whence do we have the concept of God as the highest good? Solely from the idea of moral perfection which reason formulates a priori and which it inseparably connects with the concept of a free will. Imitation has no place in moral matters, and examples serve only for encouragement. That is, they put beyond question the practicability of what the law commands, and they make visible that which the practical rule expresses more generally. But they can never justify our guiding ourselves by examples and our setting aside their true original which lies in reason.

If there is thus no genuine supreme principle of morality which does not rest merely on pure reason independently of all experience, I do not believe it is necessary even to ask whether it is well to exhibit these concepts generally (*in abstracto*), which, together with the principles belonging to them, are established a priori. At any rate, this question need not be asked if knowledge which establishes this is to be distinguished from ordinary knowledge and called philosophical. But in our times this question may perhaps be necessary. For if we collected votes as to whether pure rational knowledge separated from all experience, i.e., metaphysics of morals, or popular practical philosophy is to be preferred, it is easily guessed on which side the majority would stand.

This condescension to popular notions is certainly very commendable once the ascent to the principles of pure reason has been satisfactorily accomplished. That would mean the prior establishment of the doctrine of morals on metaphysics and then, when it is established, to procure a hearing for it through popularization. But it is extremely absurd to want to achieve popularity in the first investigation, when everything depends on the correctness of the fundamental principles. Not only can this procedure never make claim to that rarest merit of true philosophical popularity, since there is really no art in being generally comprehensible if one thereby renounces all basic insight, but it produces a disgusting jumble of patched-up observations and half-reasoned principles. Shallowpates enjoy this, for it is very useful in everyday chitchat, while the more sensible feel confused and dissatisfied without being able to help themselves. They turn their eyes away, even though philosophers, who see very well through the delusion, find little audience when they call men away for a time from this pretended popularization in order that they may rightly appear popular after they have attained a definite insight.

One need only look at the essays on morality which that popular taste favors. One will sometimes meet with the particular vocation of human nature (but occasionally also the idea of a rational nature in general), sometimes perfection, and sometimes happiness, here moral feeling, there fear of God, a little of this and a little of that in a marvelous mixture. However, it never occurs to the authors to ask whether the principles of morality are, after all, to be sought anywhere in knowledge of human nature (which we can derive only from experience). And if this is not the case, if the principles are completely a priori, free from everything empirical, and found exclusively in pure rational concepts and not at all in any other place, they never ask whether they should undertake this investigation as a separate inquiry, i.e., as pure practical philosophy or (if one may use a name so decried) a metaphysics[1] of morals. They never think of dealing with it alone and bringing it by itself to completeness, and of requiring the public, which desires popularization, to await the outcome of this undertaking.

But a completely isolated metaphysics of morals, mixed with no anthropology, no theology, no physics or hyperphysics, and even less with occult qualities (which might be called hypophysical), is not only an indispensable substrate of all theoretically sound and definite knowledge of duties; it is also a desideratum of the highest importance to the actual fulfillment of its precepts. For the pure conception of duty and of the moral law generally, with no admixture of empirical inducements, has an influence on the human heart so much more powerful than all other incentives[2] which may be derived from the empirical field that reason, in the consciousness of its dignity, despises them and gradually becomes master over them. It has this influence only through reason, which thereby first realizes that it can of itself be practical. A mixed theory of morals which is put together both from incentives of feelings and incli-

1. If one wishes, the pure philosophy of morals (metaphysics) can be distinguished from the applied (i.e., applied to human nature), just as pure mathematics and pure logic are distinguished from applied mathematics and applied logic. By this designation one is immediately reminded that moral principles are not founded on the peculiarities of human nature but must stand of themselves a priori, and that from such principles practical rules for every rational nature, and accordingly for man, must be derivable.

2. I have a letter from the late excellent [Johann Georg] Sulzer in which he asks me why the theories of virtue accomplish so little even though they contain so much that is convincing to reason. My answer was delayed in order that I might make it complete. The answer is only that the teachers themselves have not completely clarified their concepts, and when they wish to make up for this by hunting in every quarter for motives to the morally good so as to make their physic right strong, they spoil it. For the commonest observation shows that if we imagine an act of honesty performed with a steadfast soul and sundered from all view to any advantage in this or another world and even under the greatest temptations of need or allurement, it far surpasses and eclipses any similar action which was affected in the least by any foreign incentive; it elevates the soul and arouses the wish to be able to act in this way. Even moderately young children feel this impression, and one should never represent duties to them in any other way.

nations and from rational concepts must, on the other hand, make the mind vacillate between motives which cannot be brought under any principle and which can lead only accidentally to the good and often to the bad.

From what has been said it is clear that all moral concepts have their seat and origin entirely a priori in reason. This is just as much the case in the most ordinary reason as in reason which is speculative to the highest degree. It is obvious that they cannot be abstracted from any empirical and hence merely contingent cognitions. In the purity of their origin lies their worthiness to serve us as supreme practical principles, and to the extent that something empirical is added to them just this much is subtracted from their genuine influence and from the unqualified worth of actions. Furthermore, it is evident that it is not only of the greatest necessity in a theoretical point of view when it is a question of speculation but also of the utmost practical importance to derive the concepts and laws of morals from pure reason and to present them pure and unmixed, and to determine the scope of this entire practical but pure rational knowledge (the entire faculty of pure practical reason) without making the principles depend upon the particular nature of human reason as speculative philosophy may permit and even sometimes find necessary. But since moral laws should hold for every rational being as such, the principles must be derived from the universal concept of a rational being generally. In this manner all morals, which need anthropology for their application to men, must be completely developed first as pure philosophy, i.e., metaphysics, independently of anthropology (a thing which is easily done in such distinct fields of knowledge). For we know well that if we are not in possession of such a metaphysics, it is not merely futile to define accurately for the purposes of speculative judgment the moral element of duty in all actions which accord with duty, but impossible to base morals on legitimate principles for merely ordinary and practical use, especially in moral instruction; and it is only in this manner that pure moral dispositions can be produced and engrafted on men's minds for the purpose of the highest good in the world.

In this study we do not advance merely from the common moral judgment (which here is very worthy of respect) to the philosophical, as this has already been done, but we advance by natural stages from a popular philosophy (which goes no further than it can grope by means of examples) to metaphysics (which is not held back by anything empirical, and which, as it must measure out the entire scope of rational knowledge of this kind, reaches even Ideas, where examples fail us). In order to make this advance, we must follow and clearly present the practical faculty of reason from its universal rules of determination to the point where the concept of duty arises from it.

Everything in nature works according to laws. Only a rational being has the capacity of acting according to the conception of laws, i.e., according to principles. This capacity is will. Since reason is required for the derivation of actions from laws, will is nothing else than practical reason. If reason infallibly determines the will, the actions which such a being recognizes as objectively necessary are also subjectively necessary. That is, the will is a faculty of choosing only that which reason, independently of inclination, recognizes as practically necessary, i.e., as good. But if reason of itself does not sufficiently determine the will, and if the will is subjugated to subjective conditions (certain incentives) which do not always agree with objective conditions; in a word, if the will is not of itself in complete accord with reason (the actual case of men), then the actions which are recognized as objectively necessary are subjectively contingent, and the determination of such a will according to objective laws is constraint. That is, the relation of objective laws to a will which is not completely good is conceived as the determination of the will of a rational being by principles of reason to which this will is not by nature necessarily obedient.

The conception of an objective principle, so far as it constrains a will, is a command (of reason), and the formula of this command is called an *imperative*.

All imperatives are expressed by an "ought" and thereby indicate the relation of an objective law of reason to a will which is not in its subjective constitution necessarily determined by this law. This relation is that of constraint. Imperatives say that it would be good to do so or to refrain from doing something, but they say it to a will which does not always do something simply because it is presented as a good thing to do. Practical good is what determines the will by means of the conception of reason and hence not by subjective causes but, rather, objectively, i.e., on grounds which are valid for every rational being as such. It is distinguished from the pleasant as that which has an influence on the will only by means of a sensation from merely subjective causes, which hold only for the senses of this or that person and not as a principle of reason which holds for everyone.[3]

A perfectly good will, therefore, would be equally subject to objective laws (of the good), but it could not be conceived as constrained by them to act in accord with them, because, according to its own subjective constitution, it can be determined to act only through the conception of the good. Thus no imperatives hold for the divine will or, more generally, for a holy will. The "ought" is here out of place, for the volition of itself is necessarily in unison with the law. Therefore imperatives are only formulas expressing the relation of objective laws of volition in general to the subjective imperfections of the will of this or that rational being, e.g., the human will.

All imperatives command either hypothetically or categorically. The former present the practical necessity of a possible action as a means to achieving something else which one desires (or which one may possibly desire). The categorical imperative would be one which presented an action as of itself objectively necessary, without regard to any other end.

Since every practical law presents a possible action as good and thus as necessary for a subject practically determinable by reason, all imperatives are formulas of the determination of action which is necessary by the principle of a will which is in any way good. If the action is good only as a means to something else, the imperative is hypothetical; but if it is thought of as good in itself, and hence

3. The dependence of the faculty of desire on sensations is called inclination, and inclination always indicates a need. The dependence of a contingently determinable will on principles of reason, however, is called interest. An interest is present only in a dependent will which is not of itself always in accord with reason; in the divine will we cannot conceive of an interest. But even the human will can take an interest in something without thereby acting from interest. The former means the practical interest in the action; the latter, the pathological interest in the object of the action. The former indicates only the dependence of the will on principles of reason in themselves, while the latter indicates dependence on the principles of reason for the purpose of inclination, since reason gives only the practical rule by which the needs of inclination are to be aided. In the former case the action interests me, and in the latter the object of the action (so far as it is pleasant for me) interests me. In the first section we have seen that, in the case of an action performed from duty, no regard must be given to the interest in the object, but merely in the action itself and its principle in reason (i.e., the law).

as necessary in a will which of itself conforms to reason as the principle of this will, the imperative is categorical.

The imperative thus says what action possible to me would be good, and it presents the practical rule in relation to a will which does not forthwith perform an action simply because it is good, in part because the subject does not always know that the action is good and in part (when he does know it) because his maxims can still be opposed to the objective principles of practical reason.

The hypothetical imperative, therefore, says only that the action is good to some purpose, possible or actual. In the former case it is a problematical, in the latter an assertorical, practical principle. The categorical imperative, which declares the action to be of itself objectively necessary without making any reference to a purpose, i.e., without having any other end, holds as an apodictical (practical) principle.

We can think of that which is possible through the mere powers of some rational being as a possible purpose of any will. As a consequence, the principles of action, in so far as they are thought of as necessary to attain a possible purpose which can be achieved by them, are in reality infinitely numerous. All sciences have some practical part which consists of problems of some end which is possible for us and of imperatives as to how it can be reached. These can therefore generally be called imperatives of skill. Whether the end is reasonable and good is not in question at all, for the question is only of what must be done in order to attain it. The precepts to be followed by a physician in order to cure his patient and by a poisoner in order to bring about certain death are of equal value in so far as each does that which will perfectly accomplish his purpose. Since in early youth we do not know what ends may occur to us in the course of life, parents seek to let their children learn a great many things and provide for skill in the use of means to all sorts of arbitrary ends among which they cannot determine whether any one of them may later become an actual purpose of their pupil, though it is possible that he may some day have it as his actual purpose. And this anxiety is so great that they commonly neglect to form and correct their judgment on the worth of things which they may make their ends.

There is one end, however, which we may presuppose as actual in all rational beings so far as imperatives apply to them, i.e., so far as they are dependent beings; there is one purpose not only which they *can* have but which we can presuppose that they all *do* have by a necessity of nature. This purpose is happiness. The hypothetical imperative which represents the practical necessity of action as a means to the promotion of happiness is an assertorical imperative. We may not expound it as merely necessary to an uncertain and a merely possible purpose, but as necessary to a purpose which we can a priori and with assurance assume for everyone because it belongs to his essence. Skill in the choice of means to one's own highest welfare can be called prudence[4] in the narrowest sense. Thus the imperative which refers to the choice of means to one's own happiness, i.e., the precept of prudence, is still only hypothetical; the action is not absolutely commanded but commanded only as a means to another end.

Finally, there is one imperative which directly commands a certain conduct without making its condition some purpose to be reached by it. This imperative is categorical. It concerns not the material of the action and its intended result but the form and the principle from which it results. What is essentially good in it consists in the intention, the result being what it may. This imperative may be called the imperative of morality.

Volition according to these three principles is plainly distinguished by dissimilarity in the constraint to which they subject the will. In order to clarify this dissimilarity, I believe that they are most suitably named if one says that they are either rules of skill, counsels of prudence, or commands (laws) of morality, respectively. For law alone implies the concept of an unconditional and objective and hence universally valid necessity, and commands are laws which must be obeyed, even against inclination. Counsels do indeed involve necessity, but a necessity that can hold only under a subjectively contingent condition, i.e., whether this or that man counts this or that as part of his happiness; but the categorical imperative, on the other hand, is restricted by no condition. As absolutely, though practically, necessary it can be called a command in the

4. The word "prudence" may be taken in two senses, and it may bear the name of prudence with reference to things of the world and private prudence. The former sense means the skill of a man in having an influence on others so as to use them for his own purposes. The latter is the ability to unite all these purposes to his own lasting advantage. The worth of the first is finally reduced to the latter, and of one who is prudent in the former sense but not in the latter we might better say that he is clever and cunning yet, on the whole, imprudent.

strict sense. We could also call the first imperative technical (belonging to art), the second pragmatic[5] (belonging to welfare), and the third moral (belonging to free conduct as such, i.e., to morals).

The question now arises: how are all these imperatives possible? This question does not require an answer as to how the action which the imperative commands can be performed but merely as to how the constraint of the will, which the imperative expresses in the problem, can be conceived. How an imperative of skill is possible requires no particular discussion. Whoever wills the end, so far as reason has decisive influence on his action, wills also the indispensably necessary means to it that lie in his power. This proposition, in what concerns the will, is analytical; for, in willing an object as my effect, my causality as an acting cause, i.e., the use of the means, is already thought, and the imperative derives the concept of necessary actions to this end from the concept of willing this end. Synthetical propositions undoubtedly are necessary in determining the means to a proposed end, but they do not concern the ground, the act of the will, but only the way to make the object real. Mathematics teaches, by synthetical propositions only, that in order to bisect a line according to an infallible principle I must make two intersecting arcs from each of its extremities; but if I know the proposed result can be obtained only by such an action, then it is an analytical proposition that, if I fully will the effect, I must also will the action necessary to produce it. For it is one and the same thing to conceive of something as an effect which is in a certain way possible through me and to conceive of myself as acting in this way.

If it were only easy to give a definite concept of happiness, the imperatives of prudence would completely correspond to those of skill and would be likewise analytical. For it could be said in this case as well as in the former that whoever wills the end wills also (necessarily according to reason) the only means to it which are in his power. But it is a misfortune that the concept of happiness is so indefinite that, although each person wishes to attain it, he can

5. It seems to me that the proper meaning of the word "pragmatic" could be most accurately defined in this way. For sanctions which properly flow not from the law of states as necessary statutes but from provisions for the general welfare are called pragmatic. A history is pragmatically composed when it teaches prudence, i.e., instructs the world how it could provide for its interest better than, or at least as well as, has been done in the past.

never definitely and self-consistently state what it is he really wishes and wills. The reason for this is that all elements which belong to the concept of happiness are empirical, i.e., they must be taken from experience, while for the idea of happiness an absolute whole, a maximum, of well-being is needed in my present and in every future condition. Now it is impossible even for a most clear-sighted and most capable but finite being to form here a definite concept of that which he really wills. If he wills riches, how much anxiety, envy, and intrigue might he not thereby draw upon his shoulders! If he wills much knowledge and vision, perhaps it might become only an eye that much sharper to show him as more dreadful the evils which are now hidden from him and which are yet unavoidable, or to burden his desires—which already sufficiently engage him— with even more needs! If he wills a long life, who guarantees that it will not be long misery? If he wills at least health, how often has not the discomfort of the body restrained him from excesses into which perfect health would have led him? In short, he is not capable, on any principle and with complete certainty, of ascertaining what would make him truly happy; omniscience would be needed for this. He cannot, therefore, act according to definite principles so as to be happy, but only according to empirical counsels, e.g., those of diet, economy, courtesy, restraint, etc., which are shown by experience best to promote welfare on the average. Hence the imperatives of prudence cannot, in the strict sense, command, i.e., present actions objectively as practically necessary; thus they are to be taken as counsels (*consilia*) rather than as commands (*praecepta*) of reason, and the task of determining infallibly and universally what action will promote the happiness of a rational being is completely unsolvable. There can be no imperative which would, in the strict sense, command us to do what makes for happiness, because happiness is an ideal not of reason but of imagination, depending only on empirical grounds which one would expect in vain to determine an action through which the totality of consequences—which is in fact infinite—could be achieved. Assuming that the means to happiness could be infallibly stated, this imperative of prudence would be an analytical proposition, for it differs from the imperative of skill only in that its end is given while in the latter case it is merely possible. Since both, however, only command the means to that which one presupposes, the imperative which commands the willing of the means to him who wills the end is in both cases analytical. There is, consequently, no difficulty in seeing the possibility of such an imperative.

To see how the imperative of morality is possible is, then, without doubt the only question needing an answer. It is not hypothetical, and thus the objectively conceived necessity cannot be supported by presupposition, as was the case with the hypothetical imperatives. But it must not be overlooked that it cannot be shown by an example (i.e., it cannot be empirically shown) whether or not there is such an imperative; it is rather to be suspected that all imperatives which appear to be categorical may yet be hypothetical, but in a hidden way. For instance, when it is said, "Thou shalt not make a false promise," we assume that the necessity of this avoidance is not a mere counsel for the sake of escaping some other evil, so that it would read, "Thou shalt not make a false promise so that, if it comes to light, thou ruinist thy credit"; we assume rather that an action of this kind must be regarded as of itself bad and that the imperative of the prohibition is categorical. But we cannot show with certainty by any example that the will is here determined by the law alone without any other incentives, even though this appears to be the case. For it is always possible that secret fear of disgrace, and perhaps also obscure apprehension of other dangers, may have had an influence on the will. Who can prove by experience the nonexistence of a cause when experience shows us only that we do not perceive the cause? But in such a case the so-called moral imperative, which as such appears to be categorical and unconditional, would be actually only a pragmatic precept which makes us attentive to our own advantage and teaches us to consider it.

Thus we shall have to investigate purely a priori the possibility of a categorical imperative, for we do not have the advantage that experience would give us the reality of this imperative, so that the [demonstration of its] possibility would be necessary only for its explanation and not for its establishment. In the meantime, this much may at least be seen: the categorical imperative alone can be taken as a practical *law*, while all the others may be called principles of the will but not laws. This is because what is necessary merely for the attainment of an arbitrary purpose can be regarded as itself contingent, and we get rid of the precept once we give up the purpose, whereas the unconditional command leaves the will no freedom to choose the opposite. Thus it alone implies the necessity which we require of a law.

Secondly, in the case of the categorical imperative or law of morality, the cause of difficulty in discerning its possibility is very weighty. This imperative is an a priori synthetical practical proposition,[6] and, since to discern the possibility of propositions of this sort is so difficult in theoretical knowledge, it may well be gathered that it will be no less difficult in the practical.

In attacking this problem, we will first inquire whether the mere concept of a categorical imperative does not also furnish the formula containing the proposition which alone can be a categorical imperative. For even when we know the formula of the imperative, to learn how such an absolute law is possible will require difficult and special labors which we shall postpone to the last section.

If I think of a hypothetical imperative as such, I do not know what it will contain until the condition is stated [under which it is an imperative]. But if I think of a categorical imperative, I know immediately what it contains. For since the imperative contains besides the law only the necessity that the maxim[7] should accord with this law, while the law contains no condition to which it is restricted, there is nothing remaining in it except the universality of law as such to which the maxim of the action should conform; and in effect this conformity alone is represented as necessary by the imperative.

There is, therefore, only one categorical imperative. It is: Act only according to that maxim by which you can at the same time will that it should become a universal law.

---

6. I connect a priori, and hence necessarily, the action with the will without supposing as a condition that there is any inclination [to the action] (though I do so only objectively, i.e., under the idea of a reason which would have complete power over all subjective motives). This is, therefore, a practical proposition which does not analytically derive the willing of an action from some other volition already presupposed (for we do not have such a perfect will); it rather connects it directly with the concept of the will of a rational being as something which is not contained within it.

7. A maxim is the subjective principle of acting and must be distinguished from the objective principle, i.e., the practical law. The former contains the practical rule which reason determines according to the conditions of the subject (often its ignorance or inclinations) and is thus the principle according to which the subject acts. The law, on the other hand, is the objective principle valid for every rational being, and the principle by which it ought to act, i.e., an imperative.

Now if all imperatives of duty can be derived from this one imperative as a principle, we can at least show what we understand by the concept of duty and what it means, even though it remain undecided whether that which is called duty is an empty concept or not.

The universality of law according to which effects are produced constitutes what is properly called nature in the most general sense (as to form), i.e., the existence of things so far as it is determined by universal laws. [By analogy], then, the universal imperative of duty can be expressed as follows: Act as though the maxim of your action were by your will to become a universal law of nature.

We shall now enumerate some duties, adopting the usual division of them into duties to ourselves and to others and into perfect and imperfect duties.[8]

1. A man who is reduced to despair by a series of evils feels a weariness with life but is still in possession of his reason sufficiently to ask whether it would not be contrary to his duty to himself to take his own life. Now he asks whether the maxim of his action could become a universal law of nature. His maxim, however, is: For love of myself, I make it my principle to shorten my life when by a longer duration it threatens more evil than satisfaction. But it is questionable whether this principle of self-love could become a universal law of nature. One immediately sees a contradiction in a system of nature whose law would be to destroy life by the feeling whose special office is to impel the improvement of life. In this case it would not exist as nature; hence that maxim cannot obtain as a law of nature, and thus it wholly contradicts the supreme principle of all duty.

2. Another man finds himself forced by need to borrow money. He well knows that he will not be able to repay it, but he also sees that nothing will be loaned him if he does not firmly promise to repay it at a certain time. He desires to make such a promise, but he has enough conscience to ask himself whether it is not improper

8. It must be noted here that I reserve the division of duties for a future *Metaphysics of Morals* and that the division here stands as only an arbitrary one (chosen in order to arrange my examples). For the rest, by a perfect duty I here understand a duty which permits no exception in the interest of inclination; thus I have not merely outer but also inner perfect duties. This runs contrary to the usage adopted in the schools, but I am not disposed to defend it here because it is all one to my purpose whether this is conceded or not.

and opposed to duty to relieve his distress in such a way. Now, assuming he does decide to do so, the maxim of his action would be as follows: When I believe myself to be in need of money, I will borrow money and promise to repay it, although I know I shall never do so. Now this principle of self-love or of his own benefit may very well be compatible with his whole future welfare, but the question is whether it is right. He changes the pretension of self-love into a universal law and then puts the question: How would it be if my maxim became a universal law? He immediately sees that it could never hold as a universal law of nature and be consistent with itself; rather it must necessarily contradict itself. For the universality of a law which says that anyone who believes himself to be in need could promise what he pleased with the intention of not fulfilling it would make the promise itself and the end to be accomplished by it impossible; no one would believe what was promised to him but would only laugh at any such assertion as vain pretense.

3. A third finds in himself a talent which could, by means of some cultivation, make him in many respects a useful man. But he finds himself in comfortable circumstances and prefers indulgence in pleasure to troubling himself with broadening and improving his fortunate natural gifts. Now, however, let him ask whether his maxim of neglecting his gifts, besides agreeing with his propensity to idle amusement, agrees also with what is called duty. He sees that a system of nature could indeed exist in accordance with such a law, even though man (like the inhabitants of the South Sea Islands) should let his talents rust and resolve to devote his life merely to idleness, indulgence, and propagation—in a word, to pleasure. But he cannot possibly will that this should become a universal law of nature or that it should be implanted in us by a natural instinct. For, as a rational being, he necessarily wills that all his faculties should be developed, inasmuch as they are given to him for all sorts of possible purposes.

4. A fourth man, for whom things are going well, sees that others (whom he could help) have to struggle with great hardships, and he asks, "What concern of mine is it? Let each one be as happy as heaven wills, or as he can make himself; I will not take anything from him or even envy him; but to his welfare or to his assistance in time of need I have no desire to contribute." If such a way of thinking were a universal law of nature, certainly the human race

could exist, and without doubt even better than in a state where everyone talks of sympathy and good will, or even exerts himself occasionally to practice them while, on the other hand, he cheats when he can and betrays or otherwise violates the rights of man. Now although it is possible that a universal law of nature according to that maxim could exist, it is nevertheless impossible to will that such a principle should hold everywhere as a law of nature. For a will which resolved this would conflict with itself, since instances can often arise in which he would need the love and sympathy of others, and in which he would have robbed himself, by such a law of nature springing from his own will, of all hope of the aid he desires.

The foregoing are a few of the many actual duties, or at least of duties we hold to be actual, whose derivation from the one stated principle is clear. We must be able to will that a maxim of our action become a universal law; this is the canon of the moral estimation of our action generally. Some actions are of such a nature that their maxim cannot even be *thought* as a universal law of nature without contradiction, far from it being possible that one could will that it should be such. In others this internal impossibility is not found, though it is still impossible to *will* that their maxim should be raised to the universality of a law of nature, because such a will would contradict itself. We easily see that the former maxim conflicts with the stricter or narrower (imprescriptible) duty, the latter with broader (meritorious) duty. Thus all duties, so far as the kind of obligation (not the object of their action) is concerned, have been completely exhibited by these examples in their dependence on the one principle.

When we observe ourselves in any transgression of a duty, we find that we do not actually will that our maxim should become a universal law. That is impossible for us; rather, the contrary of this maxim should remain as a law generally, and we only take the liberty of making an exception to it for ourselves or for the sake of our inclination, and for this one occasion. Consequently, if we weighed everything from one and the same standpoint, namely, reason, we would come upon a contradiction in our own will, viz., that a certain principle is objectively necessary as a universal law and yet subjectively does not hold universally but rather admits exceptions. However, since we regard our action at one time from the point of view of a will wholly conformable to reason and then from that of a will affected by inclinations, there is actually no contradiction, but rather an opposition of inclination to the precept of reason (*antagonismus*). In this the universality of the principle (*universalitas*) is changed into mere generality (*generalitas*), whereby the practical principle of reason meets the maxim halfway. Although this cannot be justified in our own impartial judgment, it does show that we actually acknowledge the validity of the categorical imperative and allow ourselves (with all respect to it) only a few exceptions which seem to us to be unimportant and forced upon us.

We have thus at least established that if duty is a concept which is to have significance and actual legislation for our actions, it can be expressed only in categorical imperatives and not at all in hypothetical ones. For every application of it we have also clearly exhibited the content of the categorical imperative which must contain the principle of all duty (if there is such). This is itself very much. But we are not yet advanced far enough to prove a priori that that kind of imperative really exists, that there is a practical law which of itself commands absolutely and without any incentives, and that obedience to this law is duty.

With a view to attaining this, it is extremely important to remember that we must not let ourselves think that the reality of this principle can be derived from the particular constitution of human nature. For duty is practical unconditional necessity of action; it must, therefore, hold for all rational beings (to which alone an imperative can apply), and only for that reason can it be a law for all human wills. Whatever is derived from the particular natural situation of man as such, or from certain feelings and propensities, or even from a particular tendency of the human reason which might not hold necessarily for the will of every rational being (if such a tendency is possible), can give a maxim valid for us but not a law; that is, it can give a subjective principle by which we might act only if we have the propensity and inclination, but not an objective principle by which we would be directed to act even if all our propensity, inclination, and natural tendency were opposed to it. This is so far the case that the sublimity and intrinsic worth of the command is the better shown in a duty the fewer subjective causes there are for it and the more there are against it; the latter do not weaken the constraint of the law or diminish its validity.

Here we see philosophy brought to what is, in fact, a precarious position, which should be made fast even though it is supported by nothing in either heaven or earth. Here philosophy must show its purity as the absolute sustainer of its laws, and not as the herald of those which an implanted sense or who knows what tutelary nature whispers to it. Those may be better than no laws at all, but they can never afford fundamental principles, which reason alone dictates. These fundamental principles must originate entirely a priori and thereby obtain their commanding authority; they can expect nothing from the inclination of men but everything from the supremacy of the law and due respect for it. Otherwise they condemn man to self-contempt and inner abhorrence.

Thus everything empirical is not only wholly unworthy to be an ingredient in the principle of morality but is even highly prejudicial to the purity of moral practices themselves. For, in morals, the proper and inestimable worth of an absolutely good will consists precisely in the freedom of the principle of action from all influences from contingent grounds which only experience can furnish. We cannot too much or too often warn against the lax or even base manner of thought which seeks principles among empirical motives and laws, for human reason in its weariness is glad to rest on this pillow. In a dream of sweet illusions (in which it embraces not Juno but a cloud), it substitutes for morality a bastard patched up from limbs of very different parentage, which looks like anything one wishes to see in it, but not like virtue to anyone who has ever beheld her in her true form.[9]

The question then is: Is it a necessary law for all rational beings that they should always judge their actions by such maxims as they themselves could will to serve as universal laws? If it is such a law, it must be connected (wholly a priori) with the concept of the will of a rational being as such. But in order to discover this connection we must, however reluctantly, take a step into metaphysics, although into a region of it different from speculative philosophy,

9. To behold virtue in her proper form is nothing else than to exhibit morality stripped of all admixture of sensuous things and of every spurious adornment of reward or self-love. How much she then eclipses everything which appears charming to the senses can easily be seen by everyone with the least effort of his reason, if it be not spoiled for all abstraction.

i.e., into metaphysics of morals. In a practical philosophy it is not a question of assuming grounds for what happens but of assuming laws of what ought to happen even though it may never happen—that is to say, objective, practical laws. Hence in practical philosophy we need not inquire into the reasons why something pleases or displeases, how the pleasure of mere feeling differs from taste, and whether this is distinct from a general satisfaction of reason. Nor need we ask on what the feeling of pleasure or displeasure rests, how desires and inclinations arise, and how, finally, maxims arise from desires and inclination under the co-operation of reason. For all these matters belong to an empirical psychology, which would be the second part of physics if we consider it as philosophy of nature so far as it rests on empirical laws. But here it is a question of objectively practical laws and thus of the relation of a will to itself so far as it determines itself only by reason; for everything which has a relation to the empirical automatically falls away, because if reason of itself alone determines conduct it must necessarily do so a priori. The possibility of reason thus determining conduct must now be investigated.

The will is thought of as a faculty of determining itself to action in accordance with the conception of certain laws. Such a faculty can be found only in rational beings. That which serves the will as the objective ground of its self-determination is an end, and, if it is given by reason alone, it must hold alike for all rational beings. On the other hand, that which contains the ground of the possibility of the action, whose result is an end, is called the means. The subjective ground of desire is the incentive, while the objective ground of volition is the motive. Thus arises the distinction between subjective ends, which rest on incentives, and objective ends, which depend on motives valid for every rational being. Practical principles are formal when they disregard all subjective ends; they are material when they have subjective ends, and thus certain incentives, as their basis. The ends which a rational being arbitrarily proposes to himself as consequences of his action are material ends and are without exception only relative, for only their relation to a particularly constituted faculty of desire in the subject gives them their worth. And this worth cannot, therefore, afford any universal principles for all rational beings or valid and necessary principles for every volition. That is, they cannot give rise to any practical laws. All these relative ends, therefore, are grounds for hypothetical imperatives only.

But suppose that there were something the existence of which in itself had absolute worth, something which, as an end in itself, could be a ground of definite laws. In it and only in it could lie the ground of a possible categorical imperative, i.e., of a practical law.

Now, I say, man and, in general, every rational being exists as an end in himself and not merely as a means to be arbitrarily used by this or that will. In all his actions, whether they are directed to himself or to other rational beings, he must always be regarded at the same time as an end. All objects of inclination have only a conditional worth, for if the inclinations and the needs founded on them did not exist, their object would be without worth. The inclinations themselves as the sources of needs, however, are so lacking in absolute worth that the universal wish of every rational being must be indeed to free himself completely from them. Therefore, the worth of any objects to be obtained by our actions is at all times conditional. Beings whose existence does not depend on our will but on nature, if they are not rational beings, have only a relative worth as means and are therefore called "things"; on the other hand, rational beings are designated "persons" because their nature indicated that they are ends in themselves, i.e., things which may not be used merely as means. Such a being is thus an object of respect and, so far, restricts all [arbitrary] choice. Such beings are not merely subjective ends whose existence as a result of our action has a worth for us, but are objective ends, i.e., beings whose existence in itself is an end. Such an end is one for which no other end can be substituted, to which these beings should serve merely as means. For, without them, nothing of absolute worth could be found, and if all worth is conditional and thus contingent, no supreme practical principle for reason could be found anywhere.

Thus if there is to be a supreme practical principle and a categorical imperative for the human will, it must be one that forms an objective principle of the will from the conception of that which is necessarily an end for everyone because it is an end in itself. Hence this objective principle can serve as a universal practical law. The ground of this principle is: rational nature exists as an end in itself. Man necessarily thinks of his own existence in this way; thus far it is a subjective principle of human actions. Also every other rational being thinks of his existence by means of the same rational ground which holds also for myself;[10] thus, it is at the same time an objective principle from which, as a supreme practical ground, it must be possible to derive all laws of the will. The practical imperative, therefore, is the following: Act so that you treat humanity, whether in your own person or in that of another, always as an end and never as a means only. Let us now see whether this can be achieved.

To return to our previous examples:

First, according to the concept of necessary duty to one's self, he who contemplates suicide will ask himself whether his action can be consistent with the idea of humanity as an end in itself. If, in order to escape from burdensome circumstances, he destroys himself, he uses a person merely as a means to maintain a tolerable condition up to the end of life. Man, however, is not a thing, and thus not something to be used merely as a means; he must always be regarded in all his actions as an end in himself. Therefore, I cannot dispose of man in my own person so as to mutilate, corrupt, or kill him. (It belongs to ethics proper to define more accurately this basic principle so as to avoid all misunderstanding, e.g., as to the amputation of limbs in order to preserve myself, or to exposing my life to danger in order to save it; I must, therefore, omit them here.)

Second, as concerns necessary or obligatory duties to others, he who intends a deceitful promise to others sees immediately that he intends to use another man merely as a means, without the latter containing the end in himself at the same time. For he whom I want to use for my own purposes by means of such a promise cannot possibly assent to my mode of acting against him and cannot contain the end of this action in himself. This conflict against the principle of other men is even clearer if we cite examples of attacks on their freedom and property. For then it is clear that he who transgresses the rights of men intends to make use of the persons of others merely as a means, without considering that, as rational beings,

---

10. Here I present this proposition as a postulate, but in the last section grounds for it will be found.

they must always be esteemed at the same time as ends, i.e., only as beings who must be able to contain in themselves the end of the very same action.[11]

Third, with regard to contingent (meritorious) duty to one's self, it is not sufficient that the action not conflict with humanity in our person as an end in itself; it must also harmonize with it. Now in humanity there are capacities for greater perfection which belong to the end of nature with respect to humanity in our own person; to neglect these might perhaps be consistent with the preservation of humanity as an end in itself but not with the furtherance of that end.

Fourth, with regard to meritorious duty to others, the natural end which all men have is their own happiness. Humanity might indeed exist if no one contributed to the happiness of others, provided he did not intentionally detract from it; but this harmony with humanity as an end in itself is only negative rather than positive if everyone does not also endeavor, so far as he can, to further the ends of others. For the ends of any person, who is an end in himself, must as far as possible also be my end, if that conception of an end in itself is to have its full effect on me.

This principle of humanity and of every rational creature as an end in itself is the supreme limiting condition on freedom of the actions of each man. It is not borrowed from experience, first, because of its universality, since it applies to all rational beings generally and experience does not suffice to determine anything about them; and, secondly, because in experience humanity is not thought of (subjectively) as the end of men, i.e., as an object which we of ourselves really make our end. Rather it is thought of as the objective end which should constitute the supreme limiting condition of all subjective ends, whatever they may be. Thus this principle must arise from pure reason. Objectively the ground of all practical legislation lies (according to the first principle) in the rule and in

11. Let it not be thought that the banal *"quod tibi non vis fieri, etc.,"* could here serve as guide or principle, for it is only derived from the principle and is restricted by various limitations. It cannot be a universal law, because it contains the ground neither of duties to one's self nor of the benevolent duties to others (for many a man would gladly consent that others should not benefit him, provided only that he might be excused from showing benevolence to them). Nor does it contain the ground of obligatory duties to another, for the criminal would argue on this ground against the judge who sentences him. And so on.

the form of universality, which makes it capable of being a law (at most a natural law); subjectively, it lies in the end. But the subject of all ends is every rational being as an end in itself (by the second principle); from this there follows the third principle of the will as the supreme condition of its harmony with the universal practical reason, viz., the idea of the will of every rational being as making universal law.

By this principle all maxims are rejected which are not consistent with the universal lawgiving of will. The will is thus not only subject to the law but subject in such a way that it must be regarded also as self-legislative and only for this reason as being subject to the law (of which it can regard itself as the author).

In the foregoing mode of conception, in which imperatives are conceived universally either as conformity to law by actions—a conformity which is similar to a natural order—or as the prerogative of rational beings as such, the imperatives exclude from their legislative authority all admixture of any interest as an incentive. They do so because they were conceived as categorical. They were only assumed to be categorical, however, because we had to make such an assumption if we wished to explain the concept of duty. But that there were practical propositions which commanded categorically could not here be proved independently, just as little as it can be proved anywhere in this section. One thing, however, might have been done: to indicate in the imperative itself, by some determination which it contained, that in volition from duty the renunciation of all interest is the specific mark of the categorical imperative, distinguishing it from the hypothetical. And this is now being done in the third formulation of the principle, i.e., in the idea of the will of every rational being as a will giving universal law. A will which stands under laws can be bound to this law by an interest. But if we think of a will giving universal laws, we find that a supreme legislating will cannot possibly depend on any interest, for such a dependent will would itself need still another law which would restrict the interest of its self-love to the condition that [the maxims of the will] should be valid as universal law.

Thus the principle of every human will as a will giving universal laws in all its maxims[12] is very well adapted to being a categorical

12. I may be excused from citing examples to elucidate this principle, for those which have already illustrated the categorical imperative and its formula can here serve the same purpose.

imperative, provided it is otherwise correct. Because of the idea of universal lawgiving, it is based on no interest, and, thus of all possible imperatives, it alone can be unconditional. Or, better, converting the proposition, if there is a categorical imperative (a law for the will of every rational being), it can only command that everything be done from the maxim of its will as one which could have as its object only itself considered as giving universal laws. For only in this case are the practical principle and the imperative which the will obeys unconditional, because the will can have no interest as its foundation.

If we now look back upon all previous attempts which have ever been undertaken to discover the principle of morality, it is not to be wondered at that they all had to fail. Man was seen to be bound to laws by his duty, but it was not seen that he is subject only to his own, yet universal, legislation, and that he is only bound to act in accordance with his own will, which is, however, designed by nature to be a will giving universal laws. For if one thought of him as subject only to a law (whatever it may be), this necessarily implied some interest as a stimulus or compulsion to obedience because the law did not arise from his will. Rather, his will was constrained by something else according to a law to act in a certain way. By this strictly necessary consequence, however, all the labor of finding a supreme ground for duty was irrevocably lost, and one never arrived at duty but only at the necessity of action from a certain interest. This might be his own interest or that of another, but in either case the imperative always had to be conditional and could not at all serve as a moral command. This principle I will call the principle of *autonomy* of the will in contrast to all other principles which I accordingly count under *heteronomy*.

The concept of each rational being as a being that must regard itself as giving universal law through all the maxims of its will, so that it may judge itself and its actions from this standpoint, leads to a very fruitful concept, namely, that of a *realm of ends*.

By "realm" I understand the systematic union of different rational beings through common laws. Because laws determine ends with regard to their universal validity, if we abstract from the personal difference of rational beings and thus from all content of their private ends, we can think of a whole of all ends in systematic connection, a whole of rational beings as ends in themselves as well as of the particular ends which each may set for himself. This is a realm of ends, which is possible on the aforesaid principles. For all rational beings stand under the law that each of them should treat himself and all others never merely as means but in every case also as an end in himself. Thus there arises a systematic union of rational beings through common objective laws. This is a realm which may be called a realm of ends (certainly only an ideal), because what these laws have in view is just the relation of these beings to each other as ends and means.

A rational being belongs to the realm of ends as a member when he gives universal laws in it while also himself subject to these laws. He belongs to it as sovereign when he, as legislating, is subject to the will of no other. The rational being must regard himself always as legislative in a realm of ends possible through the freedom of the will, whether he belongs to it as a member or sovereign. He cannot maintain the latter position merely through the maxims of his will but only when he is a completely independent being without need and with power adequate to his will.

Morality, therefore, consists in the relation of every action to that legislation through which alone a realm of ends is possible. This legislation, however, must be found in every rational being. It must be able to arise from his will, whose principle then is to take no action according to any maxim which would be inconsistent with its being a universal law and thus to act only so that the will through its maxims could regard itself at the same time as universally lawgiving. If now the maxims do not by their nature already necessarily conform to this objective principle of rational beings as universally lawgiving, the necessity of acting according to that principle is called practical constraint, i.e., duty. Duty pertains not to the sovereign in the realm of ends, but rather to each member, and to each in the same degree.

The practical necessity of acting according to this principle, i.e., duty, does not rest at all on feelings, impulses, and inclinations; it rests merely on the relation of rational beings to one another, in which the will of a rational being must always be regarded as legislative, for otherwise it could not be thought of as an end in itself. Reason, therefore, relates every maxim of the will as giving universal laws to every other will and also to every action toward itself; it does so not for the sake of any other practical motive or future advantage but rather from the idea of the dignity of a rational being who obeys no law except that which he himself also gives.

In the realm of ends everything has either a *price* or a *dignity.* Whatever has a price can be replaced by something else as its equivalent; on the other hand, whatever is above all price, and therefore admits of no equivalent, has a dignity.

That which is related to general human inclinations and needs has a *market price.* That which, without presupposing any need, accords with a certain taste, i.e., with pleasure in the mere purposeless play of our faculties, has an *affective price.* But that which constitutes the condition under which alone something can be an end in itself does not have mere relative worth, i.e., a price, but an intrinsic worth, i.e., *dignity.*

Now morality is the condition under which alone a rational being can be an end in itself, because only through it is it possible to be a legislative member in the realm of ends. Thus morality and humanity, so far as it is capable of morality, alone have dignity. Skill and diligence in work have a market value; wit, lively imagination, and humor have an affective price; but fidelity in promises and benevolence on principle (not from instinct) have intrinsic worth. Nature and likewise art contain nothing which could replace their lack, for their worth consists not in effects which flow from them, nor in advantage and utility which they procure; it consists only in intentions, i.e., maxims of the will which are ready to reveal themselves in this manner through actions even though success does not favor them. These actions need no recommendation from any subjective disposition or taste in order that they may be looked upon with immediate favor and satisfaction, nor do they have need of any immediate propensity or feeling directed to them. They exhibit the will which performs them as the object of an immediate respect, since nothing but reason is required in order to impose them on the will. The will is not to be cajoled into them, for this, in the case of duties, would be a contradiction. This esteem lets the worth of such a turn of mind be recognized as dignity and puts it infinitely beyond any price, with which it cannot in the least be brought into competition or comparison without, as it were, violating its holiness.

And what is it that justifies the morally good disposition or virtue in making such lofty claims? It is nothing less than the participation it affords the rational being in giving universal laws. He is thus fitted to be a member in a possible realm of ends to which his own nature already destined him. For, as an end in himself, he is destined to be legislative in the realm of ends, free from all laws of nature and obedient only to those which he himself gives. Accordingly, his maxims can belong to a universal legislation to which he is at the same time also subject. A thing has no worth other than that determined for it by the law. The legislation which determines all worth must therefore have a dignity, i.e., unconditional and incomparable worth. For the esteem which a rational being must have for it, only the word "respect" is a suitable expression. Autonomy is thus the basis of the dignity of both human nature and every rational nature.

The three aforementioned ways of presenting the principle of morality are fundamentally only so many formulas of the very same law, and each of them unites the others in itself. There is, nevertheless, a difference in them, but the difference is more subjectively than objectively practical, for it is intended to bring an idea of reason closer to intuition (by means of a certain analogy) and thus nearer to feeling. All maxims have:

1. A form, which consists in universality; and in this respect the formula of the moral imperative required that the maxims be chosen as though they should hold as universal laws of nature.

2. A material, i.e., an end; in this respect the formula says that the rational being, as by its nature an end and thus as an end in itself, must serve in every maxim as the condition restricting all merely relative and arbitrary ends.

3. A complete determination of all maxims by the formula that all maxims which stem from autonomous legislation ought to harmonize with a possible realm of ends as with a realm of nature.[13]

There is a progression here like that through the categories of the unity of the form of the will (its universality), the plurality of material (the objects, i.e., the ends), and the all-comprehensiveness or totality of the system of ends. But it is better in moral evaluation to follow the rigorous method and to make the universal formula

13. Teleology considers nature as a realm of ends; morals regards a possible realm of ends as a realm of nature. In the former the realm of ends is a theoretical idea for the explanation of what actually is. In the latter it is a practical idea for bringing about that which is not actually real but which can become real through our conduct, and which is in accordance with this idea.

of the categorical imperative the basis: Act according to the maxim which can at the same time make itself a universal law. But if one wishes to gain a hearing for the moral law, it is very useful to bring one and the same action under the three stated principles and this, so far as possible, to bring it nearer to intuition.

We can now end where we started, with the concept of an unconditionally good will. That will is absolutely good which cannot be bad, and thus it is a will whose maxim, when made a universal law, can never conflict with itself. Thus this principle is also its supreme law: Always act according to that maxim whose universality as a law you can at the same time will. This is the only condition under which a will can never come into conflict with itself, and such an imperative is categorical. Because the validity of the will, as a universal law for possible actions, has an analogy with the universal connection of the existence of things under universal laws, which is the formal element of nature in general, the categorical imperative can also be expressed as follows: Act according to maxims which can at the same time have themselves as universal laws of nature as their object. Such, then, is the formula of an absolutely good will.

Rational nature is distinguished from others in that it proposes an end to itself. This end would be the material of every good will. Since, however, in the idea of an absolutely good will without any limiting condition of the attainment of this or that end, every end to be effected must be completely abstracted (as any particular end would make each will only relatively good), the end here is not conceived as one to be effected but as an independent end, and thus merely negatively. It is that which must never be acted against, and which must consequently never be valued as merely a means but in every volition also as an end. Now this end can never be other than the subject of all possible ends themselves, because this is at the same time the subject of a possible will which is absolutely good; for the latter cannot be made secondary to any other object without contradiction. The principle: Act with reference to every rational being (whether yourself or another) so that it is an end in itself in your maxim, is thus basically identical with the principle: Act by a maxim which involves its own universal validity for every rational being.

That in the use of means to every end I should restrict my maxim to the condition of its universal validity as a law for every subject is tantamount to saying that the subject of ends, i.e., the rational being itself, must be made the basis of all maxims of actions and must thus be treated never as a mere means but as the supreme limiting condition in the use of all means, i.e., as an end at the same time.

It follows incontestably that every rational being must be able to regard himself as an end in himself with reference to all laws which he may be subject, whatever they may be, and thus as giving universal laws. For it is just the fitness of his maxims to a universal legislation that indicates that he is an end in himself. It also follows that his dignity (his prerogative) over all merely natural beings entails that he must take his maxims from the point of view which regards himself, and hence also every other rational being, as legislative. (The rational beings are, on this account, called persons.) In this way, a world of rational beings (*mundus intelligibilis*) is possible as a realm of ends, because of the legislation belonging to all persons as members. Consequently, every rational being must act as if he, by his maxims, were at all times a legislative member in the universal realm of ends. The formal principle of these maxims is: So act as if your maxims should serve at the same time as the universal law (of all rational beings). A realm of ends is thus possible only by analogy with a realm of nature. The former, however, is possible only by maxims, i.e., self-imposed rules, while the latter is possible by laws of efficient causes of things externally necessitated. Regardless of the difference, by analogy we call the natural whole a realm of nature so far as it is related to rational beings as its end; we do so even though the natural whole is looked at as a machine. Such a realm of ends would actually be realized through maxims whose rule is prescribed to all rational beings by the categorical imperative, if they were universally obeyed. But a rational being, though he scrupulously follow this maxim, cannot for that reason expect every other rational being to be true to it; nor can he expect the realm of nature and its orderly design to harmonize with him as a fitting member of a realm of ends which is possible through himself. That is, he cannot count on its favoring his expectations of happiness. Still the law: Act according to the maxims of a universally legislative member of a merely potential realm of ends, remains in full force, because it commands categorically. And just in this lies the paradox that merely the dignity of humanity as rational nature without any end or advantage to be gained by it, and thus respect for a mere idea, should serve as the inflexible precept of the will. There is the further paradox that the sublimity of the maxims and the worthiness of every rational subject to be a legislative member in the realm of ends consist precisely in independence of the maxims from all such incentives. Otherwise he would have to be viewed as subject only to the natural law of his needs. Although the realm of nature as well as that of ends would be thought of as united under a sovereign so that the latter would no longer remain a mere idea but would receive true reality, the realm of ends would undoubtedly gain a strong urge in its favor, but its intrinsic worth would not be augmented. Regardless of this, even the one and only absolute legislator would still have to be conceived as judging the worth of rational beings only by the disinterested conduct which they prescribe to themselves merely from the idea [of dignity]. The essence of things is not changed by their external relations, and without reference to these relations a man must be judged only by what constitutes his absolute worth; and this is true whoever his judge is, even if it be the Supreme Being. Morality is thus the relation of actions to the autonomy of the will, i.e., to possible universal lawgiving by maxims of the will. The action which can be compatible with the autonomy of the will is permitted; that which does not agree with it is prohibited. The will whose maxims necessarily are in harmony with the laws of autonomy is a holy will or an absolutely good will. The dependence of a will not absolutely good on the principle of autonomy (moral constraint) is *obligation*. Hence obligation cannot be applied to a holy will. The objective necessity of an action from obligation is called *duty*.

From what has just been said, it can easily be explained how it happens that, although in the concept of duty we think of subjection to law, we do nevertheless ascribe a certain sublimity and dignity to the person who fulfills all his duties. For though there is no sublimity in him in so far as he is subject to the moral law, yet he is sublime in so far as he is legislative with reference to the law and subject to it only for this reason. We have also shown above how neither fear of nor inclination to the law is the incentive which can give a moral worth to action; only respect for it can do so. Our

own will, so far as it would act only under the condition of a
universal legislation rendered possible by its maxims—this will,
ideally possible for us, is the proper object of respect, and the dignity
of humanity consists just in its capacity of giving universal laws,
although with the condition that it is itself subject to this same
legislation.

### THE AUTONOMY OF THE WILL AS THE SUPREME
### PRINCIPLE OF MORALITY

Autonomy of the will is that property of it by which it is a law
to itself independently of any property of objects of volition. Hence
the principle of autonomy is: Never choose except in such a way
that the maxims of the choice are comprehended in the same volition
as a universal law. That this practical rule is an imperative, that is,
that the will of every rational being is necessarily bound to it as a
condition, cannot be proved by a mere analysis of the concepts
occurring in it, because it is a synthetical proposition. To prove it,
we would have to go beyond the knowledge of objects to a critical
examination of the subject, i.e., of the pure practical reason, for
this synthetical proposition which commands apodictically must be
susceptible of being known completely a priori. This matter, however, does not belong in the present section. But that the principle
of autonomy, which is now in question, is the sole principle of
morals can be readily shown by mere analysis of concepts of morality; for by this analysis we find that its principle must be a
categorical imperative and that the imperative commands neither
more nor less than this very autonomy.

### THE HETERONOMY OF THE WILL AS THE SOURCE OF
### ALL SPURIOUS PRINCIPLES OF MORALITY

If the will seeks the law which is to determine it anywhere else
than in the fitness of its maxims to its own universal legislation,
and if it thus goes outside itself and seeks this law in the property
of any of its objects, heteronomy always results. For then the will
does not give itself the law, but the object through its relation to
the will gives the law to it. This relation, whether it rests on inclination or on conceptions of reason, only admits of hypothetical

imperatives: I should do something for the reason that I will something else. The moral, and therewith categorical, imperative, on the other hand, says I should act this or that way even though I will nothing else. For example, the former says I should not lie if I wish to keep my reputation. The latter says I should not lie even though it would not cause me the least injury. The latter, therefore, must disregard every object to such an extent that it has absolutely no influence on the will, so that practical reason (will) may not merely minister to an interest not its own but rather may show its commanding authority as the supreme legislation. Thus, for instance, I should seek to further the happiness of others, not as though its realization was any concern of mine (whether because of direct inclination or of some satisfaction related to it indirectly through reason); I should do so merely because the maxim which excludes it from my duty cannot be comprehended as a universal law in one and the same volition.

## CLASSIFICATION OF ALL POSSIBLE PRINCIPLES OF MORALITY FOLLOWING FROM THE ASSUMED PRINCIPLE OF HETERONOMY

Here as everywhere in the pure use of reason, so long as a critical examination of it is lacking, human reason at first tries all possible wrong ways before it succeeds in finding the one true way.

All principles which can be taken in this point of view are either empirical or rational. The former, drawn from the principle of happiness, are based on physical or moral feeling; the latter, drawn from the principle of perfection, are based either on the rational concept of perfection as a possible result or on the concept of an independent perfection (the will of God) as the determining cause of our will.

Empirical principles are not at all suited to serve as the basis of moral laws. For if the basis of the universality by which they should be valid for all rational beings without distinction (the unconditional practical necessity which is thereby imposed upon them) is derived from a particular tendency of human nature or the accidental circumstance in which it is found, that universality is lost. But the principle of one's own happiness is the most objectionable of all. This is not merely because it is false and because experience contradicts the supposition that well-being is always proportional to good conduct, nor yet because this principle contributes nothing to the establishment of morality, inasmuch as it is a very different thing to make a man happy from making him good, and to make him prudent and farsighted for his own advantage is far from making him virtuous. Rather, it is because this principle supports morality with incentives which undermine it and destroy all its sublimity, for it puts the motives to virtue and those to vice in the same class, teaching us only to make a better calculation while obliterating the specific difference between them. On the other hand, there is the alleged special sense,[14] the moral feeling. The appeal to it is superficial, since those who cannot think expect help from feeling, even with respect to that which concerns universal laws; they do so even though feelings naturally differ so infinitely in degree that they are incapable of furnishing a uniform standard of the good and bad, and also in spite of the fact that one cannot validly judge for others by means of his own feeling. Nevertheless, the moral feeling is nearer to morality and its dignity, inasmuch as it pays virtue the honor of ascribing the satisfaction and esteem for her directly to morality, and does not, as it were, say to her face that it is not her beauty but only our advantage which attaches us to her.

Among the rational principles of morality, there is the ontological concept of perfection. It is empty, indefinite, and consequently useless for finding in the immeasurable field of possible reality the greatest possible sum which is suitable to us; and, in specifically distinguishing the reality which is here in question from all other reality, it inevitably tends to move in a circle and cannot avoid tacitly presupposing the morality which it ought to explain. Nevertheless, it is better than the theological concept, which derives morality from a most perfect divine will. It is better not merely because we cannot intuit its perfection, having rather to derive it only from our own concepts of which morality itself is foremost, but also because if we do not so derive it (and to do so would involve a most flagrant circle in explanation), the only remaining concept of

14. I count the principle of moral feeling under that of happiness, because every empirical interest promises to contribute to our well-being by the agreeableness that a thing affords, either directly and without a view to future advantage or with a view to it. We must likewise, with Hutcheson, count the principle of sympathy with the happiness of others under the moral sense which he assumed.

the divine will is made up of the attributes of desire for glory and dominion combined with the awful conceptions of might and vengeance, and any system of ethics based on them would be directly opposed to morality.

But if I had to choose between the concept of the moral sense and that of perfection in general (neither of which at any rate weakens morality, although they are not capable of serving as its foundations), I would decide for the latter, because it preserves the indefinite idea (of a will good in itself) free from corruption until it can be more narrowly defined. It at least withdraws the decision of the question from sensibility and brings it to the court of pure reason, although it does not even here decide the question.

For the rest, I think that I may be excused from a lengthy refutation of all these doctrines. It is so easy, and presumably so well understood even by those whose office requires them to decide for one of these theories (since the hearers would not tolerate suspension of judgment), that such a refutation would be only superfluous work. What interests us more, however, is to know that all these principles set up nothing other than the heteronomy of the will as the first ground of morality and thus necessarily miss their aim.

In every case in which an object of the will must be assumed as prescribing the rule which is to determine the will, the rule is nothing else but heteronomy. The imperative in this case is conditional, stating that if or because one wills this object, one should act thus or so. Therefore the imperative can never command morally, that is, categorically. The object may determine the will by means of inclination, as in the principle of one's own happiness, or by means of reason directed to objects of our possible volition in general, as in the principle of perfection; but the will in these cases never determines itself directly by the conception of the action itself but only by the incentive which the foreseen result of the action incites in the will—that is, "I ought to do something because I will something else." And here still another law must be assumed in my person as the basis of this imperative; it would be a law by which I would necessarily will that other thing; but this law would again require an imperative to restrict this maxim. Since the conception of an object commensurate to our power incites in the will an impulse according to the natural characteristic of our person, this impulse belongs to the nature of the subject (either to the sensibility, i.e., inclination and taste, or to understanding and reason, which faculties, according to the particular constitution of their nature, take pleasure in exercising themselves on an object). It follows that it would be really nature that would give the law. As a law of nature, known and proved by experience, it would be contingent and therefore unfit to be an apodictical practical rule such as the moral rule must be. Such a law always represents heteronomy of the will; the will does not give itself the law, but an external impulse gives it to the will according to the nature of the subject which is adapted to receive it.

The absolutely good will, the principle of which must be a categorical imperative, is thus undetermined with reference to any objects. It contains only the form of volition in general, and this form is autonomy. That is, the capability of the maxims of every good will to make themselves universal laws is itself the sole law which the will of every rational being imposes on itself, and it does not need to support this on any incentive or interest.

How such a synthetical practical a priori proposition is possible and why it is necessary is a problem whose solution does not lie within the boundaries of the metaphysics of morals. Moreover, we have not here affirmed its truth, and even less professed to command a proof of it. We showed only through the development of the universally received concept of morals that autonomy of the will is unavoidably connected with it, or rather that it is its foundation. Whoever, therefore, holds morality to be something real and not a chimerical idea without truth must also concede its principle which has been adduced here. Consequently, this section was merely analytical, like the first. To prove that morality is not a mere phantom of the mind—and if the categorical imperative, and with it the autonomy of the will, is true and absolutely necessary as an a priori principle, it follows that it is no phantom—requires that a synthetical use of pure practical reason is possible. But we must not venture on this use without first making a critical examination of this faculty of reason. In the last section we shall give the principal features of such an examination that will be sufficient for our purpose.

# Third Section
## *Transition from the Metaphysics of Morals to the Critical Examination of Pure Practical Reason*

As will is a kind of causality of living beings so far as they are rational, freedom would be that property of this causality by which it can be effective independently of foreign causes determining it, just as natural necessity is the property of the causality of all irrational beings by which they are determined in their activity by the influence of foreign causes.

The preceding definition of freedom is negative and therefore affords no insight into its essence. But a positive concept of freedom flows from it which is so much the richer and more fruitful. Since the concept of a causality entails that of laws according to which something, i.e., the effect, must be established through something else which we call cause, it follows that freedom is by no means lawless even though it is not a property of the will according to laws of nature. Rather, it must be a causality according to immutable laws, but of a peculiar kind. Otherwise a free will would be an absurdity. Natural necessity is, as we have seen, a heteronomy of efficient causes, for every effect is possible only according to the law that something else determines the efficient cause to its causality. What else, then, can the freedom of the will be but autonomy, i.e., the property of the will to be a law to itself? The proposition that the will is a law to itself in all its actions, however, only expresses the principle that we should act according to no other maxim than that which can also have itself as a universal law for its object. And this is just the formula of the categorical imperative and the principle of morality. Therefore a free will and a will under moral laws are identical.

Thus if freedom of the will is presupposed, morality together with its principle follows from it by the mere analysis of its concept. But the principle is nevertheless a synthetical proposition: an absolutely good will is one whose maxim can always include itself as a universal law. It is synthetical because by analysis of the concept of an absolutely good will that property of the maxim cannot be found. Such synthetical propositions, however, are possible only by the fact that both cognitions are connected through their union with a third in which both of them are to be found. The positive concept of freedom furnishes this third cognition, which cannot be, as in the case of physical causes, the nature of the sensuous world, in the concept of which we find conjoined the concepts of something as cause in relation to something else as effect. We cannot yet show directly what this third cognition is to which freedom directs us and of which we have an a priori idea, nor can we explain the deduction of the concept of freedom from pure practical reason and therewith the possibility of categorical imperative. For this some further preparation is needed.

#### FREEDOM MUST BE PRESUPPOSED AS THE PROPERTY
#### OF THE WILL OF ALL RATIONAL BEINGS

It is not enough to ascribe freedom to our will, on any grounds whatever, if we do not also have sufficient grounds for attributing it to all rational beings. For since morality serves as a law for us only as rational beings, morality must hold valid for all rational beings, and since it must be derived exclusively from the property of freedom, freedom as the property of the will of all rational beings must be demonstrated. And it does not suffice to prove it from certain alleged experiences of human nature (which is indeed impossible, as it can be proved only a priori), but we must prove it as belonging generally to the activity of rational beings endowed with a will. Now I say that every being which cannot act otherwise than under the idea of freedom is thereby really free in a practical respect. That is to say, all laws which are inseparably bound up with freedom hold for it just as if its will were proved free in itself by theoretical philosophy.[1] Now I affirm that we must necessarily grant that every rational being who has a will also has the idea of freedom and that it acts only under this idea. For in such a being we think of a reason which is practical, i.e., a reason which has causality with respect to its objects. Now, we cannot conceive of a reason which consciously responds to a bidding from the outside with respect to its judgments, for then the subject would attribute the determination of its power of judgment not to reason but to an impulse. Reason must regard itself as the author of its principles, independently of foreign influences; consequently, as practical reason or as the will of a rational being, it must regard itself as free. That is to say, the will of a rational being can be a will of its own only under the idea of freedom, and therefore in a practical point of view such a will must be ascribed to all rational beings.

### OF THE INTEREST ATTACHING TO THE
### IDEAS OF MORALITY

We have finally reduced the definite concept of morality to the idea of freedom, but we could not prove freedom to be real in ourselves and in human nature. We saw only that we must presuppose it if we would think of a being as rational and conscious of his causality with respect to actions, that is, as endowed with a will; and so we find that on the very same grounds we must ascribe to each being endowed with reason and will the property of determining himself to action under the idea of freedom.

From presupposing this idea [of freedom] there followed also consciousness of a law of action: that the subjective principles of actions, i.e., maxims, in every instance must be so chosen that they can hold also as objective, i.e., universal, principles, and thus can

---

1. I follow this method, assuming that it is sufficient for our purpose that rational beings take merely the idea of [*in der Idee*] freedom as basic to their actions, in order to avoid having also to prove freedom in its theoretical aspect. For if the latter is left unproved, the laws which would obligate a being who was really free would hold for a being who cannot act except under the idea of his own freedom. Thus we can escape here from the onus which presses on the theory.

serve as principles for the universal laws we give. But why should I subject myself as a rational being, and thereby all other beings endowed with reason, to this law? I will admit that no interest impels me to do so, for that would then give no categorical imperative. But I must nevertheless take an interest in it and see how it comes about, for this "ought" is properly a "would" that is valid for every rational being provided reason is practical for him without hindrance [i.e., exclusively determines his action]. For beings who like ourselves are affected by the senses as incentives different from reason and who do not always do that which reason for itself alone would have done, that necessity of action is expressed only as an "ought." The subjective necessity is thus distinguished from the objective.

It therefore seems that the moral law, i.e., the principle of the autonomy of the will, is, properly speaking, only presupposed in the idea of freedom, as if we could not prove its reality and objective necessity by itself. Even if that were so, we would still have gained something because we would at least have defined the genuine principle more accurately than had been done before. But with regard to its validity and to the practical necessity of subjection to it, we would not have advanced a single step, for we could give no satisfactory answer to anyone who asked us why the universal validity of our maxim as of a law had to be the restricting condition of our action. We could not tell on what is based the worth we ascribe to actions of this kind—a worth so great that there can be no higher interest, nor could we tell how it happens that man believes it is only through this that he feels his own personal worth, in contrast to which the worth of a pleasant or unpleasant condition is to be regarded as nothing.

We do find sometimes that we can take an interest in a personal quality which involves no [personal] interest in any [external] condition, provided only that [possession of] this quality makes us capable of participating in the [desired] condition in case reason were to effect the allotment of it. That is, mere worthiness to be happy even without the motive of participating in it can interest us of itself. But this judgment is in fact only the effect of the already assumed importance of moral laws (if by the idea of freedom we detach ourselves from every empirical interest). But that we ought to detach ourselves, i.e., regard ourselves as free in acting and yet as subject to certain laws, in order to find a worth merely in our person which would compensate for the loss of everything which makes our situation desirable—how this is possible and hence on what grounds the moral law obligates us we still cannot see in this way.

We must openly confess that there is a kind of circle here from which it seems there is no escape. We assume that we are free in the order of efficient causes so that we can conceive of ourselves as subject to moral laws in the order of ends. And then we think of ourselves as subject to these laws because we have ascribed freedom of the will to ourselves. This is circular because freedom and self-legislation of the will are both autonomy and thus are reciprocal concepts, and for that reason one of them cannot be used to explain the other and to furnish a ground for it. At most they can be used for the logical purpose of bringing apparently different conceptions of the same object under a single concept (as we reduce different fractions of the same value to the lowest common terms).

One recourse, however, remains open to us, namely, to inquire whether we do not assume a different standpoint when we think of ourselves as causes a priori efficient through freedom from that which we occupy when we conceive of ourselves in the light of our actions as effects which we see before our eyes.

The following remark requires no subtle reflection, and we may suppose that even the commonest understanding can make it, though it does so, after its fashion, by an obscure discernment of judgment which it calls feeling: all conceptions, like those of the senses, which come to us without our choice enable us to know the objects only as they affect us, while what they are in themselves remains unknown to us; therefore, as regards this kind of conception, even with the closest attention and clearness which understanding may ever bring to them we can attain only to knowledge of appearances and never to knowledge of things in themselves. As soon as this distinction is made (perhaps merely because of a difference noticed between conceptions which are given to us from somewhere else and to which we are passive and those which we produce only from ourselves and in which we show our own activity), it follows of itself that we must admit and assume behind the appearances something else which is not appearance, namely, things in themselves; we do so although we must admit that we cannot approach them more closely and can never know what they are in themselves, since they can never be known by us except as they affect us. This must furnish a distinction, though a crude one, between a world of sense and a world of understanding. The former, by differences in the sensuous faculties, can be very different among various observers, while the latter, which is its foundation, remains always the same. A man may not presume to know even himself as he really is by knowing himself through inner sensation. For since he does not, as it were, produce himself or derive his concept of himself a priori but only empirically, it is natural that he obtains his knowledge of himself through inner sense and consequently only through the appearance of his nature and the way in which his consciousness is affected. But beyond the characteristic of his own subject which is compounded of these mere appearances, he necessarily assumes something else as its basis, namely, his ego as it is in itself. Thus in respect to mere perception and receptivity to sensations he must count himself as belonging to the world of sense; but in respect to that which may be pure activity in himself (i.e., in respect to that which reaches consciousness directly and not by affecting the senses) he must reckon himself as belonging to the intellectual world. But he has no further knowledge of that world.

To such a conclusion, the thinking man must come with respect to all things which may present themselves to him. Presumably it is to be met with in the commonest understanding which, as is well known, is very much inclined to expect behind the objects of the senses something else invisible and acting of itself. But such an understanding soon spoils it by trying to make the invisible again sensuous, i.e., to make it an object of intuition. Thus common understanding becomes not in the least wiser.

Now man really finds in himself a faculty by which he distinguishes himself from all other things, even from himself so far as he is affected by objects. This faculty is reason. As a pure spontaneous activity it is elevated even above understanding. For though the latter is also a spontaneous activity and does not, like sense, merely contain conceptions which arise only when one is affected by things, being passive, it nevertheless cannot produce by its activity any other concepts than those which serve to bring the sensuous conceptions under rules, and thereby to unite them in one consciousness. Without this use of sensibility it would not think at all, while, on the other hand, reason shows such a pure spontaneity in the case of ideas that it far transcends everything that sensibility can give to consciousness and shows its chief occupation in distinguishing the world of sense from the world of understanding, thereby prescribing limits to the understanding itself.

For this reason a rational being must regard himself as intelligence (and not from the side of his lower powers), as belonging to the world of understanding and not to that of the senses. Thus he has two standpoints from which he can consider himself and recognize the laws of the employment of his powers and consequently of all his actions: first, as belonging to the world of sense under laws of nature (heteronomy), and, second, as belonging to the intelligible world under laws which, independent of nature, are not empirical but founded only on reason.

As a rational being and thus as belonging to the intelligible world, man cannot think of the causality of his own will except under the idea of freedom, for independence from the determining causes of the world of sense (an independence which reason must always ascribe to itself) is freedom. The concept of autonomy is inseparably connected with the idea of freedom, and with the former there is inseparably bound the universal principle of morality, which ideally is the ground of all actions of rational beings, just as natural law is the ground of all appearances.

Now we have removed the suspicion which we raised that there might be a hidden circle in our reasoning from freedom to autonomy and from the latter to the moral law. This suspicion was that we laid down the idea of freedom for the sake of the moral law in order later to derive the latter from freedom, and that we were thus unable to give any ground for the law, presenting it only as a *petitio principii* that well-disposed minds would gladly allow us but which we could never advance as a demonstrable proposition. But we now see that, if we think of ourselves as free, we transport ourselves into the intelligible world as members of it and know the autonomy of the will together with its consequence, morality; while, if we think of ourselves as obligated, we consider ourselves as belonging both to the world of sense and at the same time to the intelligible world.

HOW IS A CATEGORICAL IMPERATIVE POSSIBLE?

The rational being counts himself, qua intelligence, as belonging to the intelligible world, and only as an efficient cause belonging to it does he call his causality a will. On the other side, however, he is conscious of himself as a part of the world of sense in which his actions are found as mere appearances of that causality. But we do not discern how they are possible on the basis of that causality which we do not know; rather, those actions must be regarded as determined by other appearances, namely, desires and inclinations, belonging to the world of sense. As a mere member of the intelligible world, all my actions would completely accord with the principle of the autonomy of the pure will, and as a part only of the world of sense would they have to be assumed to conform wholly to the natural law of desires and inclinations and thus to the heteronomy of nature. (The former actions would rest on the supreme principle of morality, and the latter on that of happiness.) But since the intelligible world contains the ground of the world of sense and hence of its laws, the intelligible world is (and must be conceived as) directly legislative for my will, which belongs wholly to the intelligible world. Therefore I recognize myself qua intelligence as subject to the law of the world of understanding and to the autonomy of the will. That is, I recognize myself as subject to the law of reason which contains in the idea of freedom the law of the intelligible world, while at the same time I must acknowledge that I am a being which belongs to the world of sense. Therefore I must regard the laws of the intelligible world as imperatives for me, and actions in accord with this principle as duties.

Thus categorical imperatives are possible because the idea of freedom makes me a member of an intelligible world. Consequently, if I were a member of only that world, all my actions *would* always be in accordance with the autonomy of the will. But since I intuit myself at the same time as a member of the world of sense, my actions *ought* to conform to it, and this categorical ought presents a synthetic a priori proposition, since besides my will affected by my sensuous desires there is added the idea of exactly the same will as pure, practical of itself, and belonging to the intelligible world, which according to reason contains the supreme condition of the former [sensuously affected] will. It is similar to the manner in which concepts of the understanding, which of themselves mean nothing but lawful form in general, are added to the intuitions of the sensuous world, thus rendering possible a priori synthetic propositions on which all knowledge of a system of nature rests.

The practical use of common human reason confirms the correctness of this deduction. When we present examples of honesty of purpose, of steadfastness in following good maxims, and of sympathy and general benevolence even with great sacrifice of advantages and comfort, there is no man, not even the most malicious villain (provided he is otherwise accustomed to using his reason), who does not wish that he also might have these qualities. But because of his inclinations and impulses he cannot bring this about, yet at the same time he wishes to be free from such inclinations which are burdensome even to himself. He thus proves that, with a will free from all impulses of sensibility, he in thought transfers himself into an order of things altogether different from that of his desires in the field of sensibility. He cannot expect to obtain by that wish any gratification of desires or any condition which would satisfy his real or even imagined inclinations, for the idea itself, which elicits this wish from him, would lose its pre-eminence if he had any such expectation. He can expect only a greater inner worth of his person. He imagines himself to be this better person when he transfers himself to the standpoint of a member of the intelligible world to which he is involuntarily impelled by the idea of freedom, i.e., independence from the determining causes of the world of sense; and from this standpoint he is conscious of a good will, which on his own confession constitutes the law for his bad will as a member of the world of sense. He acknowledges the authority of this law even while transgressing it. The moral ought is therefore his own volition as a member of the intelligible world, and it is conceived by him as an ought only in so far as he regards himself at the same time as a member of the world of sense.

### ON THE EXTREME LIMIT OF ALL PRACTICAL PHILOSOPHY

In respect to their will, all men think of themselves as free. Hence arise all judgments of actions as being such as ought to have been done, although they were not done. But this freedom is not an empirical concept and cannot be such, for it still remains even though experience shows the contrary of the demands which are necessarily conceived as consequences of the supposition of freedom. On the other hand, it is equally necessary that everything which happens should be inexorably determined by natural laws, and this natural necessity is likewise no empirical concept, because it implies the concept of necessity and thus of a priori knowledge. But this concept of a system of nature is confirmed by experience, and it is inevitably presupposed if experience, which is knowledge of the objects of the senses interconnected by universal laws, is to be possible. Therefore freedom is only an idea of reason whose objective reality in itself is doubtful, while nature is a concept of the understanding which shows and necessarily must show its reality by examples in experience.

There now arises a dialectic of reason, since the freedom ascribed to the will seems to stand in contradiction to natural necessity. At this parting of the ways reason in its speculative purpose finds the way of natural necessity more well-beaten and usable than that of freedom; but in its practical purpose the footpath of freedom is the only one on which it is possible to make use of reason in our conduct. Hence it is as impossible for the subtlest philosophy as for the commonest reasoning to argue freedom away. Philosophy must therefore assume that no true contradiction will be found between freedom and natural necessity in the same human actions, for it cannot give up the concept of nature any more than that of freedom.

Hence even if we should never be able to conceive how freedom is possible, at least this apparent contradiction must be convincingly eradicated. For if even the thought of freedom contradicts itself or nature, which is equally necessary, it would have to be surrendered in competition with natural necessity.

But it would be impossible to escape this contradiction if the subject, who seems to himself free, thought of himself in the same sense or in the same relationship when he calls himself free as when he assumes that in the same action he is subject to natural law. Therefore it is an inescapable task of speculative philosophy to show at least that its illusion about the contradiction rests in the fact that we [do not] think of man in a different sense and relationship when we call him free from that in which we consider him as a part of nature and subject to its laws. It must show not only that they can very well coexist but also that they must be thought of as necessarily united in one and the same subject; for otherwise no ground could be given why we should burden reason with an idea which, though it may without contradiction be united with another that is sufficiently established, nevertheless involves us in a perplexity which sorely embarrasses reason in its speculative use. This duty is imposed only on speculative philosophy, so that it may clear the way for practical philosophy. Thus the philosopher has no choice as to whether he will remove the apparent contradiction or leave it untouched, for in the latter case the theory of it would be *bonum vacans*, into the possession of which the fatalist can rightly enter and drive all morality from its alleged property as occupying it without title.

Yet we cannot say here that we have reached the beginnings of practical philosophy. For the settlement of the controversy does not belong to practical philosophy, as the latter demands from speculative reason only that it put an end to the discord in which it entangles itself in theoretical questions, so that practical reason may have rest and security from outer attacks which could dispute with it the ground on which it desires to erect its edifice.

The title to freedom of the will claimed by common reason is based on the consciousness and the conceded presupposition of the independence of reason from merely subjectively determining causes which together constitute what belongs only to sensation, being comprehended under the general name of sensibility. Man, who in this way regards himself as intelligence, puts himself in a different order of things and in a relationship to determining grounds of an altogether different kind when he thinks of himself as intelligence with a will and thus endowed with causality, compared with that other order of things and that other set of determining grounds which become relevant when he perceives himself as a phenomenon in the world of sense (as he really also is) and submits his causality to external determination according to natural laws. Now he soon realizes that both can subsist together—indeed, that they must. For there is not the least contradiction between a thing in appearance (as belonging to the world of sense) being subject to certain laws of which it is independent as a thing or a being in itself. That it must think of itself in this twofold manner rests, with regard to the first, on the consciousness of itself as an object affected through the senses, and, with regard to what is required by the second, on the consciousness of itself as intelligence, i.e., as independent of sensuous impressions in the use of reason and thus as belonging to the intelligible world.

This is why man claims to possess a will which does not let him become accountable for what belongs merely to his desires and inclinations, but thinks of actions which can be performed only by disregarding all desires and sensuous attractions, as possible and indeed necessary for him. The causality of these actions lies in him as an intelligence and in effects and actions in accordance with principles of an intelligible world, of which he knows only that reason alone and indeed pure reason independent of sensibility gives the law in it. Moreover, since it is only as intelligence that he is his proper self (being as man only appearance of himself), he knows that those laws apply to him directly and categorically, so that that to which inclinations and impulses and hence the entire nature of the world of sense incite him cannot in the least impair the laws of his volition as an intelligence. He does not even hold himself responsible for these inclinations and impulses or attribute them to his proper self, i.e., his will, though he does ascribe to his will the indulgence which he may grant to them when he permits them an influence on his maxims to the detriment of the rational laws of his will.

When practical reason thinks itself into an intelligible world, it does in no way transcend its limits. It would do so, however, if it tried to intuit or feel itself into it. The intelligible world is only a negative thought with respect to the world of sense, which does not give reason any laws for determining the will. It is positive only in the single point that freedom as negative determination is at the same time connected with a positive faculty and even a causality of reason. This causality we call a will to act so that the principle of actions will accord with the essential characteristic of a rational cause, i.e., with the condition of the universal validity of a maxim as a law. But if it were to borrow an object of the will, i.e., a motive, from the intelligible world, it would overstep its boundaries and pretend to be acquainted with something of which it knows nothing. The concept of a world of understanding is therefore only a standpoint which reason sees itself forced to take outside of appearances, in order to think of itself as practical. If the influences of sensibility were determining for man, this would not be possible; but it is necessary unless he is to be denied the consciousness of himself as an intelligence, and thus as a rational and rationally active cause, i.e., a cause acting in freedom. This thought certainly implies the idea of an order and legislation different from that of natural mechanism which applies to the world of sense; and it makes necessary the concept of an intelligible world, the whole of rational beings as things in themselves. But it does not give us the least occasion to think of it otherwise than according to its formal condition only, i.e., the universality of the maxim of the will as law and thus the autonomy of the will, which alone is consistent with freedom. All laws, on the other hand, which are directed to an object make for heteronomy, which belongs only to natural laws and which can apply only to the world of sense.

But reason would overstep all its bounds if it undertook to explain how pure reason can be practical, which is the same problem as explaining how freedom is possible.

For we can explain nothing but what we can reduce to laws whose object can be given in some possible experience. But freedom is a mere idea, the objective reality of which can in no way be shown according to natural laws or in any possible experience. Since no example in accordance with any analogy can support it, it can never be comprehended or even imagined. It holds only as the necessary presupposition of reason in a being that believes itself conscious of a will, i.e., of a faculty different from the mere faculty of desire, or a faculty of determining itself to act as intelligence and thus according to laws of reason independently of natural instincts. But where determination according to natural laws comes to an end, there too all explanation ceases and nothing remains but defense, i.e., refutation of the objections of those who pretend to have seen more deeply into the essence of things and therefore boldly declare freedom to be impossible. We can only show them that the supposed contradiction they have discovered lies nowhere else than in their necessarily regarding man as appearance in order to make natural law valid with respect to human actions. And now when we require them to think of him qua intelligence as a thing in itself, they still persist in considering him as appearance. Obviously, then, the separation of his causality (his will) from all natural laws of the world of sense in one and the same subject is a contradiction, but this disappears when they reconsider and confess, as is reasonable, that behind the appearances things in themselves must stand as their hidden ground and that we cannot expect the laws of the activity of these grounds to be the same as those under which their appearances stand.

The subjective impossibility of explaining the freedom of the will is the same as the impossibility of discovering and explaining an interest[2] which man can take in moral laws. Nevertheless, he does actually take an interest in them, and the foundation in us of this interest we call the moral feeling. The moral feeling has been erroneously construed by some as the standard for our moral judgment, whereas it must rather be regarded as the subjective effect which the law has upon the will to which reason alone gives objective grounds.

In order to will that which reason alone prescribes to the sensuously affected rational being as that which he ought to will, certainly there is required a power of reason to instill a feeling of pleasure or satisfaction in the fulfillment of duty, and hence there must be a causality of reason to determine the sensibility in accordance with its own principles. But it is wholly impossible to discern, i.e., to make a priori conceivable, how a mere thought containing nothing sensuous is to produce a sensation of pleasure or displeasure. For that is a particular kind of causality of which, as of all causality, we cannot determine anything a priori but must consult experience only. But since experience can exemplify the relation of cause to effect only as subsisting between two objects of experience, while here pure reason by mere Ideas (which furnish no object for experience) is to be the cause of an effect which does lie in experience, an explanation of how and why the universality of the maxim as law (and hence morality) interests us is completely impossible for us as men. Only this much is certain: that it is valid for us not because it interests us (for that is heteronomy and dependence of practical reason on sensibility, i.e., on a basic feeling,

2. Interest is that by which reason becomes practical, i.e., a cause determining the will. We therefore say only of a rational being that he takes an interest in something; irrational creatures feel only sensuous impulses. A direct interest in the action is taken by reason only if the universal validity of its maxim is sufficient determining ground of the will. Only such an interest is pure. But if reason can determine the will only by means of another object of desire or under the presupposition of a particular feeling of the subject, reason takes merely an indirect interest in the action, and since reason by itself alone without experience can discover neither objects of the will nor a particular feeling which lies at its root, that indirect interest would be only empirical and not a pure interest of reason. The logical interest of reason in advancing its insights is never direct but rather presupposes purposes for which they are to be used.

and thus it could never be morally legislative), but that it interests us because it is valid for us as men, inasmuch as it has arisen from our will as intelligence and hence from our proper self; but what belongs to mere appearance is necessarily subordinated by reason to the nature of the thing in itself.

Thus the question, "How is a categorical imperative possible?" can be answered to this extent: We can cite the only presupposition under which it is alone possible. This is the Idea of freedom, and we can discern the necessity of this presupposition which is sufficient to the practical use of reason, i.e., to the conviction of the validity of this imperative and hence also of the moral law. But how this presupposition itself is possible can never be discerned by any human reason. However, on the presupposition of freedom of the will of an intelligence, its autonomy as the formal condition under which alone it can be determined is a necessary consequence. To presuppose the freedom of the will is not only quite possible, as speculative philosophy itself can prove, for it does not involve itself in a contradiction with the principle of natural necessity in the interconnection of appearances in the world of sense. But it is also unconditionally necessary that a rational being conscious of his causality through reason and thus conscious of a will different from desires should practically presuppose it, i.e., presuppose it in the idea as the fundamental condition of all his voluntary actions. Yet how pure reason, without any other incentives, wherever they may be derived, can by itself be practical, i.e., how the mere principle of the universal validity of all its maxims as laws (which would certainly be the form of a pure practical reason), without any material (object) of the will in which we might in advance take some interest, can itself furnish an incentive and produce an interest which would be called purely moral; or, in other words, how pure reason can be practical—to explain this, all human reason is wholly incompetent, and all the pains and work of seeking an explanation of it are wasted.

It is just the same as if I sought to find out how freedom itself as causality of a will is possible; for, in so doing, I would leave the philosophical basis of explanation behind, and I have no other. Certainly I could revel in the intelligible world, the world of intelligences, which still remains to me; but although I have a well-founded idea of it, still I do not have the least knowledge of it, nor can I ever attain to it by all the exertions of my natural capacity of reason. This intelligible world signifies only a something which remains when I have excluded from the determining grounds of my will everything belonging to the world of sense in order to withhold the principle of motives from the field of sensibility. I do so by limiting it and showing that it does not contain absolutely everything in itself but that outside it there is still more; but this more I do not further know. After banishing all material, i.e., knowledge of objects, from pure reason which formulates this ideal, there remain to me only the form, the practical law of universal validity of maxims, and, in conformity with this, reason in relation to a pure intelligible world as a possible effective cause, i.e., as determining the will. An incentive must here be wholly absent unless this idea of an intelligible world itself be the incentive or that in which reason primarily take an interest. But to make this conceivable is precisely the problem we cannot solve.

Here is, then, the supreme limit of all moral inquiry. To define it is very important, both in order that reason may not seek around, on the one hand, in the world of sense, in a way harmful to morals, for the supreme motive and for a comprehensible but empirical interest; and so that it will not, on the other hand, impotently flap its wings in the space (for it, an empty space) of transcendent concepts which we call the intelligible world, without being able to move from its starting point, or lose itself amid phantoms. Furthermore, the idea of a pure intelligible world as a whole of all intelligences to which we ourselves belong as rational beings (though on the other side we are at the same time members of the world of sense) is always a useful and permissible idea for the purpose of a rational faith. This is so even though all knowledge terminates at its boundary, for through the glorious ideal of a universal realm of ends-in-themselves (rational beings) a lively interest in the moral law can be awakened in us. To that realm we can belong as members only when we carefully conduct ourselves according to maxims of freedom as if they were laws of nature.

The speculative use of reason with respect to nature leads to the absolute necessity of some supreme cause of the world. The practical use of reason with respect to freedom leads also to an absolute necessity, but to the necessity only of laws of actions of a rational being as such. Now it is an essential principle of all use of reason to push its knowledge to a consciousness of its necessity, for otherwise it would not be rational knowledge. But it is also an equally essential restriction of this very same reason that it cannot discern the necessity of what is or what occurs or what ought to be done, unless a condition under which it is or occurs or ought to be done is presupposed. In this way, however, the satisfaction of reason is only further and further postponed by the constant inquiry after the condition. Therefore, reason restlessly seeks the unconditionally necessary and sees itself compelled to assume it, though it has no means by which to make it comprehensible and is happy enough if it can only discover the concept which is consistent with this presupposition. It is therefore no objection to our deduction of the supreme principle of morality, but a reproach which we must make to human reason generally, that it cannot render comprehensible the absolute necessity of an unconditional practical law (such as the categorical imperative must be). Reason cannot be blamed for being unwilling to explain it by a condition, i.e., by making some interest its basis, for the law would then cease to be moral, i.e., a supreme law of freedom. And so we do not indeed comprehend the practical unconditional necessity of the moral imperative; yet we do comprehend its incomprehensibility, which is all that can be fairly demanded of a philosophy which in its principles strives to reach the limit of human reason.

# CRITIQUE
# OF JUDGEMENT

# Preface
# to the First Edition

The faculty of knowledge from *a priori* principles may be called *pure reason,* and the general investigation into its possibility and bounds the Critique of pure reason. This is permissible although 'pure reason', as was the case with the same use of terms in our first work, is only intended to denote reason in its theoretical employment, and although there is no desire to bring under review its faculty as practical reason and its special principles as such. That Critique is, then, an investigation addressed simply to our faculty of knowing things *a priori.* Hence it makes our *cognitive faculties* its sole concern, to the exclusion of the feeling of pleasure or displeasure and the faculty of desire; and among the cognitive faculties it confines its attention to *understanding* and its *a priori* principles, to the exclusion of *judgement* and *reason,* (faculties that also belong to theoretical cognition,) because it turns out in the sequel that there is no cognitive faculty other than understanding capable of affording constitutive *a priori* principles of knowledge. Accordingly the Critique which sifts these faculties one and all, so as to try the possible claims of each of the other faculties to a share in the clear possession of knowledge from roots of its own, retains nothing but what *understanding* prescribes *a priori* as a law for nature as the complex of phenomena—the form of these being similarly furnished *a priori.* All other pure concepts it relegates to the rank of ideas, which for our faculty of theoretical cognition are transcendent: though they are not without their use nor redundant, but discharge certain functions as regulative principles. For these concepts serve partly to restrain the officious pretensions of understanding, which, presuming on its ability to supply *a priori* the conditions of the possibility of all things which it is capable of knowing, behaves as if it had thus determined these bounds as those of the possibility of all things generally, and partly also to lead understanding, in its study of nature, according to a principle of completeness, unattainable as this remains for it, and so to promote the ultimate aim of all knowledge.

Properly, therefore, it was *understanding*—which, so far as it contains constitutive *a priori* cognitive principles, has its special realm, and one, moreover, in our *faculty of knowledge*—that the Critique, called in a general way that of Pure Reason, was intended to establish in secure but particular possession against all other competitors. In the same way *reason,* which contains constitutive *a priori* principles solely in respect of the *faculty of desire,* gets its holding assigned to it by the Critique of Practical Reason.

But now comes *judgement,* which in the order of our cognitive faculties forms a middle term between understanding and reason. Has *it* also got independent *a priori* principles? If so, are they consitutive, or are they merely regulative, thus indicating no special realm? And do they give a rule *a priori* to the feeling of pleasure and displeasure, as the middle term between the faculties of cognition and desire, just as understanding prescribes laws *a priori* for the former and reason for the latter? This is the topic to which the present Critique is devoted.

A Critique of pure reason, i.e. of our faculty of judging on *a priori* principles, would be incomplete if the critical examination of judgement, which is a faculty of knowledge, and, as such, lays claim to independent principles, were not dealt with separately. Still, however, its principles cannot, in a system of pure philosophy, form a separate constituent part intermediate between the theoretical and practical divisions, but may when needful be annexed to one or other as occasion requires. For if such a system is some day worked out under the general name of Metaphysic—and its full and complete execution is both possible and of the utmost importance for the employment of reason in all departments of its activity—the critical examination of the ground for this edifice must have been previously carried down to the very depths of the foundations of the faculty of principles independent of experience, lest in some quarter it might give way, and, sinking, inevitably bring with it the ruin of all.

We may readily gather, however, from the nature of the faculty of judgement (whose correct employment is so necessary and universally requisite that it is just this faculty that is intended when we speak of sound understanding) that the discovery of a peculiar principle belonging to it—and some such it must contain in itself *a priori,* for otherwise it would not be a cognitive faculty the distinctive character of which is obvious to the most commonplace criticism—must be a task involving considerable difficulties. For this principle is one which must not be derived from *a priori* concepts, seeing that these are the property of understanding, and judgement is only directed to their application. It has, therefore, itself to furnish a concept, and one from which, properly, we get no cognition of a thing, but which it can itself employ as a rule only— but not as an objective rule to which it can adapt its judgement, because, for that, another faculty of judgement would again be required to enable us to decide whether the case was one for the application of the rule or not.

It is chiefly in those estimates that are called aesthetic, and which relate to the beautiful and sublime, whether of nature or of art, that one meets with the above difficulty about a principle (be it subjective or objective). And yet the critical search for a principle of judgement in their case is the most important item in a Critique of this faculty. For, although they do not of themselves contribute a whit to the knowledge of things, they still belong wholly to the faculty of knowledge, and evidence an immediate bearing of this faculty upon the feeling of pleasure or displeaure according to some *a priori* principle, and do so without confusing this principle with what is capable of being a determining ground of the faculty of desire, for the latter has its principles *a priori* in concepts of reason.—Logical estimates of nature, however, stand on a different footing. They deal with cases in which experience presents a conformity to law in things, which the understanding's general concept of the sensible is no longer adequate to render intelligible or explicable, and in which judgement may have recourse to itself for a principle of the reference of the natural thing to the unknowable supersensible and, indeed, must employ some such principle, though with a regard only to itself and the knowledge of nature. For in these cases the application of such an *a priori* principle for the *cognition* of what is in the world is both possible and necessary, and withal opens out prospects which are profitable for practical reason. But here there is no immediate reference to the feeling of pleasure or displeasure. But this is precisely the riddle in the principle of judgement that necessitates a separate division for this faculty in the Critique,—for there was nothing to prevent the formation of logical estimates according to concepts (from which no immediate conclusion can ever be drawn to the feeling of pleasure or displeasure) having been treated, with a critical statement of its limitations, in an appendage to the theoretical part of philosophy.

The present investigation of taste, as a faculty of aesthetic judgement, not being undertaken with a view to the formation or culture of taste, (which will pursue its course in the future, as in the past, independently of such inquiries,) but being merely directed to its transcendental aspects, I feel assured of its indulgent criticism in respect of any shortcomings on that score. But in all that is relevant to the transcendental aspect it must be prepared to stand the test of the most rigorous examination. Yet even here I venture to hope that the difficulty of unraveling a problem so involved in its nature may serve as an excuse for a certain amount of hardly avoidable obscurity in its solution, provided that the accuracy of our statement of the principle is proved with all requisite clearness. I admit that the mode of deriving the phenomena of judgement from that principle has not all the lucidity that is rightly demanded elsewhere, where the subject is cognition by concepts, and that I believe I have in fact attained in the second part of this work.

With this, then, I bring my entire critical undertaking to a close. I shall hasten to the doctrinal part, in order, as far as possible, to snatch from my advancing years what time may yet be favourable to the task. It is obvious that no separate division of Doctrine is reserved for the faculty of judgement, seeing that with judgement Critique takes the place of Theory; but, following the division of philosophy into theoretical and practical, and of pure philosophy in the same way, the whole ground will be covered by the Metaphysics of Nature and of Morals.

# Introduction

## I

## DIVISION OF PHILOSOPHY

Philosophy may be said to contain the principles of the rational cognition that concepts afford us of things (not merely, as with Logic, the principles of the form of thought in general irrespective of the Objects), and, thus interpreted, the course, usually adopted, of dividing it into *theoretical* and *practical* is perfectly sound. But this makes imperative a specific distinction on the part of the concepts by which the principles of this rational cognition get their Object assigned to them, for if the concepts are not distinct they fail to justify a division, which always presupposes that the principles belonging to the rational cognition of the several parts of the science in question are themselves mutually exclusive.

Now there are but two kinds of concepts, and these yield a corresponding number of distinct principles of the possibility of their objects. The concepts referred to are those *of nature* and that *of freedom*. By the first of these a *theoretical* cognition from *a priori* principles becomes possible. In respect of such cognition, however, the second, by its very concept, imports no more than a negative principle (that of simple antithesis), while for the determination of the will, on the other hand, it establishes fundamental principles which enlarge the scope of its activity, and which on that account are called *practical*. Hence the division of philosophy falls properly into two parts, quite distinct in their principles—a theoretical, as *Philosophy of Nature,* and a practical, as *Philosophy of Morals* (for this is what the practical legislation of reason by the concept of freedom is called). Hitherto, however, in the application of these expressions to the division of the different principles, and with them to the division of philosophy, a gross misuse of the terms has prevailed; for what is practical according to concepts of nature has been taken as identical with what is practical according to the concept of freedom, with the result that a division has been made under these heads of theoretical and practical, by which, in effect, there has been no division at all (seeing that both parts might have similar principles).

The will—for this is what is said—is the faculty of desire and, as such, is just one of the many natural causes in the world, the one, namely, which acts by concepts; and whatever is represented as possible (or necessary) through the efficacy of will is called practically possible (or necessary): the intention being to distinguish its possibility (or necessity) from the physical possibility or necessity of an effect the causality of whose cause is not determined to its production by concepts (but rather, as with lifeless matter, by mechanism, and, as with the lower animals, by instinct).—Now, the question in respect of the practical faculty: whether, that is to say, the concept, by which the causality of the will gets its rule, is a concept of nature or of freedom, is here left quite open.

The latter distinction, however, is essential. For, let the concept determining the causality be a concept of nature, and then the principles are *technically-practical;* but, let it be a concept of freedom, and they are *morally-practical.* Now, in the division of a rational science the difference between objects that require different principles for their cognition is the difference on which everything turns. Hence technically-practical principles belong to theoretical philosophy (natural science), whereas those morally-practical alone form the second part, that is, practical philosophy (ethical science).

All technically-practical rules (i.e. those of art and skill generally, or even of prudence, as a skill in exercising an influence over men and their wills) must, so far as their principles rest upon concepts, be reckoned only as corollaries to theoretical philosophy. For they only touch the possibility of things according to concepts of nature, and this embraces, not alone the means discoverable in nature for the purpose, but even the will itself (as a faculty of desire, and consequently a natural faculty), so far as it is determinable on these rules by natural motives. Still these practical rules are not called laws (like physical laws), but only precepts. This is due to the fact that the will does not stand simply under the natural concept, but also under the concept of freedom. In the latter connexion its principles are called laws, and these principles, with the addition of what follows from them, alone constitute the second or practical part of philosophy.

The solution of the problems of pure geometry is not allocated to a special part of that science, nor does the art of land-surveying merit the name of practical, in contradistinction to pure, as a second part of the general science of geometry, and with equally little, or perhaps less, right can the mechanical or chemical art of experiment or of observation be ranked as a practical part of the science of nature, or, in fine, domestic, agricultural, or political economy, the art of social intercourse, the principles of dietetics, or even general instruction as to the attainment of happiness, or as much as the control of the inclinations or the restraining of the affections with a view thereto, be denominated practical philosophy—not to mention forming these latter into a second part of philosophy in general. For, between them all, the above contain nothing more than rules of skill, which are thus only technically practical—the skill being directed to producing an effect which is possible according to natural concepts of causes and effects. As these concepts belong to theoretical philosophy they are subject to those precepts as mere corollaries of theoretical philosophy (i.e. as corollaries of natural science), and so cannot claim any place in any special philosophy called practical. On the other hand the morally practical precepts, which are founded entirely on the concept of freedom, to the complete exclusion of grounds taken from nature for the determination of the will, form quite a special kind of precepts. These, too, like the rules obeyed by nature, are, without qualification, called laws,— though they do not, like the latter, rest on sensible conditions, but upon a supersensible principle,—and they must needs have a separate part of philosophy allotted to them as their own, corresponding to the theoretical part, and termed practical philosophy.

Hence it is evident that a complex of practical precepts furnished by philosophy does not form a special part of philosophy, co-ordinate with the theoretical, by reason of its precepts being practical—for that they might be, notwithstanding that their principles were derived wholly from the theoretical knowledge of nature (as technically-practical rules). But an adequate reason only exists where their principle, being in no way borrowed from the concept of nature, which is always sensibly conditioned, rests consequently on the supersensible, which the concept of freedom alone makes cognizable by means of its formal laws, and where, therefore, they are morally-practical, i.e. not merely precepts and rules in this or that interest, but laws independent of all antecedent reference to ends or aims.

## II
### THE REALM OF PHILOSOPHY IN GENERAL

The employment of our faculty of cognition from principles, and with it philosophy, is coextensive with the applicability of *a priori* concepts.

Now a division of the complex of all the objects to which those concepts are referred for the purpose, where possible, of compassing their knowledge, may be made according to the varied competence or incompetence of our faculty in that connexion.

Concepts, so far as they are referred to objects apart from the question of whether knowledge of them is possible or not, have their field, which is determined simply by the relation in which their Object stands to our faculty of cognition in general.—The part of this field in which knowledge is possible for us, is a territory *(territorium)* for these concepts and the requisite cognitive faculty. The part of the territory over which they exercise legislative authority is the realm *(ditio)* of these concepts, and their appropriate cognitive faculty. Empirical concepts have, therefore, their territory, doubtless, in nature as the complex of all sensible objects, but they have no realm (only a dwelling-place, *domicilium*), for, although they are formed according to law, they are not themselves legislative, but the rules founded on them are empirical, and consequently contingent.

Our entire faculty of cognition has two realms, that of natural concepts and that of the concept of freedom, for through both it prescribes laws *a priori*. In accordance with this distinction, then, philosophy is divisible into theoretical and practical. But the territory upon which its realm is established, and over which it *exercises* its legislative authority, is still always confined to the complex of the objects of all possible experience, taken as no more than mere phenomena, for otherwise legislation by the understanding in respect of them is unthinkable.

The function of prescribing laws by means of concepts of nature is discharged by understanding, and is theoretical. That of prescribing laws by means of the concept of freedom is discharged by reason and is merely practical. It is only in the practical sphere that reason can prescribe laws; in respect of theoretical knowledge (of nature) it can only (as by the understanding advised in the law) deduce from given laws their logical consequences, which still always remain restricted to nature. But we cannot reverse this and say that where rules are practical reason is then and there *legislative,* since the rules might be technically practical.

Understanding and reason, therefore, have two distinct jurisdictions over one and the same territory of experience. But neither can interfere with the other. For the concept of freedom just as little disturbs the legislation of nature, as the concept of nature influences legislation through the concept of freedom.—That it is possible for us at least to think without contradiction of both these jurisdictions, and their appropriate faculties, as coexisting in the same Subject, was shown by the Critique of Pure Reason, since it disposed of the objections on the other side by detecting their dialectical illusion.

Still, how does it happen that these two different realms do not form *one* realm, seeing that, while they do not limit each other in their legislation, they continually do so in their effects in the sensible world? The explanation lies in the fact that the concept of nature represents its objects in intuition doubtless, yet not as things-in-themselves, but as mere phenomena, whereas the concept of freedom represents in its Object what is no doubt a thing-in-itself, but it does not make it untuitable, and further that neither the one nor the other is capable, therefore, of furnishing a theoretical cognition of its Object (or even of the thinking Subject) as a thing-in-itself, or, as this would be, of the supersensible—the idea of which has certainly to be introduced as the basis of the possibility of all those objects of experience, although it cannot itself ever be elevated or extended into a cognition.

Our entire cognitive faculty is, therefore, presented with an unbounded, but, also, inaccessible field—the field of the supersensible—in which we seek in vain for a territory, and on which, therefore, we can have no realm for theoretical cognition, be it for concepts of understanding or of reason. This field we must indeed occupy with ideas in the interest as well of the theoretical as the practical employment of reason, but in connexion with the laws arising from the concept of freedom we cannot procure for these ideas any but practical reality, which, accordingly, fails to advance our theoretical cognition one step towards the supersensible.

Albeit, then, between the realm of the natural concept, as the sensible, and the realm of the concept of freedom, as the supersensible, there is a great gulf fixed, so that it is not possible to pass from the former to the latter (by means of the theoretical employment of reason), just as if they were so many separate worlds, the first of which is powerless to exercise influence on the second: still the latter is *meant* to influence the former—that is to say, the concept of freedom is meant to actualize in the sensible world the end proposed by its laws; and nature must consequently also be capable of being regarded in such a way that in the conformity to law of its form it at least harmonizes with the possibility of the ends to be effectuated in it according to the laws of freedom.— There must, therefore, be a ground of the *unity* of the supersensible that lies at the basis of nature, with what the concept of freedom contains in a practical way, and although the concept of this ground neither theoretically nor practically attains to a knowledge of it, and so has no peculiar realm of its own, still it renders possible the transition from the mode of thought according to the principles of the one to that according to the principles of the other.

## III

### THE CRITIQUE OF JUDGEMENT AS A MEANS OF CONNECTING THE TWO PARTS OF PHILOSOPHY IN A WHOLE

The Critique which deals with what our cognitive faculties are capable of yielding *a priori* has properly speaking no realm in respect of Objects; for it is not a doctrine, its sole business being to investigate whether, having regard to the general bearings of our faculties, a doctrine is possible by their means, and if so, how. Its field extends to all their pretensions, with a view to confining them within their legitimate bounds. But what is shut out of the division of Philosophy may still be admitted as a principal part into the general Critique of our faculty of pure cognition, in the event, namely, of its containing principles which are not in themselves available either for theoretical or practical employment.

Concepts of nature contain the ground of all theoretical cognition *a priori* and rest, as we saw, upon the legislative authority of understanding.—The concept of freedom contains the ground of all sensuously unconditioned practical precepts *a priori,* and rests upon that of reason. Both faculties, therefore, besides their application in point of logical form to principles of whatever origin, have, in addition, their own peculiar jurisdiction in the matter of their content, and so, there being no further *(a priori)* jurisdiction above them, the division of Philosophy into theoretical and practical is justified.

But there is still further in the family of our higher cognitive faculties a middle term between understanding and reason. This is *judgement,* of which we may reasonably presume by analogy that it may likewise contain, if not a special authority to prescribe laws, still a principle peculiar to itself upon which laws are sought, although one merely subjective *a priori.* This principle, even if it has no field of objects appropriate to it as its realm, may still have some territory or other with a certain character, for which just this very principle alone may be valid.

But in addition to the above considerations there is yet (to judge by analogy) a further ground, upon which judgement may be brought into line with another arrangement of our powers of representation, and one that appears to be of even greater importance than that of its kinship with the family of cognitive faculties. For all faculties of the soul, or capacities, are reducible to three, which do not admit of any further derivation from a common ground: the *faculty of knowledge,* the *feeling of pleasure or displeasure,* and the *faculty of desire.*[1] For the faculty of cognition understanding alone is leg-

---

1. Where one has reason to suppose that a relation subsists between concepts, that are used as empirical principles, and the faculty of pure cognition *a priori,* it is worth while attempting, in consideration of this connexion, to give them a transcendental definition—a definition, that is, by pure categories, so far as these by themselves adequately indicate the distinction of the concept in question from others. This course follows that of the mathematician, who leaves the empirical data of his problem indeterminate, and only brings their relation in pure synthesis under the concepts of pure arithmetic, and thus generalizes this solution.—I have been taken to task for adopting a similar procedure (*Critique of Practical Reason,* Preface, p. 16) and fault has been found with my definition of the faculty of desire, as *a faculty which by means of its representations is the cause of the actuality of the objects of those representations:* for mere *wishes* would still be desires, and yet in their case every one is ready to abandon all claim to being able by means of them alone to call their Object into existence.—But this proves no more than the presence of desires in man by which he is in contradiction with himself. For in such a case he seeks the production of the Object by means of his representation alone, without

islative, if (as must be the case where it is considered on its own account free of confusion with the faculty of desire) this faculty, as that of *theoretical cognition,* is referred to nature, in respect of which alone (as phenomenon) it is possible for us to prescribe laws by means of *a priori* concepts of nature, which are properly pure concepts of understanding.—For the faculty of desire, as a higher faculty operating under the concept of freedom, only reason (in which alone this concept has a place) prescribes laws *a priori.*— Now between the faulties of knowledge and desire stands the feeling of pleasure, just as judgement is intermediate between understanding and reason. Hence we may, provisionally at least, assume that judgement likewise contains an *a priori* principle of its own, and that, since pleasure or displeasure is necessarily combined with the faculty of desire (be it antecedent to its principle, as with the lower desires, or, as with the higher, only supervening upon its determination by the moral law), it will effect a transition from the faculty of pure knowledge, i.e. from the realm of concepts of nature, to that of the concept of freedom, just as in its logical employment it makes possible the transition from understanding to reason.

---

any hope of its being effectual, since he is conscious that his mechanical powers (if I may so call those which are not psychological), which would have to be determined by that representation, are either unequal to the task of realizing the Object (by the intervention of means, therefore) or else are addressed to what is quite impossible as, for example, to undo the past (O *mihi praeteritos,* etc.) or, to be able to annihilate the interval that, with intolerable delay, divides us from the wished-for moment.— Now, conscious as we are in such fantastic desires of the inefficiency of our representations, (or even of their futility,) as *causes* of their objects, there is still involved in every *wish* a reference of the same as cause, and therefore the representation of its *causality,* and this is especially discernible where the wish, as *longing,* is an affection. For such affections, since they dilate the heart and render it inert and thus exhaust its powers, show that a strain is kept on being exerted and re-exerted on these powers by the representations, but that the mind is allowed continually to relapse and get languid upon recognition of the impossibility before it. Even prayers for the aversion of great, and, so far as we can see, inevitable evils, and many superstitious means for attaining ends impossible of attainment by natural means, prove the causal reference of representations to their Objects—a causality which not even the consciousness of inefficiency for producing the effect can deter from straining towards it.—But why our nature should be furnished with a propensity to consciously vain desires is a teleological problem of anthropology. It would seem that were we not to be determined to the exertion of our power before we had assured ourselves of the efficiency of our faculty for producing an Object, our power would remain to a large extent unused. For as a rule we only first learn to know our powers by making trial of them. This deceit of vain desires is therefore only the result of a beneficent disposition in our nature.

Hence, despite the fact of Philosophy being only divisible into two principal parts, the theoretical and the practical, and despite the fact of all that we may have to say of the special principles of judgement having to be assigned to its theoretical part, i.e. to rational cognition according to concepts of nature: still the Critique of pure reason, which must settle this whole question before the above system is taken in hand, so as to substantiate its possibility, consists of three parts: the Critique of pure understanding, of pure judgement, and of pure reason, which faculties are called pure on the ground of their being legislative *a priori.*

## IV

### JUDGEMENT AS A FACULTY BY WHICH LAWS ARE PRESCRIBED *A PRIORI*

Judgement in general is the faculty of thinking the particular as contained under the universal. If the universal (the rule, principle, or law,) is given, then the judgement which subsumes the particular under it *is determinant.* This is so even where such a judgement is transcendental and, as such, provides the conditions *a priori* in conformity with which alone subsumption under that universal can be effected. If, however, only the particular is given and the universal has to be found for it, then the judgement is simply *reflective.*

The determinant judgement determines under universal transcendental laws furnished by understanding and is subsumptive only; the law is marked out for it *a priori,* and it has no need to devise a law for its own guidance to enable it to subordinate the particular in nature to the universal.—But there are such manifold forms of nature, so many modifications, as it were, of the universal transcendental concepts of nature, left undetermined by the laws furnished by pure understanding *a priori* as above mentioned, and for the reason that these laws only touch the general possibility of a nature, (as an object of sense,) that there must needs also be laws in this behalf. These laws, being empirical, may be contingent as far as the light of *our* understanding goes, but still, if they are to be called laws, (as the concept of a nature requires,) they must be regarded as necessary on a principle, unknown though it be to us, of the unity of the manifold.—The reflective judgement which is compelled to ascend from the particular in nature to the universal, stands, therefore, in need of a principle. This principle it cannot borrow from experience, because what it has to do is to establish just the unity of all empirical principles under higher, though likewise empirical, principles, and thence the possibility of the systematic subordination of higher and lower. Such a transcendental principle, therefore, the reflective judgement can only give as a law from and to itself. It cannot derive it from any other quarter (as it would then be a determinant judgement). Nor can it prescribe it to nature, for reflection on the laws of nature adjusts itself to nature, and not nature to the conditions according to which we strive to obtain a concept of it,—a concept that is quite contingent in respect of these conditions.

Now the principle sought can only be this: as universal laws of nature have their ground in our understanding, which prescribes them to nature (though only according to the universal concept of it as nature), particular empirical laws must be regarded, in respect of that which is left undetermined in them by these universal laws, according to a unity such as they would have if an understanding (though it be not ours) had supplied them for the benefit of our cognitive faculties, so as to render possible a system of experience according to particular natural laws. This is not to be taken as implying that such an understanding must be actually assumed, (for it is only the reflective judgement which avails itself of this idea as a principle for the purpose of reflection and not for determining anything); but this faculty rather gives by this means a law to itself alone and not to nature.

Now the concept of an Object, so far as it contains at the same time the ground of the actuality of this Object, is called its *end,* and the agreement of a thing with that constitution of things which is only possible according to ends, is called the *finality* of its form. Accordingly the principle of judgement, in respect of the form of the things of nature under empirical laws generally, is the *finality of nature* in its multiplicity. In other words, by this concept nature is represented as if an understanding contained the ground of the unity of the manifold of its empirical laws.

The finality of nature is, therefore, a particular *a priori* concept, which has its origin solely in the reflective judgement. For we cannot ascribe to the products of nature anything like a reference of nature in them to ends, but we can only make use of this concept to reflect

upon them in respect of the nexus of phenomena in na
given according to empirical laws. Furthermore, t
entirely different from practical finality (in human a
als), though it is doubtless thought after this analogy.

V

THE PRINCIPLE OF THE FORMAL FINALITY OF NATURE IS A
TRANSCENDENTAL PRINCIPLE OF JUDGEMENT

A *transcendental* principle is one through which we represent *a
priori* the universal condition under which alone things can become
Objects of our cognition generally. A principle, on the other hand,
is called metaphysical, where it represents *a priori* the condition
under which alone Objects whose concept has to be given empirically, may become further determined *a priori.* Thus the principle
of the cognition of bodies as substances, and as changeable substances, is transcendental where the statement is that their change
must have a cause: but it is metaphysical where it asserts that their
change must have an *external* cause. For in the first case bodies
need only be thought through ontological predicates (pure concepts
of understanding), e.g. as substance, to enable the proposition to
be cognized *a priori;* whereas, in the second case, the empirical
concept of a body (as a moveable thing in space) must be introduced
to support the proposition, although, once this is done, it may be
seen quite *a priori* that the latter predicate (movement only by means
of an external cause) applies to body.—In this way, as I shall show
presently, the principle of the finality of nature (in the multiplicity
of its empirical laws) is a transcendental principle. For the concept
of Objects, regarded as standing under this principle, is only the
pure concept of objects of possible empirical cognition generally,
and involves nothing empirical. On the other hand the principle of
practical finality, implied in the idea of the *determination* of a free
*will,* would be a metaphysical principle, because the concept of a
faculty of desire, as will, has to be given empirically, i.e. is not
included among transcendental predicates. But both these principles
are, none the less, not empirical, but *a priori* principles; because
no further experience is required for the synthesis of the predicate
with the empirical concept of the subject of their judgements, but
it may be apprehended quite *a priori.*

That the concept of a finality of nature belongs to transcendental principles is abundantly evident from the maxims of judgement upon which we rely *a priori* in the investigation of nature, and which yet have to do with no more than the possibility of experience, and consequently of the knowledge of nature,—but of nature not merely in a general way, but as determined by a manifold of particular laws.—These maxims crop up frequently enough in the course of this science, though only in a scattered way. They are aphorisms of metaphysical wisdom, making their appearance in a number of rules the necessity of which cannot be demonstrated from concepts. 'Nature takes the shortest way *(lex parsimoniae)*; yet it makes no leap, either in the sequence of its changes, or in the juxtaposition of specifically different forms *(lex continui in natura)*; its vast variety in empirical laws is, for all that, unity under a few principles *(principia praeter necessitatem non sunt multiplicanda)*'; and so forth.

If we propose to assign the origin of these elementary rules, and attempt to do so on psychological lines, we go straight in the teeth of their sense. For they tell us, not what happens, i.e. according to what rule our powers of judgement actually discharge their functions, and how we judge, but how we ought to judge; and we cannot get this logical objective necessity where the principles are merely empirical. Hence the finality of nature for our cognitive faculties and their employment, which manifestly radiates from them, is a transcendental principle of judgements, and so needs also a transcendental Deduction, by means of which the ground for this mode of judging must be traced to the *a priori* sources of knowledge.

Now, looking at the grounds of the possibility of an experience, the first thing, of course, that meets us is something necessary—namely, the universal laws apart from which nature in general (as an object of sense) cannot be thought. These rest on the categories, applied to the formal conditions of all intuition possible for us, so far as it is also given *a priori*. Under these laws judgement is determinant; for it has nothing else to do than to subsume under given laws. For instance, understanding says: all change has its cause (universal law of nature); transcendental judgement has nothing further to do than to furnish *a priori* the condition of subsumption under the concept of understanding placed before it: this we get in the succession of the determinations of one and the same thing. Now for nature in general, as an object of possible experience, that law is cognized as absolutely necessary.—But besides this formal time-condition, the objects of empirical cognition are determined, or, so far as we can judge *a priori*, are determinable, in diverse ways, so that specifically differentiated natures, over and above what they have in common as things of nature in general, are further capable of being causes in an infinite variety of ways; and each of these modes must, on the concept of a cause in general, have its rule, which is a law, and, consequently, imports necessity: although owing to the constitution and limitations of our faculties of cognition we may entirely fail to see this necessity. Accordingly, in respect of nature's merely empirical laws, we must think in nature a possibility of an endless multiplicity of empirical laws, which yet are contingent so far as our insight goes, i.e. cannot be cognized *a priori*. In respect of these we estimate the unity of nature according to empirical laws, and the possibility of the unity of experience, as a system according to empirical laws, to be contingent. But, now, such a unity is one which must be necessarily presupposed and assumed, as otherwise we should not have a thoroughgoing connexion of empirical cognition in a whole of experience. For the universal laws of nature, while providing, certainly, for such a connexion among things generically, as things of nature in general, do not do so for them specifically as such particular things of nature. Hence judgement is compelled, for its own guidance, to adopt it as an *a priori* principle, that what is for human insight contingent in the particular (empirical) laws of nature contains nevertheless unity of law in the synthesis of its manifold in an intrinsically possible experience—unfathomable, though still thinkable, as such unity may, no doubt, be for us. Consequently, as the unity of law in a synthesis, which is cognized by us in obedience to a necessary aim (a need of understanding), though recognized at the same time as contingent, is represented as a finality of Objects (here of nature), so judgement, which, in respect of things under possible (yet to be discovered) empirical laws, is merely reflective, must regard nature in respect of the latter according to a *principle of finality* for our cognitive faculty, which then finds expression in the above maxims of judgement. Now this transcendental concept of a finality of nature is neither a concept of nature nor of freedom, since it attributes nothing at all to the Object, i.e. to nature, but only represents the unique mode in which we must proceed in our reflection upon the objects of nature with a view to getting a thoroughly interconnected whole of experience, and so is a subjective principle, i.e. maxim, of judgement. For this reason, too, just as if it were a lucky chance that favoured us, we are rejoiced (properly speaking relieved of a want) where we meet with such systematic unity under merely empirical laws: although we must necessarily assume the presence of such a unity, apart from any ability on our part to apprehend or prove its existence.

In order to convince ourselves of the correctness of this Deduction of the concept before us, and the necessity of assuming it as a transcendental principle of cognition, let us just bethink ourselves of the magnitude of the task. We have to form a connected experience from given perceptions of a nature containing a maybe endless multiplicity of empirical laws, and this problem has its seat *a priori* in our understanding. This understanding is no doubt *a priori* in possession of universal laws of nature, apart from which nature would be incapable of being an object of experience at all. But over and above this it needs a certain order of nature in its particular rules which are only capable of being brought to its knowledge empirically, and which, so far as it is concerned, are contingent. These rules, without which we would have no means of advance from the universal analogy of a possible experience in general to a particular, must be regarded by understanding as laws, i.e. as necessary—for otherwise they would not form an order of nature—though it be unable to cognize or ever get an insight into their necessity. Albeit, then, it can determine nothing *a priori* in respect of these (Objects), it must, in pursuit of such empirical so-called laws, lay at the basis of all reflection upon them an *a priori* principle, to the effect, namely, that a cognizable order of nature is possible according to them. A principle of this kind is expressed in the following propositions. There is in nature a subordination of genera and species comprehensible by us: Each of these genera again approximates to the others on a common principle, so that a transition may be possible from one to the other, and thereby to a higher genus: While it seems at the outset unavoidable for our understanding to assume for the specific variety of natural operations a like number of various kinds of causality, yet these may all be reduced to a small number of principles, the quest for which is our business; and so forth. This adaptation of nature to our cognitive faculties is presupposed *a priori* by judgement on behalf of its reflection upon it according to empirical laws. But understanding all the while recognizes it objectively as contingent, and it is merely judgement that attributes it to nature as transcendental finality, i.e. a finality in respect of the Subject's faculty of cognition. For, were it not for this presupposition, we should have no order of nature in accordance with empirical laws, and, consequently, no guiding-thread for an experience that has to be brought to bear upon these in all their variety, or for an investigation of them.

For it is quite conceivable that, despite all the uniformity of the things of nature according to universal laws, without which we would not have the form of general empirical knowledge at all, the specific variety of the empirical laws of nature, with their effects, might still be so great as to make it impossible for our understanding to discover in nature an intelligible order, to divide its products into genera and species so as to avail ourselves of the principles of explanation and comprehension of one for explaining and interpreting another, and out of material coming to hand in such confusion (properly speaking only infinitely multiform and ill-adapted to our power of apprehension) to make a consistent context of experience.

Thus judgement, also, is equipped with an *a priori* principle for the possibility of nature, but only in a subjective respect. By means of this it prescribes a law, not to nature (as autonomy), but to itself (as heautonomy), to guide its reflection upon nature. This law may be called *the law of the specification of nature* in respect of its empirical laws. It is not one cognized *a priori* in nature, but judgement adopts it in the interests of a natural order, cognizable by our understanding, in the division which it makes of nature's universal laws when it seeks to subordinate to them a variety of particular laws. So when it is said that nature specifies its universal laws on a principle of finality for our cognitive faculties, i.e. of suitability for the human understanding and its necessary function of finding the universal for the particular presented to it by perception, and again for varieties (which are, of course, common for each species) connexion in the unity of principle, we do not thereby either prescribe a law to nature, or learn one from it by observation—although the principle in question may be confirmed by this means. For it is not a principle of the determinant but merely of the reflective judgement. All that is intended is that, no matter what is the order and disposition of nature in respect of its universal laws, we must investigate its empirical laws throughout on that principle and the maxims founded thereon, because only so far as that principle applies can we make any headway in the employment of our understanding in experience, or gain knowledge.

## VI

### THE ASSOCIATION OF THE FEELING OF PLEASURE WITH THE CONCEPT OF THE FINALITY OF NATURE

The conceived harmony of nature in the manifold of its particular laws with our need of finding universality of principles for it must, so far as our insight goes, be deemed contingent, but withal indispensable for the requirements of our understanding, and, consequently, a finality by which nature is in accord with our aim, but only so far as this is directed to knowledge.—The universal laws of understanding, which are equally laws of nature, are, although arising from spontaneity, just as necessary for nature as the laws of motion applicable to matter. Their origin does not presuppose any regard to our cognitive faculties, seeing that it is only by their means that we first come by any conception of the meaning of a knowledge of things (of nature), and they of necessity apply to nature as Object of our cognition in general. But it is contingent, so far as we can see, that the order of nature in its particular laws, with their wealth of at least possible variety and heterogeneity transcending all our powers of comprehension, should still in actual fact be commensurate with these powers. To find out this order is an undertaking on the part of our understanding, which pursues it with a regard to a necessary end of its own, that, namely, of introducing into nature unity of principle. This end must, then, be attributed to nature by judgement, since no law can be here prescribed to it by understanding.

The attainment of every aim is coupled with a feeling of pleasure. Now where such attainment has for its condition a representation *a priori*—as here a principle for the reflective judgement in general—the feeling of pleasure also is determined by a ground which is *a priori* and valid for all men: and that, too, merely by virtue of the reference of the Object to our faculty of cognition. As the concept of finality here takes no cognizance whatever of the faculty of desire, it differs entirely from all practical finality of nature.

As a matter of fact, we do not, and cannot, find in ourselves the slightest effect on the feeling of pleasure from the coincidence of perceptions with the laws in accordance with the universal concepts of nature (the Categories), since in their case understanding necessarily follows the bent of its own nature without ulterior aim. But, while this is so, the discovery, on the other hand, that two or more empirical heterogeneous laws of nature are allied under one principle that embraces them both, is the ground of a very appreciable pleasure, often even of admiration, and such, too, as does not wear off even though we are already familiar enough with its object. It is true that we no longer notice any decided pleasure in the comprehensibility of nature, or in the unity of its divisions into genera and species, without which the empirical concepts, that afford us our knowledge of nature in its particular laws, would not be possible. Still it is certain that the pleasure appeared in due course, and only by reason of the most ordinary experience being impossible without it, has it become gradually fused with simple cognition, and no longer arrests particular attention.—Something, then, that makes us attentive in our estimate of nature to its finality for our understanding—an endeavour to bring, where possible, its heterogeneous laws under higher, though still always empirical, laws—is required, in order that, on meeting with success, pleasure may be felt in this their accord with our cognitive faculty, which accord is regarded by us as purely contingent. As against this a representation of nature would be altogether displeasing to us, were we to be forewarned by it that, on the least investigation carried beyond the commonest experience, we should come in contact with such a heterogeneity of its laws as would make the union of its particular laws under universal empirical laws impossible for our understanding. For this would conflict with the principle of the subjectively final specification of nature in its genera, and with our own reflective judgement in respect thereof.

Yet this presupposition of judgement is so indeterminate on the question of the extent of the prevalence of that ideal finality of nature for our cognitive faculties, that if we are told that a more

searching or enlarged knowledge of nature, derived from observation, must eventually bring us into contact with a multiplicity of
laws that no human understanding could reduce to a principle, we
can reconcile ourselves to the thought. But still we listen more gladly
to others who hold out to us the hope that the more intimately we
come to know the secrets of nature, or the better we are able to
compare it with external members as yet unknown to us, the more
simple shall we find it in its principles, and the further our experience
advances the more harmonious shall we find it in the apparent
heterogeneity of its empirical laws. For our judgement makes it
imperative upon us to proceed on the principle of the conformity
of nature to our faculty of cognition, so far as that principle extends,
without deciding—for the rule is not given to us by a determinant
judgement—whether bounds are anywhere set to it or not. For
while in respect of the rational employment of our cognitive faculty
bounds may be definitely determined, in the empirical field no such
determination of bounds is possible.

## VII
### THE AESTHETIC REPRESENTATION
### OF THE FINALITY OF NATURE

That which is purely subjective in the representation of an Object,
i.e. what constitutes its reference to the Subject, not to the object,
is its aesthetic quality. On the other hand, that which in such a
representation serves, or is available, for the determination of the
object (for the purpose of knowledge), is its logical validity. In the
cognition of an object of sense both sides are presented conjointly.
In the sense-representation of external things the Quality of space
in which we intuite them is the merely subjective side of my representation of them (by which what the things are in themselves as
Objects is left quite open), and it is on account of that reference
that the object in being intuited in space is also thought merely as
a phenomenon. But despite its purely subjective Quality, space is
still a constituent of the knowledge of things as phenomena. *Sensation* (here external) also agrees in expressing a merely subjective
side of our representations of external things, but one which is
properly their matter (through which we are given something with
real existence), just as space is the mere *a priori* form of the pos-

sibility of their intuition; and so sensation is, none the less, also employed in the cognition of external Objects.

But that subjective side of a representation *which is incapable of becoming an element of cognition,* is the *pleasure* or *displeasure* connected with it; for through it I cognize nothing in the object of the representation, although it may easily be the result of the operation of some cognition or other. Now the finality of a thing, so far as represented in our perception of it, is in no way a quality of the object itself (for a quality of this kind is not one that can be perceived), although it may be inferred from a cognition of things. In the finality, therefore, which is prior to the cognition of an Object, and which, even apart from any desire to make use of the representation of it for the purpose of a cognition, is yet immediately connected with it, we have the subjective quality belonging to it that is incapable of becoming a constituent of knowledge. Hence we only apply the term 'final' to the object on account of its representation being immediately coupled with the feeling of pleasure: and this representation itself is an aesthetic representation of the finality.—The only question is whether such a representation of finality exists at all.

If pleasure is connected with the mere apprehension *(apprehensio)* of the form of an object of intuition, apart from any reference it may have to a concept for the purpose of a definite cognition, this does not make the representation referable to the Object, but solely to the Subject. In such a case the pleasure can express nothing but the conformity of the Object to the cognitive faculties brought into play in the reflective judgement, and so far as they are in play, and hence merely a subjective formal finality of the Object. For that apprehension of forms in the imagination can never take place without the reflective judgement, even when it has no intention of so doing, comparing them at least with its faculty of referring intuitions to concepts. If, now, in this comparison, imagination (as the faculty of intuitions *a priori*) is undesignedly brought into accord with understanding, (as the faculty of concepts,) by means of a given representation, and a feeling of pleasure is thereby aroused, then the object must be regarded as final for the reflective judgement. A judgement of this kind is an aesthetic judgement upon the finality of the Object, which does not depend upon any present concept of the object, and does not provide one. When the form of an object (as opposed to the matter of its repesentation, as sensation) is, in the mere act of reflecting upon it, without regard to any concept to be obtained from it, estimated as the ground of a pleasure in the representation of such an Object, then this pleasure is also judged to be combined necessarily with the representation of it, and so not merely for the Subject apprehending this form, but for all in general who pass judgement. The object is then called beautiful; and the faculty of judging by means of such a pleasure (and so also with universal validity) is called taste. For since the ground of the pleasure is made to reside merely in the form of the object for reflection generally, consequently not in any sensation of the object, and without any reference, either, to any concept that might have something or other in view, it is with the conformity to law in the empirical employment of judgement generally (unity of imagination and understanding) in the Subject, and with this alone, that the representation of the Object in reflection, the conditions of which are universally valid *a priori,* accords. And, as this accordance of the object with the faculties of the Subject is contingent, it gives rise to a representation of a finality on the part of the object in respect of the cognitive faculties of the Subject.

Here, now, is a pleasure which—as is the case with all pleasure or displeasure that is not brought about through the agency of the concept of freedom (i.e. through the antecedent determination of the higher faculty of desire by means of pure reason)—no concepts could ever enable us to regard as necessarily connected with the representation of an object. It must always be only through reflective perception that it is cognized as conjoined with the representation of an object. It must always be only through reflective perception that it is cognized as conjoined with this representation. As with all empirical judgements, it is, consequently, unable to announce objective necessity or lay claim to *a priori* validity. But, then, the judgement of taste in fact only lays claim, like every other empirical judgement, to be valid for every one, and, despite its inner contingency this is always possible. The only point that is strange or out of the way about it, is that it is not an empirical concept, but a feeling of pleasure (and so not a concept at all), that is yet exacted from every one by the judgement of taste, just as if it were a predicate united to the cognition of the Object, and that is meant to be conjoined with its representation.

A singular empirical judgement, as, for example, the judgement of one who perceives a movable drop of water in a rock-crystal, rightly looks to every one finding the fact as stated, since the judgement has been formed according to the universal conditions of the determinant judgement under the laws of a possible experience generally. In the same way one who feels pleasure in simple reflection on the form of an object, without having any concept in mind, rightly lays claim to the agreement of every one, although this judgement is empirical and a singular judgement. For the ground of this pleasure is found in the universal, though subjective, condition of reflective judgements, namely the final harmony of an object (be it a product of nature or of art) with the mutual relation of the faculties of cognition, (imagination and understanding,) which are requisite for every empirical cognition. The pleasure in judgements of taste is, therefore, dependent doubtless on an empirical representation, and cannot be united *a priori* to any concept (one cannot determine *a priori* what object will be in accordance with taste or not—one must find out the object that is so); but then it is only made the determining ground of this judgement by virtue of our consciousness of its resting simply upon reflection and the universal, though only subjective, conditions of the harmony of that reflection with the knowledge of objects generally, for which the form of the Object is final.

This is why judgements of taste are subjected to a Critique in respect of their possibility. For their possibility presupposes an *a priori* principle, although that principle is neither a cognitive principle for understanding nor a practical principle for the will, and is thus in no way determinant *a priori*.

Susceptibility to pleasure arising from reflection on the forms of things (whether of nature or of art) betokens, however, not only a finality on the part of Objects in their relation to the reflective judgement in the Subject, in accordance with the concept of nature, but also, conversely, a finality on the part of the Subject, answering to the concept of freedom, in respect of the form, or even formlessness, of objects. The result is that the aesthetic judgement refers not merely, as a judgement of taste, to the beautiful, but also, as springing from a higher intellectual feeling, to the *sublime*. Hence the above-mentioned Critique of Aesthetic Judgement must be divided on these lines into two main parts.

## VIII
### THE LOGICAL REPRESENTATION
### OF THE FINALITY OF NATURE

There are two ways in which finality may be represented in an object given in experience. It may be made to turn on what is purely subjective. In this case the object is considered in respect of its form as present in *apprehension (apprehensio)* prior to any concept; and the harmony of this form with the cognitive faculties, promoting the combination of the intuition with concepts for cognition generally, is represented as a finality of the form of the object. Or, on the other hand, the representation of finality may be made to turn on what is objective, in which case it is represented as the harmony of the form of the object with the possibility of the thing itself according to an antecedent concept of it containing the ground of this form. We have seen that the representation of the former kind of finality rests on the pleasure immediately felt in mere reflection on the form of the object. But that of the latter kind of finality, as it refers the form of the Object, not to the Subject's cognitive faculties engaged in its apprehension, but to a definite cognition of the object under a given concept, has nothing to do with a feeling of pleasure in things, but only with understanding and its estimate of them. Where the concept of an object is given, the function of judgement, in its employment of that concept for cognition, consists in *presentation (exhibitio),* i.e. in placing beside the concept an intuition corresponding to it. Here it may be that our own imagination is the agent employed, as in the case of art, where we realize a preconceived concept of an object which we set before ourselves as an end. Or the agent may be nature in its technic, (as in the case of organic bodies,) when we read into it our own concept of an end to assist our estimate of its product. In this case what is represented is not a mere *finality* of nature in the form of the thing, but this very product as a *natural end.*—Although our concept that nature, in its empirical laws, is subjectively final in its forms is in no way a concept of the Object, but only a principle of judgement for providing itself with concepts in the vast multiplicity of nature, so that it may be able to take its bearings, yet on the analogy of an end, as it were a regard to our cognitive faculties is here attributed to nature. *Natural beauty* may, therefore, be looked on as the *pre-*

*sentation* of the concept of formal, i.e. merely subjective, finality and *natural ends* as the presentation of the concept of a real, i.e. objective, finality. The former of these we estimate by taste (aesthetically by means of the feeling of pleasure), the latter by understanding and reason (logically according to concepts).

On these considerations is based the division of the Critique of Judgement into that of the *aesthetic* and the *teleological* judgement. By the first is meant the faculty of estimating formal finality (otherwise called subjective) by the feeling of pleasure or displeasure, by the second the faculty of estimating the real finality (objective) of nature by understanding and reason.

In a Critique of Judgement the part dealing with aesthetic judgement is essentially relevant, as it alone contains a principle introduced by judgement completely *a priori* as a basis of its reflection upon nature. This is the principle of nature's formal finality for our cognitive faculties in its particular (empirical) laws—a principle without which understanding could not feel itself at home in nature: whereas no reason is assignable *a priori,* nor is so much as the possibility of one apparent from the concept of nature as an object of experience, whether in its universal or in its particular aspects, why there should be objective ends of nature, i.e. things only possible as natural ends. But it is only judgement that, without being itself possessed *a priori* of a principle in that behalf, in actually occurring cases (of certain products) contains the rule for making use of the concept of ends in the interest of reason, after that the above transcendental principle has already prepared understanding to apply to nature the concept of an end (at least in respect of its form).

But the transcendental principle by which a finality of nature, in its subjective reference to our cognitive faculties, is represented in the form of a thing as a principle of its estimation, leaves quite undetermined the question of where and in what cases we have to make our estimate of the object as a product according to a principle of finality, instead of simply according to universal laws of nature. It resigns to the *aesthetic* judgement the task of deciding the conformity of this product (in its form) to our cognitive faculties as a question of taste (a matter which the aesthetic judgement decides, not by any harmony with concepts, but by feeling). On the other hand judgement as teleologically employed assigns the determinate conditions under which something (e.g. an organized body) is to be estimated after the idea of an end of nature. But it can adduce no principle from the concept of nature, as an object of experience, to give it its authority to ascribe *a priori* to nature a reference to ends or even only indeterminately to assume them from actual experience in the case of such products. The reason of this is that in order to be able merely empirically to cognize objective finality in a certain object, many particular experiences must be collected and reviewed under the unity of their principle.—Aesthetic judgement is, therefore, a special faculty of estimating according to a rule, but not according to concepts. The teleological is not a special faculty, but only general reflective judgement proceeding, as it always does in theoretical cognition, according to concepts, but in respect of certain objects of nature, following special principles— those, namely, of a judgement that is merely reflective and does not determine Objects. Hence, as regards its application, it belongs to the theoretical part of philosophy, and on account of its special principles, which are not determinant, as principles belonging to doctrine have to be, it must also form a special part of the Critique. On the other hand the aesthetic judgement contributes nothing to the cognition of its objects. Hence it must *only* be allocated to the Critique of the judging Subject and of its faculties of knowledge so far as these are capable of possessing *a priori* principles, be their use (theoretical or practical) otherwise what it may—a Critique which is the propaedeutic of all philosophy.

## IX

### JOINDER OF THE LEGISLATIONS OF UNDERSTANDING AND REASON BY MEANS OF JUDGEMENT

Understanding prescribes laws *a priori* for nature as an Object of sense, so that we may have a theoretical knowledge of it in a possible experience. Reason prescribes laws *a priori* for freedom and its peculiar causality as the supersensible in the Subject, so that we may have a purely practical knowledge. The realm of the concept of nature under the one legislation, and that of the concept of freedom under the other, are completely cut off from all reciprocal influence, that they might severally (each according to its own principles) exert upon the other, by the broad gulf that divides the supersensible from phenomena. The concept of freedom determines nothing in respect of the theoretical cognition of nature; and the concept of nature likewise nothing in respect of the practical laws of freedom. To that extent, then, it is not possible to throw a bridge from the one realm to the other.—Yet although the determining grounds of causality according to the concept of freedom (and the practical rule that this contains) have no place in nature, and the sensible cannot determine the supersensible in the Subject; still the converse is possible (not, it is true, in respect of the knowledge of nature, but of the consequences arising from the supersensible and bearing on the sensible). So much indeed is implied in the concept of a causality by freedom, the *operation* of which, in conformity with the formal laws of freedom, is to take effect in the world. The word *cause,* however, in its application to the supersensible only signifies the *ground* that determines the causality of things of nature to an effect in conformity with their appropriate natural laws, but at the same time also in unison with the formal principle of the laws of reason—a ground which, while its possibility is impenetrable, may still be completely cleared of the charge of contradiction that it is alleged to involve.[2] The effect in accordance with the concept of freedom is the final end which (or the manifestation of which in the sensible world) is to exist, and this presupposes the condition of the possibility of that end in nature (i.e. in the nature of the Subject as a being of the sensible world, namely, as man). It is so presupposed *a priori,* and without regard to the practical, by judgement. This faculty, with its concept of a *finality* of nature, provides us with the mediating concept between

2. One of the various supposed contradictions in this complete distinction of the causality of nature from that through freedom, is expressed in the objection that when I speak of *hindrances* opposed by nature to causality according to laws of freedom (moral laws) or of *assistance* lent to it by nature, I am all the time admitting an *influence* of the former upon the latter. But the misinterpretation is easily avoided, if attention is only paid to the meaning of the statement. The resistance or furtherance is not between nature and freedom, but between the former as phenomenon and *the effects* of the latter as phenomena in the world of sense. Even the causality of freedom (of pure and practical reason) is the causality of a natural cause subordinated to freedom (a causality of the Subject regarded as man, and consequently as a phenomenon), and one, the ground of whose determination is contained in the intelligible, that is thought under freedom, in a manner that is not further or otherwise explicable (just as in the case of that intelligible that forms the supersensible substrate of nature).

concepts of nature and the concept of freedom—a concept that makes possible the transition from the pure theoretical [legislation of understanding] to the pure practical [legislation of reason] and from conformity to law in accordance with the former to final ends according to the latter. For through that concept we cognize the possibility of the final end that can only be actualized in nature and in harmony with its laws.

Understanding, by the possibility of its supplying *a priori* laws for nature, furnishes a proof of the fact that nature is cognized by us only as phenomenon, and in so doing points to its having a supersensible substrate; but this substrate it leaves quite *undetermined*. Judgement by the *a priori* principle of its estimation of nature according to its possible particular laws provides this supersensible substrate (within as well as without us) with *determinability through the intellectual faculty*. But reason gives *determination* to the same *a priori* by its practical law. Thus judgement makes possible the transition from the realm of the concept of nature to that of the concept of freedom.

In respect of the faculties of the soul generally, regarded as higher faculties, i.e. as faculties containing an autonomy, understanding is the one that contains the *constitutive a priori* principles for the *faculty of cognition* (the theoretical knowledge of nature). The *feeling of pleasure and displeasure* is provided for by the judgement in its independence from concepts and from sensations that refer to the determination of the faculty of desire and would thus be capable of being immediately practical. For the *faculty of desire* there is reason, which is practical without mediation of any pleasure of whatsoever origin, and which determines for it, as a higher faculty, the final end that is attended at the same time with pure intellectual delight in the Object.—Judgement's concept of a finality of nature falls, besides, under the head of natural concepts, but only as a regulative principle of the cognitive faculties—although the aesthetic judgement on certain objects (of nature or of art) which occasions that concept, is a constitutive principle in respect of the feeling of pleasure or displeasure. The spontaneity in the play of the cognitive faculties whose harmonious accord contains the ground of this pleasure, makes the concept in question, in its consequences, a suitable mediating link connecting the realm of the concept of nature with that of the concept of freedom, as this accord at the same time promotes the sensibility of the mind for moral feeling. The following table may facilitate the review of all the above faculties in their systematic unity.[3]

| *List of Mental Faculties* | *Cognitive Faculties* |
|---|---|
| Cognitive faculties | Understanding |
| Feeling of pleasure and displeasure | Judgement |
| Faculty of desire | Reason |
| | |
| *A priori Principles* | *Application* |
| Conformity to law | Nature |
| Finality | Art |
| Final End | Freedom |

3. It has been thought somewhat suspicious that my divisions in pure philosophy should almost always come out threefold. But it is due to the nature of the case. If a division is to be *a priori* it must be either analytic, according to the law of contradiction—and then it is always twofold (quodlibet ens est aut A aut non A)—or else it is *synthetic.* If it is to be derived in the latter case from *a priori* concepts (not, as in mathematics, from the *a priori* intuition corresponding to the concept,) then, to meet the requirements of synthetic unity in general, namely (1) a condition, (2) a conditioned, (3) the concept arising from the union of the conditioned with its condition, the division must of necessity be trichotomous.

# Analytic of the Beautiful

## First Moment
## of the Judgement of Taste[1]:
## Moment of Quality

### § 1
#### THE JUDGEMENT OF TASTE IS AESTHETIC

If we wish to discern whether anything is beautiful or not, we do not refer the representation of it to the Object by means of understanding with a view to cognition, but by means of the imagination (acting perhaps in conjunction with understanding) we refer the representation to the Subject and its feeling of pleasure or displeasure. The judgement of taste, therefore, is not a cognitive judgement, and so not logical, but is aesthetic—which means that it is one whose determining ground *cannot be other than subjective*. Every reference of representations is capable of being objective, even that of sensations (in which case it signifies the real in an empirical representation). The one exception to this is the feeling of pleasure or displeasure. This denotes nothing in the object, but is a feeling

---

1. The definition of taste here relied upon is that it is the faculty of estimating the beautiful. But the discovery of what is required for calling an object beautiful must be reserved for the analysis of judgements of taste. In my search for the moments to which attention is paid by this judgement in its reflection, I have followed the guidance of the logical functions of judging (for a judgement of taste always involves a reference to understanding). I have brought the moment of quality first under review, because this is what the aesthetic judgement on the beautiful looks to in the first instance.

which the Subject has of itself and of the manner in which it is affected by the representation.

To apprehend a regular and appropriate building with one's cognitive faculties, be the mode of representation clear or confused, is quite a different thing from being conscious of this representation with an acompanying sensation of delight. Here the representation is referred wholly to the Subject, and what is more to its feeling of life—under the name of the feeling of pleasure or displeasure—and this forms the basis of a quite separate faculty of discriminating and estimating, that contributes nothing to knowledge. All it does is to compare the given representation in the Subject with the entire faculty of representations of which the mind is conscious in the feeling of its state. Given representations in a judgement may be empirical, and so aesthetic; but the judgement which is pronounced by their means is logical, provided it refers them to the Object. Conversely, be the given representations even rational, but referred in a judgement solely to the Subject (to its feeling), they are always to that extent aesthetic.

## § 2

### THE DELIGHT WHICH DETERMINES THE JUDGEMENT OF TASTE IS INDEPENDENT OF ALL INTEREST

The delight which we connect with the representation of the real existence of an object is called interest. Such a delight, therefore, always involves a reference to the faculty of desire, either as its determining ground, or else as necessarily implicated with its determining ground. Now, where the question is whether something is beautiful, we do not want to know, whether we, or any one else, are, or even could be, concerned in the real existence of the thing, but rather what estimate we form of it on mere contemplation (intuition or reflection). If any one asks me whether I consider that the palace I see before me is beautiful, I may, perhaps, reply that I do not care for things of that sort that are merely made to be gaped at. Or I may reply in the same strain as that Iroquois *sachem* who said that nothing in Paris pleased him better than the eating-houses. I may even go a step further and inveigh with the vigour of a *Rousseau* against the vanity of the great who spend the sweat of the people on such superfluous things. Or, in fine, I may quite easily persuade myself that if I found myself on an uninhabited island, without hope of ever again coming among men, and could conjure such a palace into existence by a mere wish, I should still not trouble to do so, so long as I had a hut there that was comfortable enough for me. All this may be admitted and approved; only it is not the point now at issue. All one wants to know is whether the mere representation of the object is to my liking, no matter how indifferent I may be to the real existence of the object of this representation. It is quite plain that in order to say that the object *is beautiful,* and to show that I have taste, everything turns on the meaning which I can give to this representation, and not on any factor which makes me dependent on the real existence of the object. Every one must allow that a judgement on the beautiful which is tinged with the slightest interest, is very partial and not a pure judgement of taste. One must not be in the least prepossessed in favour of the real existence of the thing, but must preserve complete indifference in this respect, in order to play the part of judge in matters of taste.

This proposition, which is of the utmost importance, cannot be better explained than by contrasting the pure disinterested[2] delight which appears in the judgement of taste with that allied to an interest—especially if we can also assure ourselves that there are no other kinds of interest beyond those presently to be mentioned.

## § 3
### DELIGHT IN THE AGREEABLE IS COUPLED WITH INTEREST

*That is* agreeable *which the senses find pleasing in sensation.* This at once affords a convenient opportunity for condemning and directing particular attention to a prevalent confusion of the double meaning of which the word 'sensation' is capable. All delight (as is said or thought) is itself sensation (of a pleasure). Consequently everything that pleases, and for the very reason that it pleases, is agreeable—and according to its different degrees, or its relations to other agreeable sensations, is attractive, charming, delicious, enjoyable, etc. But if this is conceded, then impressions of sense, which

2. A judgement upon an object of our delight may be wholly *disinterested* but withal very *interesting,* i.e. it relies on no interest, but it produces one. Of this kind are all pure moral judgements. But, of themselves, judgements of taste do not even set up any interest whatsoever. Only in society is it *interesting* to have taste—a point which will be explained in the sequel.

determine inclination, or principles of reason, which determine the will, or mere contemplated forms of intuition, which determine judgement, are all on a par in everything relevant to their effect upon the feeling of pleasure, for this would be agreeableness in the sensation of one's state; and since, in the last resort, all the elaborate work of our faculties must issue in and unite in the practical as its goal, we could credit our faculties with no other appreciation of things and the worth of things, than that consisting in the gratification which they promise. How this is attained is in the end immaterial; and, as the choice of the means is here the only thing that can make a difference, men might indeed blame one another for folly or imprudence, but never for baseness or wickedness; for they are all, each according to his own way of looking at things, pursuing one goal, which for each is the gratification in question.

When a modification of the feeling of pleasure or displeasure is termed sensation, this expression is given quite a different meaning to that which it bears when I call the representation of a thing (through sense as receptivity pertaining to the faculty of knowledge) sensation. For in the latter case the representation is referred to the Object, but in the former it is referred solely to the Subject and is not available for any cognition, not even for that by which the Subject *cognizes* itself.

Now in the above definition the word sensation is used to denote an objective representation of sense; and, to avoid continually running the risk of misinterpretation, we shall call that which must always remain purely subjective, and is absolutely incapable of forming a representation of an object, by the familiar name of feeling. The green colour of the meadows belongs to *objective* sensation, as the perception of an object of sense; but its agreeableness to *subjective* sensation, by which no object is represented: i.e. to feeling, through which the object is regarded as an Object of delight (which involves no cognition of the object).

Now, that a judgement on an object by which its agreeableness is affirmed, expresses an interest in it, is evident from the fact that through sensation it provokes a desire for similar objects, consequently the delight presupposes, not the simple judgement about it, but the bearing its real existence has upon my state so far as affected by such an Object. Hence we do not merely say of the agreeable that it *pleases,* but that it *gratifies.* I do not accord it a simple approval, but inclination is aroused by it, and where agree-

ableness is of the liveliest type a judgement on the character of the
Object is so entirely out of place, that those who are always intent
only on enjoyment (for that is the word used to denote intensity of
gratification) would fain dispense with all judgement.

## § 4

### DELIGHT IN THE GOOD IS COUPLED WITH INTEREST

That is *good* which by means of reason commends itself by its
mere concept. We call that *good for something* (useful) which only
pleases as a means; but that which pleases on its own account we
call *good in itself*. In both cases the concept of an end is implied,
and consequently the relation of reason to (at least possible) willing,
and thus a delight in the *existence* of an Object or action, i.e. some
interest or other.

To deem something good, I must always know what sort of a
thing the object is intended to be, i.e. I must have a concept of it.
That is not necessary to enable me to see beauty in a thing. Flowers,
free patterns, lines aimlessly intertwining—technically termed foliage,—have no signification, depend upon no definite concept, and
yet please. Delight in the beautiful must depend upon the reflection
on an object precursory to some (not definitely determined) concept.
It is thus also differentiated from the agreeable, which rests entirely
upon sensation.

In many cases, no doubt, the agreeable and the good seem convertible terms. Thus it is commonly said that all (especially lasting)
gratification is of itself good; which is almost equivalent to saying
that to be permanently agreeable and to be good are identical. But
it is readily apparent that this is merely a vicious confusion of words,
for the concepts appropriate to these expressions are far from in-
terchangeable. The agreeable, which, as such, represents the object
solely in relation to sense, must in the first instance be brought
under principles of reason through the concept of an end, to be, as
an object of will, called good. But that the reference to delight is
wholly different where what gratifies is at the same time called
*good*, is evident from the fact that with the good the question always
is whether it is mediately or immediately good, i.e. useful or good
in itself; whereas with the agreeable this point can never arise, since
the word always means what pleases immediately—and it is just
the same with what I call beautiful.

Even in everyday parlance a distinction is drawn between the agreeable and the good. We do not scruple to say of a dish that stimulates the palate with spices and other condiments that it is agreeable—owning all the while that it is not good: because, while it immediately *satisfies* the senses, it is mediately displeasing, i.e. in the eye of reason that looks ahead to the consequences. Even in our estimate of health this same distinction may be traced. To all that possess it, it is immediately agreeable—at least negatively, i.e. as remoteness of all bodily pains. But, if we are to say that it is good, we must further apply to reason to direct it to ends, that is, we must regard it as a state that puts us in a congenial mood for all we have to do. Finally, in respect of happiness every one believes that the greatest aggregate of the pleasures of life, taking duration as well as number into account, merits the name of a true, nay even of the highest, good. But reason sets its face against this too. Agreeableness is enjoyment. But if this is all that we are bent on, it would be foolish to be scrupulous about the means that procure it for us—whether it be obtained passively by the bounty of nature or actively and by the work of our own hands. But that there is any intrinsic worth in the real existence of a man who merely lives for *enjoyment,* however busy he may be in this respect, even when in so doing he serves others—all equally with himself intent only on enjoyment—as an excellent means to that one end, and does so, moreover, because through sympathy he shares all their gratifications,—this is a view to which reason will never let itself be brought round. Only by what a man does heedless of enjoyment, in complete freedom and independently of what he can procure passively from the hand of nature, does he give to his existence, as the real existence of a person, an absolute worth. Happiness, with all its plethora of pleasures, is far from being an unconditioned good.[3]

But, despite all this difference between the agreeable and the good, they both agree in being invariably coupled with an interest in their object. This is true, not alone of the agreeable, § 3, and of the mediately good, i.e. the useful, which pleases as a means to some pleasure, but also of that which is good absolutely and from every point of view, namely the moral good which carries with it

3. An obligation to enjoyment is a patent absurdity. And the same, then, must also be said of a supposed obligation to actions that have merely enjoyment for their aim, no matter how spiritually this enjoyment may be refined in thought (or embellished), and even if it be a mystical, so-called heavenly, enjoyment.

the highest interest. For the good is the Object of will, i.e. of a rationally determined faculty of desire. But to will something, and to take a delight in its existence, i.e. to take an interest in it, are identical.

## § 5

### COMPARISON OF THE THREE SPECIFICALLY DIFFERENT KINDS OF DELIGHT

Both the Agreeable and the Good involve a reference to the faculty of desire, and are thus attended, the former with a delight pathologically conditioned (by stimuli), the latter with a pure practical delight. Such delight is determined not merely by the representation of the object, but also by the represented bond of connexion between the Subject and the real existence of the object. It is not merely the object, but also its real existence, that pleases. On the other hand the judgement of taste is simply *contemplative,* i.e. it is a judgement which is indifferent as to the existence of an object, and only decides how its character stands with the feeling of pleasure and displeasure. But not even is this contemplation itself directed to concepts; for the judgement of taste is not a cognitive judgement (neither a theoretical one nor a practical), and hence, also, is not *grounded* on concepts, nor yet *intentionally directed* to them.

The agreeable, the beautiful, and the good thus denote three different relations of representations to the feeling of pleasure and displeasure, as a feeling in respect of which we distinguish different objects or modes of representation. Also, the corresponding expressions which indicate our satisfaction in them are different. The *agreeable* is what GRATIFIES a man; the *beautiful* what simply PLEASES him; the *good* what is ESTEEMED *(approved)*, i.e. that on which he sets an objective worth. Agreeableness is a significant factor even with irrational animals; beauty has purport and significance only for human beings, i.e. for beings at once animal and rational (but not merely for them as rational—intelligent beings—but only for them as at once animal and rational); whereas the good is good for every rational being in general;—a proposition which can only receive its complete justification and explanation in the sequel. Of all these three kinds of delight, that of taste in the beautiful may be said to be the one and only disinterested and *free* delight; for, with it, no interest, whether of sense or reason, extorts approval.

And so we may say that delight, in the three cases mentioned, is related to *inclination,* to *favour,* or to *respect.* For FAVOUR is the only free liking. An object of inclination, and one which a law of reason imposes upon our desire, leaves us no freedom to turn anything into an object of pleasure. All interest presupposes a want, or calls one forth; and, being a ground determining approval, deprives the judgement on the object of its freedom.

So far as the interest of inclination in the case of the agreeable goes, every one says: Hunger is the best sauce; and people with a healthy appetite relish everything, so long as it is something they can eat. Such delight, consequently, gives no indication of taste having anything to say to the choice. Only when men have got all they want can we tell who among the crowd has taste or not. Similarly there may be correct habits (conduct) without virtue, politeness without good-will, propriety without honour, etc. For where the moral law dictates, there is, objectively, no room left for free choice as to what one has to do; and to show taste in the way one carries out these dictates, or in estimating the way others do so, is a totally different matter from displaying the moral frame of one's mind. For the latter involves a command and produces a need of something, whereas moral taste only plays with the objects of delight without devoting itself sincerely to any.

### Definition of the Beautiful Derived from the First Moment

*Taste* is the faculty of estimating an object or a mode of representation by means of a delight or aversion *apart from any interest.* The object of such a delight is called *beautiful.*

# Second Moment of the Judgement of Taste: Moment of Quantity

## § 6

### THE BEAUTIFUL IS THAT WHICH, APART FROM CONCEPTS, IS REPRESENTED AS THE OBJECT OF A UNIVERSAL DELIGHT

This definition of the beautiful is deducible from the foregoing definition of it as an object of delight apart from any interest. For where any one is conscious that his delight in an object is with him independent of interest, it is inevitable that he should look on the object as one containing a ground of delight for all men. For, since the delight is not based on any inclination of the Subject (or on any other deliberate interest), but the Subject feels himself completely *free* in respect of the liking which he accords to the object, he can find as reason for his delight no personal conditions to which his own subjective self might alone be party. Hence he must regard it as resting on what he may also presuppose in every other person; and therefore he must believe that he has reason for demanding a similar delight from every one. Accordingly he will speak of the beautiful as if beauty were a quality of the object and the judgement logical (forming a cognition of the Object by concepts of it); although it is only aesthetic, and contains merely a reference of the representation of the object to the Subject;—because it still bears this resemblance to the logical judgement, that it may be presupposed to be valid for all men. But this universality cannot spring from concepts. For from concepts there is no transition to the feeling of pleasure or displeasure (save in the case of pure practical laws, which, however, carry an interest with them; and such an interest does not attach to the pure judgement of taste). The result is that the judgement of taste, with its attendant consciousness of detachment from all interest, must involve a claim to validity for all men, and must do so apart from universality attached to Objects, i.e. there must be coupled with it a claim to subjective universality.

## § 7

### COMPARISON OF THE BEAUTIFUL WITH THE AGREEABLE AND THE GOOD BY MEANS OF THE ABOVE CHARACTERISTIC

As regards the *agreeable* every one concedes that his judgement, which he bases on a private feeling, and in which he declares that an object pleases him, is restricted merely to himself personally. Thus he does not take it amiss if, when he says that Canary-wine is agreeable, another corrects the expression and reminds him that he ought to say: It is agreeable *to me*. This applies not only to the taste of the tongue, the palate, and the throat, but to what may with any one be agreeable to eye or ear. A violet colour is to one soft and lovely: to another dull and faded. One man likes the tone of wind instruments, another prefers that of string instruments. To quarrel over such points with the idea of condemning another's judgement as incorrect when it differs from our own, as if the opposition between the two judgements were logical, would be folly. With the agreeable, therefore, the axiom holds good: *Every one has his own taste* (that of sense).

The beautiful stands on quite a different footing. It would, on the contrary, be ridiculous if any one who plumed himself on his taste were to think of justifying himself by saying: This object (the building we see, the dress that person has on, the concert we hear, the poem submitted to our criticism) is beautiful *for me*. For if it merely pleases *him,* he must not call it *beautiful*. Many things may for him possess charm and agreeableness—no one cares about that; but when he puts a thing on a pedestal and calls it beautiful, he demands the same delight from others. He judges not merely for himself, but for all men, and then speaks of beauty as if it were a property of things. Thus he says the *thing* is beautiful; and it is not as if he counted on others agreeing in his judgement of liking owing to his having found them in such agreement on a number of occasions, but he *demands* this agreement of them. He blames them if they judge differently, and denies them taste, which he still requires of them as something they ought to have; and to this extent it is not open to men to say: Every one has his own taste. This would be equivalent to saying that there is no such thing at all as taste, i.e. no aesthetic judgement capable of making a rightful claim upon the assent of all men.

Yet even in the case of the agreeable we find that the estimates men form do betray a prevalent agreement among them, which leads to our crediting some with taste and denying it to others, and that, too, not as an organic sense but as a critical faculty in respect of the agreeable generally. So of one who knows how to entertain his guests with pleasures (of enjoyment through all the senses) in such a way that one and all are pleased, we say that he has taste. But the universality here is only understood in a comparative sense; and the rules that apply are, like all empirical rules, *general* only, not *universal,*—the latter being what the judgement of taste upon the beautiful deals or claims to deal in. It is a judgement in respect of sociability so far as resting on empirical rules. In respect of the good it is true that judgements also rightly assert a claim to validity for every one; but the good is only represented as an Object of universal delight *by means of a concept,* which is the case neither with the agreeable nor the beautiful.

## § 8

### IN A JUDGEMENT OF TASTE THE UNIVERSALITY OF DELIGHT IS ONLY REPRESENTED AS SUBJECTIVE

This particular form of the universality of an aesthetic judgement, which is to be met with in a judgement of taste, is a significant feature, not for the logician certainly, but for the transcendental philosopher. It calls for no small effort on his part to discover its origin, but in return it brings to light a property of our cognitive faculty which, without this analysis, would have remained unknown.

First, one must get firmly into one's mind that by the judgement of taste (upon the beautiful) the delight in an object is imputed to *every one,* yet without being founded on a concept (for then it would be the good), and that this claim to universality is such an essential factor of a judgement by which we describe anything as *beautiful,* that were it not for its being present to the mind it would never enter into any one's head to use this expression, but everything that pleased without a concept would be ranked as agreeable. For in respect of the agreeable every one is allowed to have his own opinion, and no one insists upon others agreeing with his judgement of taste, which is what is invariably done in the judgement of taste about beauty. The first of these I may call the taste of sense, the second, the taste of reflection: the first laying down judgements merely private, the second, on the other hand, judgements ostensibly of general validity (public), but both alike being aesthetic (not practical) judgements about an object merely in respect of the bearings of its representation on the feeling of pleasure or displeasure. Now it does seem strange that while with the taste of sense it is not alone experience that shows that its judgement (of pleasure or displeasure in something) is not universally valid, but every one willingly refrains from imputing this agreement to others (despite the frequent actual prevalence of a considerable consensus of general opinion even in these judgements), the taste of reflection, which, as experience teaches, has often enough to put up with a rude dismissal of its claims to universal validity of its judgement (upon the beautiful), can (as it actually does) find it possible for all that, to formulate judgements capable of demanding this agreement in its universality. Such agreement it does in fact require from every one for each of its judgements of taste,—the persons who pass these judgements not quarrelling over the possibility of such a claim, but only failing in particular cases to come to terms as to the correct application of this faculty.

First of all we have here to note that a universality which does not rest upon concepts of the Object (even though these are only empirical) is in no way logical, but aesthetic, i.e. does not involve any objective quantity of the judgement, but only one that is subjective. For this universality I use the expression *general validity*, which denotes the validity of the reference of a representation, not to the cognitive faculties, but to the feeling of pleasure or displeasure for every Subject. (The same expression, however, may also be employed for the logical quantity of the judgement, provided we add *objective* universal validity, to distinguish it from the merely subjective validity which is always aesthetic.)

Now a judgement that has *objective universal validity* has always got the subjective also, i.e. if the judgement is valid for everything which is contained under a given concept, it is valid also for all who represent an object by means of this concept. But from a *subjective universal validity*, i.e. the aesthetic, that does not rest on any concept, no conclusion can be drawn to the logical; because judgements of that kind have no bearing upon the Object. But for this very reason the aesthetic universality attributed to a judgement must also be of a special kind, seeing that it does not join the predicate of beauty to the concept of the *Object* taken in its entire logical sphere, and yet does extend this predicate over the whole sphere of *judging Subjects*.

In their logical quantity all judgements of taste are *singular* judgements. For, since I must present the object immediately to my feeling of pleasure or displeasure, and that, too, without the aid of concepts, such judgements cannot have the quantity of judgements with objective general validity. Yet by taking the singular representation of the Object of the judgement of taste, and by comparison converting it into a concept according to the conditions determining that judgement, we can arrive at a logically universal judgement. For instance, by a judgement of taste I describe the rose at which I am looking as beautiful. The judgement, on the other hand, resulting from the comparison of a number of singular representations: Roses in general are beautiful, is no longer pronounced as a purely aesthetic judgement, but as a logical judgement founded on one that is aesthetic. Now the judgement, 'The rose is agreeable' (to smell) is also, no doubt, an aesthetic and singular judgement, but then it is not one of taste but of sense. For it has this point of difference from a judgement of taste, that the latter imports an *aesthetic quantity* of universality, i.e. of validity for every one which is not to be met with in a judgement upon the agreeable. It is only judgements upon the good which, while also determining the delight in an object, possess logical and not mere aesthetic universality; for it is as involving a cognition of the Object that they are valid of it, and on that account valid for every one.

In forming an estimate of Objects merely from concepts, all representation of beauty goes by the board. There can, therefore, be no rule according to which any one is to be compelled to recognize anything as beautiful. Whether a dress, a house, or a flower is beautiful is a matter upon which one declines to allow one's judgement to be swayed by any reasons or principles. We want to get a look at the Object with our own eyes, just as if our delight depended on sensation. And yet, if upon so doing, we call the object beautiful, we believe ourselves to be speaking with a universal voice, and lay claim to the concurrence of every one, whereas no private sensation would be decisive except for the observer alone and *his* liking.

Here, now, we may perceive that nothing is postulated in the judgement of taste but such a *universal voice* in respect of delight that is not mediated by concepts; consequently, only the *possibility* of an aesthetic judgement capable of being at the same time deemed valid for every one. The judgement of taste itself does not *postulate* the agreement of every one (for it is only competent for a logically universal judgement to do this, in that it is able to bring forward reasons); it only *imputes* this agreement to every one, as an instance of the rule in respect of which it looks for confirmation, not from concepts, but from the concurrence of others. The universal voice is, therefore, only an idea—resting upon grounds the investigation of which is here postponed. It may be a matter of uncertainty whether a person who thinks he is laying down a judgement of taste is, in fact, judging in conformity with that idea; but that this idea is what is contemplated in his judgement, and that, consequently, it is meant to be a judgement of taste, is proclaimed by his use of the expression 'beauty.' For himself he can be certain on the point from his mere consciousness of the separation of everything belonging to the agreeable and the good from the delight remaining to him; and this is all for which he promises himself the agreement of every one—a claim which, under these conditions, he would also be warranted in making, were it not that he frequently sinned against them, and thus passed an erroneous judgement of taste.

## § 9

### INVESTIGATION OF THE QUESTION OF THE RELATIVE PRIORITY IN A JUDGEMENT OF TASTE OF THE FEELING OF PLEASURE AND THE ESTIMATING OF THE OBJECT

The solution of this problem is the key to the Critique of taste, and so is worthy of all attention.

Were the pleasure in a given object to be the antecedent, and were the universal communicability of this pleasure to be all that the judgement of taste is meant to allow to the representation of the object, such a sequence would be self-contradictory. For a pleasure of that kind would be nothing but the feeling of mere agreeableness to the senses, and so, from its very nature, would possess no more than private validity, seeing that it would be immediately dependent on the representation through which the object *is given*.

Hence it is the universal capacity for being communicated incident to the mental state in the given representation which, as the subjective condition of the judgement of taste, must be fundamental, with the pleasure in the object as its consequent. Nothing, however, is capable of being universally communicated but cognition and representation so far as appurtenant to cognition. For it is only as thus appurtenant that the representation is objective, and it is this alone that gives it a universal point of reference with which the power of representation of every one is obliged to harmonize. If, then, the determining ground of the judgement as to this universal communicability of the representation is to be merely subjective, that is to say, is to be conceived independently of any concept of the object, it can be nothing else than the mental state that presents itself in the mutual relation of the powers of representation so far as they refer a given representation *to cognition in general.*

The cognitive powers brought into play by this representation are here engaged in a free play, since no definite concept restricts them to a particular rule of cognition. Hence the mental state in this representation must be one of a feeling of the free play of the powers of representation in a given representation for a cognition in general. Now a representation, whereby an object is given, involves, in order that it may become a source of cognition at all, *imagination* for bringing together the manifold of intuition, and *understanding* for the unity of the concept uniting the representations. This state of *free play* of the cognitive faculties attending a representation by which an object is given must admit of universal communication: because cognition, as a definition of the Object with which given representations (in any Subject whatever) are to accord, is the one and only representation which is valid for every one.

As the subjective universal communicability of the mode of representation in a judgement of taste is to subsist apart from the presupposition of any definite concept, it can be nothing else than the mental state present in the free play of imagination and understanding (so far as these are in mutual accord, as is requisite for *cognition in general*): for we are conscious that this subjective relation suitable for a cognition in general must be just as valid for every one, and consequently as universally communicable, as is any determinate cognition, which always rests upon that relation as its subjective condition.

Now this purely subjective (aesthetic) estimating of the object, or of the representation through which it is given, is antecedent to the pleasure in it, and is the basis of this pleasure in the harmony of the cognitive faculties. Again, the above-described universality of the subjective conditions of estimating objects forms the sole foundation of this universal subjective validity of the delight which we connect with the representation of the object that we call beautiful.

That an ability to communicate one's mental state, even though it be only in respect of our cognitive faculties, is attended with a pleasure, is a fact which might easily be demonstrated from the natural propensity of mankind to social life, i.e. empirically and psychologically. But what we have here in view calls for something more than this. In a judgement of taste the pleasure felt by us is exacted from every one else as necessary, just as if, when we call something beautiful, beauty was to be regarded as a quality of the object forming part of its inherent determination according to concepts; although beauty is for itself, apart from any reference to the feeling of the Subject, nothing. But the discussion of this question must be reserved until we have answered the further one of whether, and how, aesthetic judgements are possible *a priori.*

At present we are exercised with the lesser question of the way in which we become conscious, in a judgement of taste, of a reciprocal subjective common accord of the powers of cognition. Is it aesthetically by sensation and our mere internal sense? Or is it intellectually by consciousness of our intentional activity in bringing these powers into play?

Now if the given representation occasioning the judgement of taste were a concept which united understanding and imagination in the estimate of the object so as to give a cognition of the Object, the consciousness of this relation would be intellectual (as in the objective schematism of judgement dealt with in the Critique). But, then, in that case the judgement would not be laid down with respect to pleasure and displeasure, and so would not be a judgement of taste. But, now, the judgement of taste determines the Object, independently of concepts, in respect of delight and of the predicate of beauty. There is, therefore, no other way for the subjective unity of the relation in question to make itself known than by sensation. The quickening of both faculties (imagination and understanding) to an indefinite, but yet, thanks to the given representation, harmonious activity, such as belongs to cognition generally, is the sensation whose universal communicability is postulated by the judgement of taste. An objective relation can, of course, only be thought, yet in so far as, in respect of its conditions, it is subjective, it may be felt in its effect upon the mind, and, in the case of a relation (like that of the powers of representation to a faculty of cognition generally) which does not rest on any concept, no other consciousness of it is possible beyond that through sensation of its effect upon the mind—an effect consisting in the more facile play

of both mental powers (imagination and understanding) as quick-
ened by their mutual accord. A representation which is singular
and independent of comparison with other representations, and,
being such, yet accords with the conditions of the universality that
is the general concern of understanding, is one that brings the cognitive faculties into that proportionate accord which we require for
all cognition and which we therefore deem valid for every one who
is so constituted as to judge by means of understanding and sense
conjointly (i.e. for every man).

### Definition of the Beautiful Drawn
### from the Second Moment

The *beautiful* is that which, apart from a concept, pleases universally.

# Third Moment
# of Judgements of Taste: Moment of
# the *Relation* of the Ends Brought
# Under Review in Such Judgements

## § 10
### FINALITY IN GENERAL

Let us define the meaning of 'an end' in transcendental terms
(i.e. without presupposing anything empirical, such as the feeling
of pleasure). An end is the object of a concept so far as this concept
is regarded as the cause of the object (the real ground of its possibility); and the causality of a *concept* in respect of its *Object* is
finality *(forma finalis)*. Where, then, not the cognition of an object
merely, but the object itself (its form or real existence) as an effect,
is thought to be possible only through a concept of it, there we
imagine an end. The representation of the effect is here the determining ground of its cause and takes the lead of it. The consciousness of the causality of a representation in respect of the state of
the Subject as one tending *to preserve a continuance* of that state,
may here be said to denote in a general way what is called pleasure;

whereas displeasure is that representation which contains the ground for converting the state of the representations into their opposite (for hindering or removing them).

The faculty of desire, so far as determinable only through concepts, i.e. so as to act in conformity with the representation of an end, would be the will. But an Object, or state of mind, or even an action may, although its possibility does not necessarily presuppose the representation of an end, be called final simply on account of its possibility being only explicable and intelligible for us by virtue of an assumption on our part of a fundamental causality according to ends, i.e. a will that would have so ordained it according to a certain represented rule. Finality, therefore, may exist apart from an end, in so far as we do not locate the causes of this form in a will, but yet are able to render the explanation of its possibility intelligible to ourselves only by deriving it from a will. Now we are not always obliged to look with the eye of reason into what we observe (i.e. to consider it in its possibility). So we may at least observe a finality of form, and trace it in objects—though by reflection only—without resting it on an end (as the material of the *nexus finalis*).

## § 11

### THE SOLE FOUNDATION OF THE JUDGEMENT OF TASTE IS
### THE *FORM OF FINALITY* OF AN OBJECT
### (OR MODE OF REPRESENTING IT)

Whenever an end is regarded as a source of delight it always imports an interest as determining ground of the judgement on the object of pleasure. Hence the judgement of taste cannot rest on any subjective end as its ground. But neither can any representation of an objective end, i.e. of the possibility of the object itself on principles of final connexion, determine the judgement of taste, and, consequently, neither can any concept of the good. For the judgement of taste is an aesthetic and not a cognitive judgement, and so does not deal with any *concept* of the nature or of the internal or external possibility, by this or that cause, of the object, but simply with the relative bearing of the representative powers so far as determined by a representation.

Now this relation, present when an object is characterized as beautiful, is coupled with the feeling of pleasure. This pleasure is by the judgement of taste pronounced valid for every one; hence an agreeableness attending the representation is just as incapable of containing the determining ground of the judgement as the representation of the perfection of the object or the concept of the good. We are thus left with the subjective finality in the representation of an object, exclusive of any end (objective or subjective)— consequently the bare form of finality in the representation whereby an object is *given* to us, so far as we are conscious of it—as that which is alone capable of constituting the delight which, apart from any concept, we estimate as universally communicable, and so of forming the determining ground of the judgement of taste.

## § 12

### THE JUDGEMENT OF TASTE RESTS UPON *A PRIORI* GROUNDS

To determine *a priori* the connexion of the feeling of pleasure or displeasure as an effect, with some representation or other (sensation or concept) as its cause, is utterly impossible; for that would be a causal relation which, (with objects of experience,) is always one that can only be cognized *a posteriori* and with the help of experience. True, in the Critique of Practical Reason we did actually derive *a priori* from universal moral concepts the feeling of respect (as a particular and peculiar modification of this feeling which does not strictly answer either to the pleasure or displeasure which we receive from empirical objects). But there we were further able to cross the border of experience and call in aid a causality resting on a supersensible attribute of the Subject, namely that of freedom. But even there it was not this *feeling* exactly that we deduced from the idea of the moral as cause, but from this was derived simply the determination of the will. But the mental state present in the determination of the will by any means is at once in itself a feeling of pleasure and identical with it, and so does not issue from it as an effect. Such an effect must only be assumed where the concept of the moral as a good precedes the determination of the will by the law; for in that case it would be futile to derive the pleasure combined with the concept from this concept as a mere cognition.

Now the pleasure in aesthetic judgements stands on a similar

footing: only that here it is merely contemplative and dc
about an interest in the Object; whereas in the moral
is practical. The consciousness of mere formal finalit,
of the cognitive faculties of the Subject attending a representation
whereby an object is given, is the pleasure itself, because it involves
a determining ground of the Subject's activity in respect of the
quickening of its cognitive powers, and thus an internal causality
(which is final) in respect of cognition generally, but without being
limited to a definite cognition, and consequently a mere form of
the subjective finality of a representation in an aesthetic judgement.
This pleasure is also in no way practical, neither resembling that
from the pathological ground of agreeableness nor that from the
intellectual ground of the represented good. But still it involves an
inherent causality, that, namely, of *preserving a continuance* of the
state of the representation itself and the active engagement of the
cognitive powers without ulterior aim. We *dwell* on the contemplation of the beautiful because this contemplation strengthens and
reproduces itself. The case is analogous (but analogous only) to the
way we linger on a charm in the representation of an object which
keeps arresting the attention, the mind all the while remaining passive.

## § 13

### THE PURE JUDGEMENT OF TASTE IS INDEPENDENT OF CHARM
### AND EMOTION

Every interest vitiates the judgement of taste and robs it of its
impartiality. This is especially so where instead of, like the interest
of reason, making finality take the lead of the feeling of pleasure,
it grounds it upon this feeling—which is what always happen in
aesthetic judgements upon anything so far as it gratifies or pains.
Hence judgements so influenced can either lay no claim at all to a
universally valid delight, or else must abate their claim in proportion as sensations of the kind in question enter into the determining grounds of taste. Taste that requires an added element
of *charm* and *emotion* for its delight, not to speak of adopting
this as the measure of its approval, has not yet emerged from
barbarism.

And yet charms are frequently not alone ranked with beauty

(which ought properly to be a question merely of the form) as supplementary to the aesthetic universal delight, but they have been accredited as intrinsic beauties, and consequently the matter of delight passed off for the form. This is a misconception which, like many others that have still an underlying element of truth, may be removed by a careful definition of these concepts.

A judgement of taste which is uninfluenced by charm or emotion, (though these may be associated with the delight in the beautiful,) and whose determining ground, therefore, is simply finality of form, is *a pure judgement of taste*.

## § 14

### EXEMPLIFICATION

Aesthetic, just like theoretical (logical) judgements, are divisible into empirical and pure. The first are those by which agreeableness or disagreeableness, the second those by which beauty, is predicated of an object or its mode of representation. The former are judgements of sense (material aesthetic judgements), the latter (as formal) alone judgements of taste proper.

A judgement of taste, therefore, is only pure so far as its determining ground is tainted with no merely empirical delight. But such a taint is always present where charm or emotion have a share in the judgement by which something is to be described as beautiful.

Here now there is a recrudescence of a number of specious pleas that go the length of putting forward the case that charm is not merely a necessary ingredient of beauty, but is even of itself sufficient to merit the name of beautiful. A mere colour, such as the green of a plot of grass, or a mere tone (as distinguished from sound or noise), like that of a violin, is described by most people as in itself beautiful, notwithstanding the fact that both seem to depend merely on the matter of the representations—in other words, simply on sensation, which only entitles them to be called agreeable. But it will at the same time be observed that sensations of colour as well as of tone are only entitled to be immediately regarded as beautiful where, in either case, they are *pure*. This is a determination which at once goes to their form, and it is the only one which these representations possess that admits with certainty of being universally communicated. For it is not to be assumed that even the quality of the sensations agrees in all Subjects, and we can hardly take it for granted that the agreeableness of a colour, or of the tone of a musical instrument, which we judge to be preferable to that of another, is given a like preference in the estimate of every one.

Assuming with *Euler* that colours are isochronous vibrations *(pulsus)* of the aether, as tones are of the air set in vibration by sound, and, what is most important, that the mind not alone perceives by sense their effect in stimulating the organs, but also, by reflection, the regular play of the impressions, (and consequently the form in which different representations are united,)—which I, still, in no way doubt—then colour and tone would not be mere sensations. They would be nothing short of formal determinations of the unity of a manifold of sensations, and in that case could even be ranked as intrinsic beauties.

But the purity of a simple mode of sensation means that its uniformity is not disturbed or broken by any foreign sensation. It belongs merely to the form; for abstraction may there be made from the quality of the mode of such sensation (what colour or tone, if any, it represents). For this reason all simple colours are regarded as beautiful so far as pure. Composite colors have not this advantage, because, not being simple, there is no standard for estimating whether they should be called pure or impure.

But as for the beauty ascribed to the object on account of its form, and the supposition that it is capable of being enhanced by charm, this is a common error and one very prejudicial to genuine, uncorrupted, sincere taste. Nevertheless charms may be added to beauty to lend to the mind, beyond a bare delight, an adventitious interest in the representation of the object, and thus to advocate taste and its cultivation. This applies especially where taste is as yet crude and untrained. But they are positively subversive of the judgement of taste, if allowed to obtrude themselves as grounds of estimating beauty. For so far are they from contributing to beauty, that it is only where taste is still weak and untrained, that, like aliens, they are admitted as a favour, and only on terms that they do not violate that beautiful form.

In painting, sculpture, and in fact in all the formative arts, in architecture and horticulture, so far as fine arts, the *design* is what is essential. Here it is not what gratifies in sensation but merely what pleases by its form, that is the fundamental prerequisite for taste. The colours which give brilliancy to the sketch are part of the charm. They may no doubt, in their own way, enliven the object for sensation, but make it really worth looking at and beautiful they cannot. Indeed, more often than not the requirements of the beautiful form restrict them to a very narrow compass, and, even where charm is admitted, it is only this form that gives them a place of honour.

All form of objects of sense (both of external and also, mediately, of internal sense) is either *figure* or *play*. In the latter case it is either play of figures (in space: mimic and dance), or mere play of sensations (in time). The *charm* of colours, or of the agreeable tones of instruments, may be added: but the *design* in the former and the *composition* in the latter constitute the proper object of the pure judgement of taste. To say that the purity alike of colours and of tones, or their variety and contrast, seem to contribute to beauty, is by no means to imply that, because in themselves agreeable, they therefore yield an addition to the delight in the form and one on a par with it. The real meaning rather is that they make this form more clearly, definitely, and completely intuitable, and besides stimulate the representation by their charm, as they excite and sustain the attention directed to the object itself.

Even what is called *ornamentation (parerga)*, i.e. what is only an adjunct, and not an intrinsic constituent in the complete representation of the object, in augmenting the delight of taste does so only by means of its form. Thus it is with the frames of pictures or the drapery on statues, or the colonnades of palaces. But if the ornamentation does not itself enter into the composition of the beautiful form—if it is introduced like a gold frame merely to win approval for the picture by means of its charm—it is then called *finery* and takes away from the genuine beauty.

Emotion—a sensation where an agreeable feeling is produced merely by means of a momentary check followed by a more powerful outpouring of the vital force—is quite foreign to beauty. Sublimity (with which the feeling of emotion is connected) requires, however, a different standard of estimation from that relied upon by taste. A pure judgement of taste has, then, for its determining ground neither charm nor emotion, in a word, no sensation as matter of the aesthetic judgement.

## § 15

### THE JUDGEMENT OF TASTE IS ENTIRELY INDEPENDENT OF THE CONCEPT OF PERFECTION

*Objective* finality can only be cognized by means of a reference of the manifold to a definite end, and hence only through a concept. This alone makes it clear that the beautiful, which is estimated on the ground of a mere formal finality, i.e. a finality apart from an end, is wholly independent of the representation of the good. For the latter presupposes an objective finality, i.e. the reference of the object to a definite end.

Objective finality is either external, i.e. the *utility,* or internal, i.e. the *perfection,* of the object. That the delight in an object on account of which we call it beautiful is incapable of resting on the representation of its utility, is abundantly evident from the two preceding articles; for in that case, it would not be an immediate delight in the object, which latter is the essential condition of the judgement upon beauty. But in an objective, internal finality, i.e. perfection, we have what is more akin to the predicate of beauty, and so this has been held even by philosophers of reputation to be convertible with beauty, though subject to the qualification: *where it is thought in a confused way.* In a Critique of taste it is of the utmost importance to decide whether beauty is really reducible to the concept of perfection.

For estimating objective finality we always require the concept of an end, and, where such finality has to be, not an external one (utility), but an internal one, the concept of an internal end containing the ground of the internal possibility of the object. Now an end is in general that, the *concept* of which may be regarded as the ground of the possibility of the object itself. So in order to represent an objective finality in a thing we must first have a concept of *what sort of a thing it is to be.* The agreement of the manifold in a thing with this concept (which supplies the rule of its synthesis) is the *qualitative perfection* of the thing. *Quantitative* perfection is entirely distinct from this. It consists in the completeness of anything after its kind, and is a mere concept of quantity (of totality). In its case the question of *what the thing is to be* is regarded as definitely disposed of, and we only ask whether it is possessed of *all* the requisites that go to make it such. What is formal in the representation of a thing, i.e. the agreement of its manifold with a unity (i.e. irrespective of what it is to be) does not, of itself, afford us any cognition whatsoever of objective finality. For since abstraction is made from this unity as *end* (what the thing is to be) nothing is left but the subjective finalty of the representations in the mind of the Subject intuiting. This gives a certain finality of the representative state of the Subject, in which the Subject feels itself quite at home in its effort to grasp a given form in the imagination, but no perfection of any Object, the latter not being here thought through any concept. For instance, if in a forest I light upon a plot of grass, round which trees stand in a circle, and if I do not then form any repesentation of an end, as that it is meant to be used, say, for country dances, then not the least hint of a concept of perfection is given by the mere form. To suppose a formal *objective* finality that is yet devoid of an end, i.e. the mere form of a *perfection* (apart from any matter or *concept* of that to which the agreement relates, even though there was the mere general idea of a conformity to law) is a veritable contradiction.

Now the judgement of taste is an aesthetic judgement, i.e. one resting on subjective grounds. No concept can be its determining ground, and hence not one of a definite end. Beauty, therefore, as a formal subjective finality, involves no thought whatsoever of a perfection of the object, as a would-be formal finality which yet, for all that, is objective: and the distinction between the concepts of the beautiful and the good, which represents both as differing only in their logical form, the first being merely a confused, the second a clearly defined, concept of perfection, while otherwise alike in content and origin, all goes for nothing: for then there would be no *specific* difference between them, but the judgement of taste would be just as much a cognitive judgement as one by which something is described as good—just as the man in the street, when he says that deceit is wrong, bases his judgement on confused, but the philosopher on clear grounds, while both appeal in reality to identical principles of reason. But I have already stated that an aesthetic judgement is quite unique, and affords absolutely no, (not even a confused,) knowledge of the Object. It is only through a logical judgement that we get knowledge. The aesthetic judgement, on the other hand, refers the representation, by which an Object is given, solely to the Subject, and brings to our notice no quality of the object, but only the final form in the determination of the powers of representation engaged upon it. The judgement is called aesthetic for the very reason that its determining ground cannot be a concept, but is rather the feeling (of the internal sense) of the concert in the play of the mental powers as a thing only capable of being felt. If, on the other hand, confused concepts, and the objective judgement based on them, are going to be called aesthetic, we shall find ourselves with an understanding judging by sense, or a sense representing its objects by concepts—a mere choice of contradictions. The faculty of concepts, be they confused or be they clear, is understanding; and although understanding has (as in all judgements) its rôle in the judgement of taste, as an aesthetic judgement, its rôle there is not that of a faculty for cognizing an object, but of a faculty for determining that judgement and its representation (without a concept) according to its relation to the Subject and its internal feeling, and for doing so in so far as that judgement is possible according to a universal rule.

## § 16

### A JUDGEMENT OF TASTE BY WHICH AN OBJECT IS DESCRIBED AS BEAUTIFUL UNDER THE CONDITION OF A DEFINITE CONCEPT IS NOT PURE

There are two kinds of beauty: free beauty *(pulchritudo vaga),* or beauty which is merely dependent *(pulchritudo adhaerens).* The first presupposes no concept of what the object should be; the second does presuppose such a concept and, with it, an answering perfection of the object. Those of the first kind are said to be (self-subsisting) beauties of this thing or that thing; the other kind of beauty, being attached to a concept (conditioned beauty), is ascribed to Objects which come under the concept of a particular end.

Flowers are free beauties of nature. Hardly any one but a botanist knows the true nature of a flower, and even he, while recognizing in the flower the reproductive organ of the plant, pays no attention to this natural end when using his taste to judge of its beauty. Hence no perfection of any kind—no internal finality, as something to which the arrangement of the manifold is related—underlies this judgement. Many birds (the parrot, the humming-bird, the bird of paradise), and a number of crustacea, are self-subsisting beauties

which are not appurtenant to any object defined with respect to its
end, but please freely and on their own account. So designs à la
grecque, foliage for framework or on wall-papers, etc., have no
intrinsic meaning; they represent nothing—no Object under a definite concept—and are free beauties. We may also rank in the same
class what in music are called fantasias (without a theme), and,
indeed, all music that is not set to words.

In the estimate of a free beauty (according to mere form) we
have the pure judgement of taste. No concept is here presupposed
of any end for which the manifold should serve the given Object,
and which the latter, therefore, should represent—an incumbrance
which would only restrict the freedom of the imagination that, as
it were, is at play in the contemplation of the outward form.

But the beauty of man (including under this head that of a man,
woman, or child), the beauty of a horse, or of a building (such as
a church, palace, arsenal, or summer-house), presupposes a concept
of the end that defines what the thing has to be, and consequently
a concept of its perfection; and is therefore merely appendant beauty.
Now, just as it is a clog on the purity of the judgement of taste to
have the agreeable (of sensation) joined with beauty to which properly only the form is relevant, so to combine the good with beauty,
(the good, namely, of the manifold to the thing itself according to
its end,) mars its purity.

Much might be added to a building that would immediately
please the eye, were it not intended for a church. A figure might be
beautified with all manner of flourishes and light but regular lines,
as is done by the New Zealanders with their tattooing, were we
dealing with anything but the figure of a human being. And here
is one whose rugged features might be softened and given a more
pleasing aspect, only he has got to be a man, or is, perhaps, a
warrior that has to have a warlike appearance.

Now the delight in the manifold of a thing, in a reference to the
internal end that determines its possibility, is a delight based on a
concept, whereas delight in the beautiful is such as does not presuppose any concept, but is immediately coupled with the representation through which the object is given (not through which it
is thought). If, now, the judgement of taste in respect of the latter
delight is made dependent upon the end involved in the former
delight as a judgement of reason, and is thus placed under a restriction, then it is no longer a free and pure judgement of taste.

Taste, it is true, stands to gain by this combination of intellectual delight with the aesthetic. For it becomes fixed, and, while not universal, it enables rules to be prescribed for it in respect of certain definite final Objects. But these rules are then not rules of taste, but merely rules for establishing a union of taste with reason, i.e. of the beautiful with the good—rules by which the former becomes available as an intentional instrument in respect of the latter, for the purpose of bringing that temper of the mind which is self-sustaining and of subjective universal validity to the support and maintenance of that mode of thought which, while possessing objective universal validity, can only be preserved by a resolute effort. But, strictly speaking, perfection neither gains by beauty, nor beauty by perfection. The truth is rather this, when we compare the representation through which an object is given to us with the Object (in respect of what it is meant to be) by means of a concept, we cannot help reviewing it also in respect of the sensation in the Subject. Hence there results a gain to the *entire faculty* of our representative power when harmony prevails between both states of mind.

In respect of an object with a definite internal end, a judgement of taste would only be pure where the person judging either has no concept of this end, or else makes abstraction from it in his judgement. But in cases like this, although such a person should lay down a correct judgement of taste, since he would be estimating the object as a free beauty, he would still be found fault with by another who saw nothing in its beauty but a dependent quality (i.e. who looked to the end of the object) and would be accused by him of false taste, though both would, in their own way, be judging correctly: the one according to what he had present to his senses, the other according to what was present in his thoughts. This distinction enables us to settle many disputes about beauty on the part of critics; for we may show them how one side is dealing with free beauty, and the other with that which is dependent: the former passing a pure judgement of taste, the latter one that is applied intentionally.

## § 17
### THE IDEAL OF BEAUTY

There can be no objective rule of taste by which what is beautiful may be defined by means of concepts. For every judgement from that source is aesthetic, i.e. its determining ground is the feeling of the Subject, and not any concept of an Object. It is only throwing away labour to look for a principle of taste that affords a universal criterion of the beautiful by definite concepts; because what is sought is a thing impossible and inherently,contradictory. But in the universal communicability of the sensation (of delight or aversion)— a communicability, too, that exists apart from any concept—in the accord, so far as possible, of all ages and nations as to this feeling in the representation of certain objects, we have the empirical criterion, weak indeed and scarce sufficient to raise a presumption, of the derivation of a taste, thus confirmed by examples, from grounds deep-seated and shared alike by all men, underlying their agreement in estimating the forms under which objects are given to them.

For this reason some products of taste are looked on as *exemplary*—not meaning thereby that by imitating others taste may be acquired. For taste must be an original faculty; whereas one who imitates a model, while showing skill commensurate with his success, only displays taste as himself a critic of this model.[4] Hence it follows that the highest model, the archetype of taste, is a mere idea, which each person must beget in his own consciousness, and according to which he must form his estimate of everything that is an Object of taste, or that is an example of critical taste, and even of universal taste itself. Properly speaking, an *idea* signifies a concept of reason, and an *ideal* the representation of an individual existence as adequate to an idea. Hence this archetype of taste—which rests indeed, upon reason's indeterminate idea of a maximum, but is not, however, capable of being represented by means of concepts, but only in an individual presentation—may more appropriately be called the ideal of the beautiful. While not having this ideal in our possession, we still strive to beget it within us. But it is bound to be merely an ideal of the imagination, seeing that it rests, not upon concepts, but upon the presentation—the faculty of presentation being the imagination.—Now, how do we arrive at such an ideal

4. Models of taste with respect to the arts of speech must be composed in a dead and learned language; the first, to prevent their having to suffer the changes that inevitably overtake living ones, making dignified expressions become degraded, common ones antiquated, and ones newly coined after a short currency obsolete; the second to ensure its having a grammar that is not subject to the caprices of fashion, but has fixed rules of its own.

of beauty? Is it *a priori* or empirically? Further, what species of the beautiful admits of an ideal?

First of all, we do well to observe that the beauty for which an ideal has to be sought cannot be a beauty that is *free and at large,* but must be one *fixed* by a concept of objective finality. Hence it cannot belong to the Object of an altogether pure judgement of taste, but must attach to one that is partly intellectual. In other words, where an ideal is to have place among the grounds upon which any estimate is formed, then beneath grounds of that kind there must lie some idea of reason according to determinate concepts, by which the end underlying the internal possibility of the object is determined *a priori.* An ideal of beautiful flowers, of a beautiful suite of furniture, or of a beautiful view, is unthinkable. But, it may also be impossible to represent an ideal of a beauty dependent on definite ends, e.g. a beautiful residence, a beautiful tree, a beautiful garden, etc., presumably because their ends are not sufficiently defined and fixed by their concept, with the result that their finality is nearly as free as with beauty that is quite *at large.* Only what has in itself the end of its real existence—only *man* that is able himself to determine his ends by reason, or, where he has to derive them from external perception, can still compare them with essential and universal ends, and then further pronounce aesthetically upon their accord with such ends, only he, among all objects in the world, admits, therefore, of an ideal of *beauty,* just as humanity in his person, as intelligence, alone admits of the ideal of *perfection.*

Two factors are here involved. *First,* there is the aesthetic *normal idea,* which is an individual intuition (of the imagination). This represents the norm by which we judge of a man as a member of a particular animal species. *Secondly,* there is the *rational idea.* This deals with the ends of humanity so far as capable of sensuous representation, and converts them into a principle for estimating his outward form, through which these ends are revealed in their phenomenal effect. The normal idea must draw from experience the constituents which it requires for the form of an animal of a particular kind. But the greatest finality in the construction of this form—that which would serve as a universal norm for forming an estimate of each individual of the species in question—the image that, as it were, forms an intentional basis underlying the technic

> which no separate individual, but only the race as a
equate, has its seat merely in the idea of the judging
it is, with all its proportions, an aesthetic idea, and,
as such, capable of being fully presented *in concreto* in a model
image. Now, how is this effected? In order to render the process
to some extent intelligible (for who can wrest nature's whole secret
from her?), let us attempt a psychological explanation.

It is of note that the imagination, in a manner quite incomprehensible to us, is able on occasion, even after a long lapse of time,
not alone to recall the signs for concepts, but also to reproduce the
image and shape of an object out of a countless number of others
of a different, or even of the very same, kind. And, further, if the
mind is engaged upon comparisons, we may well suppose that it
can in actual fact, though the process is unconscious, superimpose
as it were one image upon another, and from the coincidence of a
number of the same kind arrive at a mean contour which serves as
a common standard for all. Say, for instance, a person has seen a
thousand full-grown men. Now if he wishes to judge normal size
determined upon a comparative estimate, then imagination (to my
mind) allows a great number of these images (perhaps the whole
thousand) to fall one upon the other, and, if I may be allowed to
extend to the case the analogy of optical presentation, in the space
where they come most together, and within the contour where the
place is illuminated by the greatest concentration of colour, one
gets a perception of the *average size,* which alike in height and
breadth is equally removed from the extreme limits of the greatest
and smallest statures; and this is the stature of a beautiful man.
(The same result could be obtained in a mechanical way, by taking
the measures of all the thousand, and adding together their heights,
and their breadths [and thicknesses], and dividing the sum in each
case by a thousand.) But the power of imagination does all this by
means of a dynamical effect upon the organ of internal sense, arising
from the frequent apprehension of such forms. If, again, for our
average man we seek on similar lines for the average head, and for
this the average nose, and so on, then we get the figure that underlies
the normal idea of a beautiful man in the country where the comparison is instituted. For this reason a Negro must necessarily (under
these empirical conditions) have a different normal idea of the beauty
of forms from what a white man has, and the Chinaman one dif-

ferent from the European. And the process would be just the same with the *model* of a beautiful horse or dog (of a particular breed).— This *normal idea* is not derived from proportions taken from experience *as definite rules:* rather is it according to this idea that rules for forming estimates first become possible. It is an intermediate between all singular intuitions of individuals, with their manifold variations—a floating image for the whole genus, which nature has set as an archetype underlying those of her products that belong to the same species, but which in no single case she seems to have completely attained. But the normal idea is far from giving the complete *archetype* of *beauty* in the genus. It only gives the form that constitutes the indispensable condition of all beauty, and, consequently, only *correctness* in the presentation of the genus. It is, as the famous *Doryphorus* of *Polycletus* was called, the *rule* (and *Myron*'s Cow might be similarly employed for its kind). It cannot, for that very reason, contain anything specifically characteristic; for otherwise it would not be the *normal idea* for the genus. Further, it is not by beauty that its presentation pleases, but merely because it does not contradict any of the conditions under which alone a thing belonging to this genus can be beautiful. The presentation is merely academically correct.[5]

But the *ideal* of the beautiful is still something different from its *normal idea.* For reasons already stated it is only to be sought in the *human figure.* Here the ideal consists in the expression of the *moral,* apart from which the object would not please at once universally and positively (not merely negatively in a presentation academically correct). The visible expression of moral ideas that govern men inwardly can, of course, only be drawn from experience; but their combination with all that our reason connects with the morally

---

5. It will be found that a perfectly regular face—one that a painter might fix his eye on for a model—ordinarily conveys nothing. This is because it is devoid of anything characteristic, and so the idea of the race is expressed in it rather than the specific qualities of a person. The exaggeration of what is characteristic in this way, i.e. exaggeration violating the normal idea (the finality of the race), is called *caricature.* Also experience shows that these quite regular faces indicate as a rule internally only a mediocre type of man; presumably—if one may assume that nature in its external form expresses the proportions of the internal—because, where none of the mental qualities exceed the proportion requisite to constitute a man free from faults, nothing can be expected in the way of what is called *genius,* in which nature seems to make a departure from its wonted relations of the mental powers in favour of some special one.

good in the idea of the highest finality—benevolence, purity, strength, or equanimity, etc.—may be made, as it were, visible in bodily manifestation (as effect of what is internal), and this embodiment involves a union of pure ideas of reason and great imaginative power, in one who would even form an estimate of it, not to speak of being the author of its presentation. The correctness of such an ideal of beauty is evidenced by its not permitting any sensuous charm to mingle with the delight in its Object, in which it still allows us to take a great interest. This fact in turn shows that an estimate formed according to such a standard can never be purely aesthetic, and that one formed according to an ideal of beauty cannot be a simple judgement of taste.

### Definition of the Beautiful Derived from This Third Moment

*Beauty* is the form of *finality* in an object, so far as perceived in it *apart from the representation of an end.*[6]

# Fourth Moment
# of the Judgement of Taste: Moment of the Modality of the Delight in the Object

### § 18
#### NATURE OF THE MODALITY IN A JUDGEMENT OF TASTE

I may assert in the case of every representation that the synthesis of a pleasure with the representation (as a cognition) is at least

6. As telling against this explanation, the instance may be adduced, that there are things in which we see a form suggesting adaptation to an end, without any end being cognized in them—as, for example, the stone implements frequently obtained from sepulchral tumuli and supplied with a hole, as if for [inserting] a handle; and although these by their shape manifestly indicate a finality, the end of which is unknown, they are not on that account described as beautiful. But the very fact of their being regarded as art-products involves an immediate recognition that their shape is attributed to some purpose or other and to a definite end. For this reason there is no immediate delight whatever in their contemplation. A flower, on the other hand, such as a tulip, is regarded as beautiful, because we meet with a certain finality in its perception, which, in our estimate of it, is not referred to any end whatever.

*possible*. Of what I call *agreeable* I assert that it *actually* causes pleasure in me. But what we have in mind in the case of the *beautiful* is a *necessary* reference on its part to delight. However, this necessity is of a special kind. It is not a theoretical objective necessity—such as would let us cognize *a priori* that every one *will feel* this delight in the object that is called beautiful by me. Nor yet is it a practical necessity, in which case, thanks to concepts of a pure rational will in which free agents are supplied with a rule, this delight is the necessary consequence of an objective law, and simply means that one ought absolutely (without ulterior object) to act in a certain way. Rather, being such a necessity as is thought in an aesthetic judgement, it can only be termed *exemplary*. In other words it is a necessity of the assent of *all* to a judgement regarded as exemplifying a universal rule incapable of formulation. Since an aesthetic judgement is not an objective or cognitive judgement, this necessity is not derivable from definite concepts, and so is not apodictic. Much less is it inferable from universality of experience (of a thorough-going agreement of judgements about the beauty of a certain object). For, apart from the fact that experience would hardly furnish evidences sufficiently numerous for this purpose, empirical judgements do not afford any foundation for a concept of the necessity of these judgements.

## § 19

### THE SUBJECTIVE NECESSITY ATTRIBUTED TO A JUDGEMENT OF TASTE IS CONDITIONED

The judgement of taste exacts agreement from every one; and a person who describes something as beautiful insists that every one *ought* to give the object in question his approval and follow suit in describing it as beautiful. The *ought* in aesthetic judgements, therefore, despite an accordance with all the requisite data for passing judgement, is still only pronounced conditionally. We are suitors for agreement from every one else, because we are fortified with a ground common to all. Further, we would be able to count on this agreement, provided we were always assured of the correct subsumption of the case under that ground as the rule of approval.

## § 20

THE CONDITION OF THE NECESSITY ADVANCED BY A JUDGEMENT
OF TASTE IS THE IDEA OF A COMMON SENSE

Were judgements of taste (like cognitive judgements) in possession of a definite objective principle, then one who in his judgement
followed such a principle would claim unconditioned necessity for
it. Again, were they devoid of any principle, as are those of the
mere taste of sense, then no thought of any necessity on their part
would enter one's head. Therefore they must have a subjective
principle, and one which determines what pleases or displeases, by
means of feeling only and not through concepts, but yet with universal validity. Such a principle, however, could only be regarded
as a *common sense*. This differs essentially from common understanding, which is also sometimes called common sense *(sensus
communis):* for the judgement of the latter is not one by feeling,
but always one by concepts, though usually only in the shape of
obscurely represented principles.

The judgement of taste, therefore, depends on our presupposing
the existence of a common sense. (But this is not to be taken to
mean some external sense, but the effect arising from the free play
of our powers of cognition.) Only under the presupposition, I re-
peat, of such a common sense, are we able to lay down a judgement
of taste.

## § 21

HAVE WE REASON FOR PRESUPPOSING A COMMON SENSE?

Cognitions and judgements must, together with their attendant
conviction, admit of being universally communicated; for otherwise
a correspondence with the Object would not be due to them. They
would be a conglomerate constituting a mere subjective play of the
powers of representation, just as scepticism would have it. But if
cognitions are to admit of communication, then our mental state,
i.e. the way the cognitive powers are attuned for cognition generally,
and, in fact, the relative proportion suitable for a representation
(by which an object is given to us) from which cognition is to result,
must also admit of being universally communicated, as, without
this, which is the subjective condition of the act of knowing, knowl-

edge, as an effect, would not arise. And this is always what actually happens where a given object, through the intervention of sense, sets the imagination at work in arranging the manifold, and the imagination, in turn, the understanding in giving to this arrangement the unity of concepts. But this disposition of the cognitive powers has a relative proportion differing with the diversity of the Objects that are given. However, there must be one in which this internal ratio suitable for quickening (one faculty by the other) is best adapted for both mental powers in respect of cognition (of given objects) generally; and this disposition can only be determined through feeling (and not by concepts). Since, now, this disposition itself must admit of being universally communicated, and hence also the feeling of it (in the case of a given representation), while again, the universal communicability of a feeling presupposes a common sense: it follows that our assumption of it is well founded. And here, too, we do not have to take our stand on psychological observations, but we assume a common sense as the necessary condition of the universal communicability of our knowledge, which is presupposed in every logic and every principle of knowledge that is not one of scepticism.

## § 22

### THE NECESSITY OF THE UNIVERSAL ASSENT THAT IS THOUGHT IN A JUDGEMENT OF TASTE, IS A SUBJECTIVE NECESSITY WHICH, UNDER THE PRESUPPOSITION OF A COMMON SENSE, IS REPRESENTED AS OBJECTIVE

In all judgements by which we describe anything as beautiful we tolerate no one else being of a different opinion, and in taking up this position we do not rest our judgement upon concepts, but only on our feeling. Accordingly we introduce this fundamental feeling not as a private feeling, but as a public sense. Now, for this purpose, experience cannot be made the ground of this common sense, for the latter is invoked to justify judgements containing an 'ought'. The assertion is not that every one *will* fall in with our judgement, but rather that every one *ought* to agree with it. Here I put forward my judgement of taste as an example of the judgement of common sense, and attribute to it on that account *exemplary* validity. Hence common sense is a mere ideal norm. With this as presupposition, a judgement that accords with it, as well as the delight in an Object expressed in that judgement, is rightly converted into a rule for every one. For the principle, while it is only subjective, being yet assumed as subjectively universal (a necessary idea for every one), could, in what concerns the consensus of different judging Subjects, demand universal assent like an objective principle, provided we were assured of our subsumption under it being correct.

This indeterminate norm of a common sense is, as a matter of fact, presupposed by us; as is shown by our presuming to lay down judgements of taste. But does such a common sense in fact exist as a constitutive principle of the possibility of experience, or is it formed for us as a regulative principle by a still higher principle of reason, that for higher ends first seeks to beget in us a common sense? Is taste, in other words, a natural and original faculty, or is it only the idea of one that is artificial and to be acquired by us, so that a judgement of taste, with its demand for universal assent, is but a requirement of reason for generating such a con*sensus,* and does the 'ought', i.e. the objective necessity of the coincidence of the feeling of all with the particular feeling of each, only betoken the possibility of arriving at some sort of unanimity in these matters, and the judgement of taste only adduce an example of the application of this principle? These are questions which as yet we are neither willing nor in a position to investigate. For the present we have only to resolve the faculty of taste into its elements, and to unite these ultimately in the idea of a common sense.

### Definition of the Beautiful Drawn from the Fourth Moment

The beautiful is that which, apart from a concept, is cognized as object of a *necessary* delight.

### General Remark on the First Section of the Analytic

The result to be extracted from the foregoing analysis is in effect this: that everything runs up into the concept of taste as a critical faculty by which an object is estimated in reference to the *free conformity to law* of the imagination. If, now, imagination must in the judgement of taste be regarded in its freedom, then, to begin with, it is not taken as reproductive, as in its subjection to the laws of association, but as productive and exerting an activity of its own (as originator of arbitrary forms of possible intuitions). And although in the apprehension of a given object of sense it is tied down to a definite form of this Object and, to that extent, does not enjoy free play, (as it does in poetry,) still it is easy to conceive that the object may supply ready-made to the imagination just such a form of the arrangement of the manifold, as the imagination, if it were left to itself, would freely project in harmony with the general *conformity to law of the understanding.* But that the *imagination* should be both *free* and *of itself conformable to law,* i.e. carry autonomy with it, is a contradiction. The understanding alone gives the law. Where, however, the imaginaton is compelled to follow a course laid down by a definite law, then what the form of the product is to be is determined by concepts; but, in that case, as already shown, the delight is not delight in the beautiful, but in the good, (in perfection, though it be no more than formal perfection), and the judgement is not one due to taste. Hence it is only a conformity to law without a law, and a subjective harmonizing of the imagination and the understanding without an objective one—which latter would mean that the representation was referred to a definite concept of the object—that can consist with the free conformity to law of the understanding (which has also been called finality apart from an end) and with the specific character of a judgement of taste.

Now geometrically regular figures, a circle, a square, a cube, and the like, are commonly brought forward by critics of taste as the most simple and unquestionable examples of beauty. And yet the very reason why they are called regular, is because the only way of representing them is by looking on them as mere presentations of a determinate concept by which the figure has its rule (according to which alone it is possible) prescribed for it. One or other of these two views must, therefore, be wrong: either the verdict of the critics that attributes beauty to such figures, or else our own, which makes finality apart from any concept necessary for beauty.

One would scarce think it necessary for a man to have taste to take more delight in a circle than in a scrawled outline, in an equilateral and equiangular quadrilateral than in one that is all lopsided, and, as it were, deformed. The requirements of common understanding ensure such a preference without the least demand upon taste. Where some purpose is perceived, as, for instance, that of forming an estimate of the area of a plot of land, or rendering intelligible the relation of divided parts to one another and to the whole, then regular figures, and those of the simplest kind, are needed; and the delight does not rest immediately upon the way the figure strikes the eye, but upon its serviceability for all manner of possible purposes. A room with the walls making oblique angles, a plot laid out in a garden in a similar way, even any violation of symmetry, as well in the figure of animals (e.g. being one-eyed) as in that of buildings, or of flower-beds, is displeasing because of its perversity of form, not alone in a practical way in respect of some definite use to which the thing may be put, but for an estimate that looks to all manner of possible purposes. With the judgement of taste the case is different. For, when it is pure, it combines delight or aversion immediately with the bare *contemplation* of the object irrespective of its use or of any end.

The regularity that conduces to the concept of an object is, in fact, the indispensable condition *(conditio sine qua non)* of grasping the object as a single representation and giving to the manifold its determinate form. This determination is an end in respect of knowledge; and in this connexion it is invariably coupled with delight (such as attends the accomplishment of any, even problematical, purpose). Here, however, we have merely the value set upon the solution that satisfies the problem, and not a free and indeterminately final entertainment of the mental powers with what is called beautiful. In the latter case understanding is at the service of imagination, in the former this relation is reversed.

With a thing that owes its possibility to a purpose, a building, or even an animal, its regularity, which consists in symmetry, must express the unity of the intuition accompanying the concept of its end, and belongs with it to cognition. But where all that is intended is the maintenance of a free play of the powers of representation (subject, however, to the condition that there is to be nothing for understanding to take exception to), in ornamental gardens, in the decoration of rooms, in all kinds of furniture that shows good taste, etc., regularity in the shape of constraint is to be avoided as far as possible. Thus English taste in gardens, and fantastic taste in furniture, push the freedom of imagination to the verge of what is grotesque—the idea being that in this divorce from all constraint of rules the precise instance is being afforded where taste can exhibit its perfection in projects of the imagination to the fullest extent.

All stiff regularity (such as borders on mathematical regularity) is inherently repugnant to taste, in that the contemplation of it affords us no lasting entertainment. Indeed, where it has neither cognition nor some definite practical end expressly in view, we get heartily tired of it. On the other hand, anything that gives the imagination scope for unstudied and final play is always fresh to us. We do not grow to hate the very sight of it. *Marsden* in his description of Sumatra observes that the free beauties of nature so surround the beholder on all sides that they cease to have much attraction for him. On the other hand he found a pepper garden full of charm, on coming across it in mid-forest with its rows of parallel stakes on which the plant twines itself. From all this he infers that wild, and in its appearance quite irregular beauty, is only pleasing as a change to one whose eyes have become surfeited with regular beauty. But he need only have made the experiment of passing one day in his pepper garden to realize that once the regularity has enabled the understanding to put itself in accord with the order that is its constant requirement, instead of the object diverting him any longer, it imposes an irksome constraint upon the imagination: whereas nature subject to no constraint of artificial rules, and lavish, as it there is, in its luxuriant variety can supply constant food for his taste.—Even a bird's song, which we can reduce to no musical rule, seems to have more freedom in it, and thus to be richer for taste, than the human voice singing in accordance with all the rules that the art of music prescribes; for we grow tired much sooner of frequent and lengthy repetitions of the latter. Yet here most likely our sympathy with the mirth of a dear little creature is confused with the beauty of its song, for if exactly imitated by man (as has been sometimes done with the notes of the nightingale) it would strike our ear as wholly destitute of taste.

Further, beautiful objects have to be distinguished from beautiful views of objects (where the distance often prevents a clear perception). In the latter case taste appears to fasten, not so much on what the imagination *grasps* in this field, as on the incentive it receives to indulge in poetic fiction, i.e. in the peculiar fancies with which the mind entertains itself as it is being continually stirred by the variety that strikes the eye. It is just as when we watch the changing shapes of the fire or of a rippling brook: neither of which are things of beauty, but they convey a charm to the imagination, because they sustain its free play.

# Analytic of the Sublime

## § 23
### TRANSITION FROM THE FACULTY OF ESTIMATING THE BEAUTIFUL TO THAT OF ESTIMATING THE SUBLIME

The beautiful and the sublime agree on the point of pleasing on their own account. Further they agree in not presupposing either a judgement of sense or one logically determinant, but one of reflection. Hence it follows that the delight does not depend upon a sensation, as with the agreeable, nor upon a definite concept, as does the delight in the good, although it has, for all that, an indeterminate reference to concepts. Consequently the delight is connected with the mere presentation or faculty of presentation, and is thus taken to express the accord, in a given intuition, of the faculty of presentation, or the imagination, with the *faculty of concepts* that belongs to understanding or reason, in the sense of the former assisting the latter. Hence both kinds of judgements are *singular,* and yet such as profess to be universally valid in respect of every Subject, despite the fact that their claims are directed merely to the feeling of pleasure and not to any knowledge of the object.

There are, however, also important and striking differences between the two. The beautiful in nature is a question of the form of the object, and this consists in limitation, whereas the sublime is to be found in an object even devoid of form, so far as it immediately involves, or else by its presence provokes, a representation of *limitlessness,* yet with a super-added thought of its totality. Accordingly the beautiful seems to be regarded as a presentation of an indeterminate concept of understanding, the sublime as a presentation of an indeterminate concept of reason. Hence the delight is in the former case coupled with the representation of *Quality*, but in this case with that of *Quantity*. Moreover, the former delight is very different from the latter in kind. For the beautiful is directly attended with a feeling of the furtherance of life, and is thus compatible with charms and a playful imagination. On the other hand, the feeling of the sublime is a pleasure that only arises indirectly, being brought about by the feeling of a momentary check to the vital forces followed at once by a discharge all the more powerful, and so it is an emotion that seems to be no sport, but dead earnest in the affairs of the imagination. Hence charms are repugnant to it; and, since the mind is not simply attracted by the object, but is also alternately repelled thereby, the delight in the sublime does not so much involve positive pleasure as admiration or respect, i.e. merits the name of a negative pleasure.

But the most important and vital distinction between the sublime and the beautiful is certainly this: that if, as is allowable, we here confine our attention in the first instance to the sublime in Objects of nature, (that of art being always restricted by the conditions of an agreement with nature,) we observe that whereas natural beauty (such as is self-subsisting) conveys a finality in its form making the object appear, as it were, preadapted to our power of judgement, so that it thus forms of itself an object of our delight, that which, without our indulging in any refinements of thought, but, simply in our apprehension of it, excites the feeling of the sublime, may appear, indeed, in point of form to contravene the ends of our power of judgement, to be ill-adapted to our faculty of presentation, and to be, as it were, an outrage on the imagination, and yet it is judged all the more sublime on that account.

From this it may be seen at once that we express ourselves on the whole inaccurately if we term any *Object of nature* sublime, although we may with perfect propriety call many such objects beautiful. For how can that which is apprehended as inherently contra-final be noted with an expression of approval? All that we can say is that the object lends itself to the presentation of a sublimity discoverable in the mind. For the sublime, in the strict sense of the word, cannot be contained in any sensuous form, but rather concerns ideas of reason, which, although no adequate presentation of them is possible, may be excited and called into the mind by that very inadequacy itself which does admit of sensuous presentation. Thus the broad ocean agitated by storms cannot be called sublime. Its aspect is horrible, and one must have stored one's mind in advance with a rich stock of ideas, if such an intuition is to raise it to the pitch of a feeling which is itself sublime—sublime because the mind has been incited to abandon sensibility, and employ itself upon ideas involving higher finality.

Self-subsisting natural beauty reveals to us a technic of nature which shows it in the light of a system ordered in accordance with laws the principle of which is not to be found within the range of our entire faculty of understanding. This principle is that of a finality relative to the employment of judgement in respect of phenomena which have thus to be assigned, not merely to nature regarded as aimless mechanism, but also to nature regarded after the analogy of art. Hence it gives a veritable extension, not, of course, to our knowledge of Objects of nature, but to our conception of nature itself—nature as mere mechanism being enlarged to the conception of nature as art—an extension inviting profound inquiries as to the possibility of such a form. But in what we are wont to call sublime in nature there is such an absence of anything leading to particular objective principles and corresponding forms of nature, that it is rather in its chaos, or in its wildest and most irregular disorder and desolation, provided it gives signs of magnitude and power, that nature chiefly excites the ideas of the sublime. Hence we see that the concept of the sublime in nature is far less important and rich in consequences than that of its beauty. It gives on the whole no indication of anything final in nature itself, but only in the possible *employment* of our intuitions of it in inducing a feeling in our own selves of a finality quite independent of nature. For the beautiful in nature we must seek a ground external to ourselves, but for the sublime one merely in ourselves and the attitude of mind that introduces sublimity into the representation of nature. This is a very needful preliminary remark. It entirely separates the ideas of the sublime from that of a finality of *nature,* and makes the theory of the sublime a mere appendage to the aesthetic estimate of the finality of nature, because it does not give a representation of any particular form in nature, but involves no more than the development of a final employment by the imagination of its own representation.

## § 24

### SUBDIVISION OF AN INVESTIGATION OF THE FEELING
### OF THE SUBLIME

In the division of the moments of an aesthetic estimate of objects in respect of the feeling of the sublime, the course of the Analytic will be able to follow the same principle as in the analysis of judgements of taste. For, the judgement being one of the aesthetic reflective judgement, the delight in the sublime, just like that in the beautiful, must in its *Quantity* by shown to be universally valid, in its *Quality* independent of interest, in its *Relation* subjective finality, and the latter, in its *Modality,* necessary. Hence the method here will not depart from the lines followed in the preceding section: unless something is made of the point that there, where the aesthetic Judgement bore on the form of the Object, we began with the investigation of its Quality, whereas here, considering the formlessness that may belong to what we call Sublime, we begin with that of its Quantity, as first moment of the aesthetic judgement on the sublime—a divergence of method the reason for which is evident from § 23.

But the analysis of the sublime obliges a division not required by that of the beautiful, namely one into the *mathematically* and the *dynamically* sublime.

For the feeling of the sublime involves as its characteristic feature a mental *movement* combined with the estimate of the object, whereas taste in respect of the beautiful presupposes that the mind is in *restful* contemplation, and preserves it in this state. But this movement has to be estimated as subjectively final (since the sublime pleases). Hence it is referred through the imagination either to the *faculty of cognition* or to that of *desire;* but to whichever faculty the reference is made the finality of the given representation is estimated only in respect of these faculties (apart from end or interest). Accordingly the first is attributed to the Object as a *mathematical,* the second as a *dynamical,* affection of the imagination. Hence we get the above double mode of representing an Object as sublime.

## A. *The Mathematically Sublime*

### § 25
#### DEFINITION OF THE TERM 'SUBLIME'

*Sublime* is the name given to what is *absolutely great*. But to be great and to be a magnitude are entirely different concepts (*magnitudo* and *quantitas*). In the same way to *assert without qualification (simpliciter)* that something is great, is quite a different thing from saying that it is *absolutely great (absolute, non comparative magnum)*. The latter is *what is beyond all comparison great.*— What, then, is the meaning of the assertion that anything is great, or small, or of medium size? What is indicated is not a pure concept of understanding, still less an intuition of sense; and just as little is it a concept of reason, for it does not import any principle of cognition. It must, therefore, be a concept of judgement, or have its source in one, and must introduce as basis of the judgement a subjective finality of the representation with reference to the power of judgement. Given a multiplicity of the homogeneous together constituting one thing, and we may at once cognize from the thing itself that it is a *magnitude (quantum)*. No comparison with other things is required. But to determine *how great* it is always requires something else, which itself has magnitude, for its measure. Now, since in the estimate of magnitude we have to take into account not merely the multiplicity (number of units) but also the magnitude of the unit (the measure), and since the magnitude of this unit in turn always requires something else as its measure and as the standard of its comparison, and so on, we see that the computation of the magnitude of phenomena is, in all cases, utterly incapable of affording us any absolute concept of a magnitude, and can, instead, only afford one that is always based on comparison.

If, now, I assert without qualification that anything is great, it would seem that I have nothing in the way of a comparison present to my mind, or at least nothing involving an objective measure, for no attempt is thus made to determine how great the object is. But, despite the standard of comparison being merely subjective, the claim of the judgement is none the less one to universal agreement; the judgements: 'That man is beautiful' and 'He is tall' do not purport to speak only for the judging Subject, but, like theoretical judgements, they demand the assent of every one.

206 · Immanuel Kant

Now in a judgement that without qualification describes anything as great, it is not merely meant that the object has a magnitude, but greatness is ascribed to it pre-eminently among many other objects of a like kind, yet without the extent of this pre-eminence being determined. Hence a standard is certainly laid at the basis of the judgement, which standard is presupposed to be one that can be taken as the same for every one, but which is available only for an aesthetic estimate of the greatness, and not for one that is logical (mathematically determined), for the standard is a merely subjective one underlying the reflective judgement upon the greatness. Furthermore, this standard may be empirical, as, let us say, the average size of the men known to us, of animals of a certain kind, of trees, of houses, of mountains, and so forth. Or it may be a standard given *a priori,* which by reason of the imperfections of the judging Subject is restricted to subjective conditions of presentation *in concreto:* as, in the practical sphere, the greatness of a particular virtue, or of public liberty and justice in a country; or, in the theoretical sphere, the greatness of the accuracy or inaccuracy of an experiment or measurement, etc.

Here, now, it is of note that, although we have no interest whatever in the Object, i.e. its real existence may be a matter of no concern to us, still its mere greatness, regarded even as devoid of form, is able to convey a universally communicable delight and so involve the consciousness of a subjective finality in the employment of our cognitive faculties, but not, be it remembered, a delight in the Object, for the latter may be formless, but, in contradistinction to what is the case with the beautiful, where the reflective judgement finds itself set to a key that is final in respect of cognition generally, a delight in an extension affecting the imagination itself.

If (subject as above) we say of an object, without qualification, that it is great, this is not a mathematically determinant, but a mere reflective judgement upon its representation, which is subjectively final for a particular employment of our cognitive faculties in the estimation of magnitude, and we then always couple with the representation a kind of respect, just as we do a kind of contempt with what we call absolutely small. Moreover, the estimate of things as great or small extends to everything, even to all their qualities. Thus we call even their beauty great or small. The reason of this is to be found in the fact that we have only got to present a thing in intuition, as the precept of judgement directs, (consequently to represent it aesthetically,) for it to be in its entirety a phenomenon, and hence a quantum.

If, however, we call anything not alone great, but, without qualification, absolutely, and in every respect (beyond all comparison) great, that is to say, sublime, we soon perceive that for this it is not permissible to seek an appropriate standard outside itself, but merely in itself. It is a greatness comparable to itself alone. Hence it comes that the sublime is not to be looked for in the things of nature, but only in our own ideas. But it must be left to the Deduction to show in which of them it resides.

The above definition may also be expressed in this way: *that is sublime in comparison with which all else is small.* Here we readily see that nothing can be given in nature, no matter how great we may judge it to be, which, regarded in some other relation, may not be degraded to the level of the infinitely little, and nothing so small which in comparison with some still smaller standard may not for our imagination be enlarged to the greatness of a world. Telescopes have put within our reach an abundance of material to go upon in making the first observation, and microscopes the same in making the second. Nothing, therefore, which can be an object of the senses is to be termed sublime when treated on this footing. But precisely because there is a striving in our imagination towards progress *ad infinitum,* while reason demands absolute totality, as a real idea, that same inability on the part of our faculty for the estimation of the magnitude of things of the world of sense to attain to this idea, is the awakening of a feeling of a supersensible faculty within us; and it is the use to which judgement naturally puts particular objects on behalf of this latter feeling, and not the object of sense, that is absolutely great, and every other contrasted employment small. Consequently it is the disposition of soul evoked by a particular representation engaging the attention of the reflective judgement, and not the Object, that is to be called sublime.

The foregoing formulae defining the sublime may, therefore, be supplemented by yet another: *The sublime is that, the mere capacity of thinking which evidences a faculty of mind transcending every standard of sense.*

## § 26

THE ESTIMATION OF THE MAGNITUDE OF NATURAL THINGS
REQUISITE FOR THE IDEA OF THE SUBLIME

The estimation of magnitude by means of concepts of number
(or their signs in algebra) is mathematical, but that in mere intuition
(by the eye) is aesthetic. Now we can only get definite concepts of
*how great* anything is by having recourse to numbers (or, at any
rate, by getting approximate measurements by means of numerical
series progressing *ad infinitum*), the unit being the measure; and to
this extent all logical estimation of magnitude is mathematical. But,
as the magnitude of the measure has to be assumed as a known
quantity, if, to form an estimate of this, we must again have recourse
to numbers involving another standard for their unit, and consequently must again proceed mathematically, we can never arrive at
a first or fundamental measure, and so cannot get any definite
concept of a given magnitude. The estimation of the magnitude of
the fundamental measure must, therefore, consist merely in the
immediate grasp which we can get of it in intuition, and the use to
which our imagination can put this in presenting the numerical
concepts: i.e. all estimation of the magnitude of objects of nature
is in the last resort aesthetic (i.e. subjectively and not objectively
determined).

Now for the mathematical estimation of magnitude there is, of
course, no greatest possible (for the power of numbers extends to
infinity), but for the aesthetic estimation there certainly is, and of
it I say that where it is considered an absolute measure beyond
which no greater is possible subjectively (i.e. for the judging Subject), it then conveys the idea of the sublime, and calls forth that
emotion which no mathematical estimation of magnitudes by numbers can evoke (unless in so far as the fundamental aesthetic measure
is kept vividly present to the imagination): because the latter presents only the relative magnitude due to comparison with others of
a like kind, whereas the former presents magnitude absolutely, so
far as the mind can grasp it in an intuition.

To take in a quantum intuitively in the imagination so as to be
able to use it as a measure, or unit for estimating magnitude by
numbers, involves two operations of this faculty: *apprehension (apprehensio)* and *comprehension (comprehensio aesthetica)*. Appre-

hension presents no difficulty: for this process can be carried on *ad infinitum;* but with the advance of apprehension comprehension becomes more difficult at every step and soon attains its maximum, and this is the aesthetically greatest fundamental measure for the estimation of magnitude. For if the apprehension has reached a point beyond which the representations of sensuous intuition in the case of the parts first apprehended begin to disappear from the imagination as this advances to the apprehension of yet others, as much, then, is lost at one end as is gained at the other, and for comprehension we get a maximum which the imagination cannot exceed.

This explains Savary's observations in his account of Egypt, that in order to get the full emotional effect of the size of the Pyramids we must avoid coming too near just as much as remaining too far away. For in the latter case the representation of the apprehended parts (the tiers of stones) is but obscure, and produces no effect upon the aesthetic judgement of the Subject. In the former, however, it takes the eye some time to complete the apprehension from the base to the summit; but in this interval the first tiers always in part disappear before the imagination has taken in the last, and so the comprehension is never complete.—The same explanation may also sufficiently account for the bewilderment, or sort of perplexity, which, as is said, seizes the visitor on first entering St. Peter's in Rome. For here a feeling comes home to him of the inadequacy of his imagination for presenting the idea of a whole within which that imagination attains its maximum, and, in its fruitless efforts to extend this limit, recoils upon itself, but in so doing succumbs to an emotional delight.

At present I am not disposed to deal with the ground of this delight, connected, as it is, with a representation in which we would least of all look for it—a representation, namely, that lets us see its own inadequacy, and consequently its subjective want of finality for our judgement in the estimation of magnitude—but confine myself to the remark that if the aesthetic judgement is to be *pure* (*unmixed with any teleological judgement* which, as such, belongs to reason), and if we are to give a suitable example of it for the Critique of *aesthetic* judgement, we must not point to the sublime in works of art, e.g. buildings, statues and the like, where a human end determines the form as well as the magnitude, nor yet in things of nature, *that in their very concept import a definite end,* e.g. animals of a recognized natural order, but in rude nature merely as involving magnitude (and only in this so far as it does not convey any charm or any emotion arising from actual danger). For in a representation of this kind nature contains nothing monstrous (nor what is either magnificent or horrible)—the magnitude apprehended may be increased to any extent provided imagination is able to grasp it all in one whole. An object is *monstrous* where by its size it defeats the end that forms its concept. The *colossal* is the mere presentation of a concept which is almost too great for presentation, i.e. borders on the relatively monstrous; for the end to be attained by the presentation of a concept is made harder to realize by the intuition of the object being almost too great for our faculty of apprehension.—A pure judgement upon the sublime must, however, have no end belonging to the Object as its determining ground, if it is to be aesthetic and not to be tainted with any judgement of understanding or reason.

Since whatever is to be a source of pleasure, apart from interest, to the merely reflective judgement must involve in its representation subjective, and, as such, universally valid finality—though here, however, no finality of the *form* of the object underlies our estimate of it (as it does in the case of the beautiful)—the question arises, What is this subjective finality, and what enables it to be prescribed as a norm so as to yield a ground for universally valid delight in the mere estimation of magnitude, and that, too, in a case where it is pushed to the point at which our faculty of imagination breaks down in presenting the concept of a magnitude, and proves unequal to its task?

In the successive aggregation of units requisite for the representation of magnitudes the imagination of itself advances *ad infinitum* without let or hindrance—understanding, however, conducting it by means of concepts of number for which the former must supply the schema. This procedure belongs to the logical estimation of magnitude, and, as such, is doubtless something objectively final according to the concept of an end (as all measurement is), but it is not anything which for the aesthetic judgement is final or pleasing. Further, in this intentional finality there is nothing compelling us to tax the utmost powers of the imagination, and drive it as far as ever it can reach in its presentations, so as to enlarge the size of the measure, and thus make the single intuition holding the many in one (the *comprehension*) as great as possible. For in the estimation of magnitude by the understanding (arithmetic) we get just as far, whether the comprehension of the units is pushed to the number 10 (as in the decimal scale) or only to 4 (as in the quaternary); the further production of magnitude being carried out by the successive aggregation of units, or, if the quantum is given in intuition, by apprehension, merely progressively (not comprehensively), according to an adopted principle of progression. In this mathematical estimation of magnitude understanding is as well served and as satisfied whether imagination selects for the unit a magnitude which one can take in at a glance, e.g. a foot, or a perch, or else a German mile, or even the earth's diameter, the apprehension of which is indeed possible, but not its comprehension in an intuition of the imagination (i.e. it is not possible by means of a *comprehensio aesthetica*, though quite so by means of a *comprehensio logica* in a numerical concept). In each case the logical estimation of magnitude advances *ad infinitum* with nothing to stop it.

The mind, however, hearkens now to the voice of reason, which for all given magnitudes—even for those which can never be completely apprehended, though (in sensuous representation) estimated as completely given—requires totality, and consequently comprehension in *one* intuition, and which calls for a *presentation* answering to all the above members of a progressively increasing numerical series, and does not exempt even the infinite (space and time past) from this requirement, but rather renders it inevitable for us to regard this infinite (in the judgement of common reason) as *completely given* (i.e. given in its totality).

But the infinite is absolutely (not merely comparatively) great. In comparison with this all else (in the way of magnitudes of the same order) is small. But the point of capital importance is that the mere ability even to think it as a *whole* indicates a faculty of mind transcending every standard of sense. For the latter would entail a comprehension yielding as unit a standard bearing to the infinite a definite ratio expressible in numbers, which is impossible. Still the *mere ability even to think* the given infinite without contradiction, is something that requires the presence in the human mind of a faculty that is itself supersensible. For it is only through this faculty and its idea of a noumenon, which latter, while not itself admitting of any intuition, is yet introduced as substrate underlying the intuition of the world as mere phenomenon, that the infinite of the world of sense, in the pure intellectual estimation of magnitude, is *completely* comprehended *under* a concept, although in the mathematical estimation *by means of numerical concepts* it can never be completely thought. Even a faculty enabling the infinite of supersensible intuition to be regarded as given (in its intelligible substrate), transcends every standard of sensibility, and is great beyond all comparison even with the faculty of mathematical estimation: not, of course, from a theoretical point of view that looks to the interests of our faculty of knowledge, but as a broadening of the mind that from another (the practical) point of view feels itself empowered to pass beyond the narrow confines of sensibility.

Nature, therefore, is sublime in such of its phenomena as in their intuition convey the idea of their infinity. But this can only occur through the inadequacy of even the greatest effort of our imagination in the estimation of the magnitude of an object. But, now, in the case of the mathematical estimation of magnitude imagination is quite competent to supply a measure equal to the requirements of any object. For the numerical concepts of the understanding can by progressive synthesis make any measure adequate to any given magnitude. Hence it must be the *aesthetic* estimation of magnitude in which we get at once a feeling of the effort towards a comprehension that exceeds the faculty of imagination for mentally grasping the progressive apprehension in a whole of intuition, and, with it, a perception of the inadequacy of this faculty, which has no bounds to its progress, for taking in and using for the estimation of magnitude a fundamental measure that understanding could turn to account without the least trouble. Now the proper unchangeable fundamental measure of nature is its absolute whole, which, with it, regarded as a phenomenon, means infinity comprehended. But, since this fundamental measure is a self-contradictory concept, (owing to the impossibility of the absolute totality of an endless progression,) it follows that where the size of a natural Object is such that the imagination spends its whole faculty of comprehension upon it in vain, it must carry our concept of nature to a supersensible substrate (underlying both nature and our faculty of thought) which is great beyond every standard of sense. Thus, instead of the object, it is rather the cast of the mind in appreciating it that we have to estimate as *sublime*.

Therefore, just as the aesthetic judgement in its estimate of the beautiful refers the imagination in its free play to the *understanding,* to bring out its agreement with the *concepts* of the latter in general (apart from their determination): so in its estimate of a thing as sublime it refers that faculty to *reason* to bring out its subjective accord with *ideas* of reason (indeterminately indicated), i.e. to induce a temper of mind conformable to that which the influence of definite (practical) ideas would produce upon feeling, and in common accord with it.

This makes it evident that true sublimity must be sought only in the mind of the judging Subject, and not in the Object of nature that occasions this attitude by the estimate formed of it. Who would apply the term 'sublime' even to shapeless mountain masses towering one above the other in wild disorder, with their pyramids of ice, or to the dark tempestuous ocean, or such like things? But in the contemplation of them, without any regard to their form, the mind abandons itself to the imagination and to a reason placed, though quite apart from any definite end, in conjuction therewith, and merely broadening its view, and it feels itself elevated in its own estimate of itself on finding all the might of imagination still unequal to its ideas.

We get examples of the mathematically sublime of nature in mere intuition in all those instances where our imagination is afforded, not so much a greater numerical concept as a large unit as measure (for shortening the numerical series). A tree judged by the height of man gives, at all events, a standard for a mountain; and, supposing this is, say, a mile high, it can serve as unit for the number expressing the earth's diameter, so as to make it intuitable; similarly the earth's diameter for the known planetary system; this again for the system of the Milky Way; and the immeasurable host of such systems, which go by the name of nebulae, and most likely in turn themselves form such a system, holds out no prospect of a limit. Now in the aesthetic estimate of such an immeasurable whole, the sublime does not lie so much in the greatness of the number, as in the fact that in our onward advance we always arrive at proportionately greater units. The systematic division of the cosmos conduces to this result. For it represents all that is great in nature as in turn becoming little; or, to be more exact, it represents our imagination in all its boundlessness, and with it nature, as sinking into insignificance before the ideas of reason, once their adequate presentation is attempted.

§ 27

QUALITY OF THE DELIGHT IN OUR ESTIMATE OF THE SUBLIME

The feeling of our incapacity to attain to an idea *that is a law for us,* is RESPECT. Now the idea of the comprehension of any phenomenon whatever, that may be given us, in a whole of intuition, is an idea imposed upon us by a law of reason, which recognizes no definite, universally valid and unchangeable measure except the absolute whole. But our imagination, even when taxing itself to the uttermost on the score of this required comprehension of a given object in a whole of intuition, (and so with a view to the presentation of the idea of reason,) betrays its limits and its inadequacy, but still, at the same time, its proper vocation of making itself adequate to the same as a law. Therefore the feeling of the sublime in nature is respect for our own vocation, which we attribute to an Object of nature by a certain subreption (substitution of a respect for the Object in place of one for the idea of humanity in our own self—the Subject); and this feeling renders, as it were, intuitable the supremacy of our cognitive faculties on the rational side over the greatest faculty of sensibility.

The feeling of the sublime is, therefore, at once a feeling of displeasure, arising from the inadequacy of imagination in the aesthetic estimation of magnitude to attain to its estimation by reason, and a simultaneously awakened pleasure, arising from this very judgement of the inadequacy of the greatest faculty of sense being in accord with ideas of reason, so far as the effort to attain to these is for us a law. It is, in other words, for us a law (of reason), which goes to make us what we are, that we should esteem as small in comparison with ideas of reason everything which for us is great in nature as an object of sense; and that which makes us alive to the feeling of this supersensible side of our being harmonizes with the law. Now the greatest effort of the imagination in the presentation of the unit for the estimation of magnitude involves in itself a reference to something *absolutely great,* consequently a reference also to the law of reason that this alone is to be adopted as the supreme measure of what is great. Therefore the inner perception of the inadequacy of every standard of sense to serve for the rational estimation of magnitude is a coming into accord with reason's laws, and a displeasure that makes us alive to the feeling of the super-sensible side of our being, according to which it is final, and consequently a pleasure, to find every standard of sensibility falling short of the ideas of reason.

The mind feels itself *set in motion* in the representation of the sublime in nature; whereas in the aesthetic judgement upon what is beautiful therein it is in *restful* contemplation. This movement, especially in its inception, may be compared with a vibration, i.e. with a rapidly alternating repulsion and attraction produced by one and the same Object. The point of excess for the imagination (towards which it is driven in the apprehension of the intuition) is like an abyss in which it fears to lose itself; yet again for the rational idea of the supersensible it is not excessive, but conformable to law, and directed to drawing out such an effort on the part of the imagination: and so in turn as much a source of attraction as it was repellent to mere sensibility. But the judgement itself all the while steadfastly preserves its aesthetic character, because it represents, without being grounded on any definite concept of the Object, merely the subjective play of the mental powers (imagination and reason) as harmonious by virtue of their very contrast. For just as in the estimate of the beautiful imagination and *understanding* by their concert generate subjective finality of the mental faculties, so imagination and *reason* do so here by their conflict—that is to say they induce a feeling of our possessing a pure and self-sufficient reason, or a faculty for the estimation of magnitude, whose pre-eminence can only be made intuitively evident by the inadequacy of that faculty which in the presentation of magnitudes (of objects of sense) is itself unbounded.

Measurement of a space (as apprehension) is at the same time a description of it, and so an objective movement in the imagination and a progression. On the other hand the comprehension of the manifold in the unity, not of thought, but of intuition, and consequently the comprehension of the successively apprehended parts at one glance, is a retrogression that removes the time-condition in the progression of the imagination, and renders *co-existence* intuitable. Therefore, since the time-series is a condition of the internal sense and of an intuition, it is a subjective movement of the imagination by which it does violence to the internal sense—a violence which must be proportionately more striking the greater the quantum which the imagination comprehends in one intuition. The effort, therefore, to receive in a single intuition a measure for magnitudes which it takes an appreciable time to apprehend, is a mode of representation which, subjectively considered, is contra-final, but, objectively, is requisite for the estimation of magnitude, and is consequently final. Here the very same violence that is wrought on the Subject through the imagination is estimated as final *for the whole province* of the mind.

The *quality* of the feeling of the sublime consists in its being, in respect of the faculty of forming aesthetic estimates, a feeling of displeasure at an object, which yet, at the same time, is represented as being final—a representation which derives its possibility from the fact that the Subject's very incapacity betrays the consciousness of an unlimited faculty of the same Subject, and that the mind can only form an aesthetic estimate of the latter faculty by means of that incapacity.

In the case of the logical estimation of magnitude the impossibility of ever arriving at absolute totality by the progressive measurement of things of the sensible world in time and space was cognized as an objective impossibility, i.e. one of *thinking* the infinite as given, and not as simply subjective, i.e. an incapacity for *grasping* it; for nothing turns there on the amount of the comprehension in one intuition, as measure, but everything depends on a numerical concept. But in an aesthetic estimation of magnitude the numerical concept must drop out of count or undergo a change. The only thing that is final for such estimation is the comprehension on the part of imagination in respect of the unit of measure (the concept of a law of the successive production of the concept of magnitude being consequently avoided).—If, now, a magnitude begins to tax the utmost stretch of our faculty of comprehension in an intuition, and still numerical magnitudes—in respect of which we are conscious of the boundlessness of our faculty—call upon the imagination for aesthetic comprehension in a greater unit, the mind then gets a feeling of being aesthetically confined within bounds. Nevertheless, with a view to the extension of imagination necessary for adequacy with what is unbounded in our faculty of reason, namely the idea of the absolute whole, the attendant displeasure, and, consequently, the want of finality in our faculty of imagination, is still represented as final for ideas of reason and their animation. But in this very way the aesthetic judgement itself is subjectively final for reason as source of ideas, i.e. of such an intellectual comprehension as makes all aesthetic comprehension small, and the object is received as sublime with a pleasure that is only possible through the mediation of a displeasure.

## B. *The Dynamically Sublime in Nature*

### § 28

#### NATURE AS MIGHT

*Might* is a power which is superior to great hindrances. It is termed *dominion* if it is also superior to the resistance of that which itself possesses might. Nature considered in an aesthetic judgement as might that has no dominion over us, is *dynamically sublime*.

If we are to estimate nature as dynamically sublime, it must be represented as a source of fear (though the converse, that every object that is a source of fear is, in our aesthetic judgement, sublime, does not hold). For in forming an aesthetic estimate (no concept being present) the superiority to hindrances can only be estimated according to the greatness of the resistance. Now that which we strive to resist is an evil, and, if we do not find our powers commensurate to the task, an object of fear. Hence the aesthetic judgement can only deem nature a might, and so dynamically sublime, in so far as it is looked upon as an object of fear.

But we may look upon an object as *fearful,* and yet not be afraid *of* it, if, that is, our estimate takes the form of our simply *picturing to ourselves* the case of our wishing to offer some resistance to it, and recognizing that all such resistance would be quite futile. So the righteous man fears God without being afraid of Him, because he regards the case of his wishing to resist God and His commandments as one which need cause *him* no anxiety. But in every such case, regarded by him as not intrinsically impossible, he cognizes Him as One to be feared.

One who is in a state of fear can no more play the part of a judge of the sublime of nature than one captivated by inclination and appetite can of the beautiful. He flees from the sight of an object filling him with dread; and it is impossible to take delight in terror that is seriously entertained. Hence the agreeableness arising from the cessation of an uneasiness is a *state of joy.* But this, depending upon deliverance from a danger, is a rejoicing accompanied with a resolve never again to put oneself in the way of the danger: in fact we do not like bringing back to mind how we felt on that occasion—not to speak of going in search of an opportunity for experiencing it again.

Bold, overhanging, and, as it were, threatening rocks, thunderclouds piled up the vault of heaven, borne along with flashes and peals, volcanoes in all their violence of destruction, hurricanes leaving desolation in their track, the boundless ocean rising with rebellious force, the high waterfall of some mighty river, and the like, make our power of resistance of trifling moment in comparison with their might. But, provided our own position is secure, their aspect is all the more attractive for its fearfulness; and we readily call these objects sublime, because they raise the forces of the soul above the height of vulgar commonplace, and discover within us a power of resistance of quite another kind, which gives us courage to be able to measure ourselves against the seeming omnipotence of nature.

In the immeasurableness of nature and the incompetence of our faculty for adopting a standard proportionate to the aesthetic estimation of the magnitude of its *realm,* we found our own limitation. But with this we also found in our rational faculty another nonsensuous standard, one which has that infinity itself under it as unit, and in comparison with which everything in nature is small, and so found in our minds a pre-eminence over nature even in its immeasurability. Now in just the same way the irresistibility of the might of nature forces upon us the recognition of our physical helplessness as beings of nature, but at the same time reveals a faculty of estimating ourselves as independent of nature, and discovers a pre-eminence above nature that is the foundation of a self-preservation of quite another kind from that which may be assailed and brought into danger by external nature. This saves humanity in our own person from humiliation, even though as mortal men we have to submit to external violence. In this way external nature is not estimated in our aesthetic judgement as sublime so far as exciting fear, but rather because it challenges our power (one not of nature) to regard as small those things of which we are wont to be solicitous (worldly goods, health, and life), and hence to regard its might (to which in these matters we are no doubt subject) as exercising over us and our personality no such rude dominion that we should bow down before it, once the question becomes one of our highest principles and of our asserting or forsaking them. Therefore nature is here called sublime merely because it raises the imagination to a presentation of those cases in which the mind can make itself sensible of the appropriate sublimity of the sphere of its own being, even above nature.

This estimation of ourselves loses nothing by the fact that we must see ourselves safe in order to feel this soul-stirring delight— a fact from which it might be plausibly argued that, as there is no seriousness in the danger, so there is just as little seriousness in the sublimity of our faculty of soul. For here the delight only concerns the *province* of our faculty disclosed in such a case, so far as this faculty has its root in our nature; notwithstanding that its development and exercise is left to ourselves and remains an obligation. Here indeed there is truth—no matter how conscious a man, when he stretches his reflection so far abroad, may be of his actual present helplessness.

This principle has, doubtless, the appearance of being too far-fetched and subtle, and so of lying beyond the reach of an aesthetic judgement. But observation of men proves the reverse, and that it may be the foundation of the commonest judgements, although one is not always conscious of its presence. For what is it that, even to the savage, is the object of the greatest admiration? It is a man who is undaunted, who knows no fear, and who, therefore, does not give way to danger, but sets manfully to work with full deliberation. Even where civilization has reached a high pitch there remains this special reverence for the soldier; only that there is then further required of him that he should also exhibit all the virtues of peace— gentleness, sympathy and even becoming thought for his own person; and for the reason that in this we recognize that his mind is above the threats of danger. And so, comparing the statesman and the general, men may argue as they please as to the pre-eminent respect which is due to either above the other; but the verdict of the aesthetic judgement is for the latter. War itself, provided it is conducted with order and a sacred respect for the rights of civilians, has something sublime about it, and gives nations that carry it on in such a manner a stamp of mind only the more sublime the more numerous the dangers to which they are exposed, and which they are able to meet with fortitude. On the other hand, a prolonged peace favours the predominance of a mere commercial spirit, and with it a debasing self-interest, cowardice, and effeminacy, and tends to degrade the character of the nation.

So far as sublimity is predicated of might, this solution of the concept of it appears at variance with the fact that we are wont to represent God in the tempest, the storm, the earthquake, and the like, as presenting Himself in His wrath, but at the same time also in His sublimity, and yet here it would be alike folly and presumption to imagine a pre-eminence of our minds over the operations and, as it appears, even over the direction of such might. Here, instead of a feeling of the sublimity of our own nature, submission, prostration, and a feeling of utter helplessness seem more to constitute the attitude of mind befitting the manifestation of such an object, and to be that also more customarily associated with the idea of it on the occasion of a natural phenomenon of this kind. In religion, as a rule, prostration, adoration with bowed head, coupled with contrite, timorous posture and voice, seems to be the only becoming demeanour in presence of the Godhead, and accordingly most nations have assumed and still observe it. Yet this cast of mind is far from being intrinsically and necessarily involved in the idea of the *sublimity* of a religion and of its object. The man that is actually in a state of fear, finding in himself good reason to be so, because he is conscious of offending with his evil disposition against a might directed by a will at once irresistible and just, is far from being in the frame of mind for admiring divine greatness, for which a temper of calm reflection and a quite free judgement are required. Only when he becomes conscious of having a disposition that is upright and acceptable to God, do those operations of might serve to stir within him the idea of the sublimity of this Being, so far as he recognizes the existence in himself of a sublimity of disposition consonant with His will, and is thus raised above the dread of such operations of nature, in which he no longer sees God pouring forth the vials of the wrath. Even humility, taking the form of an un-

compromising judgement upon his shortcomings, which, ʌ
consciousness of good intentions, might readily be glossed
the ground of the frailty of human nature, is a sublime temper of
the mind voluntarily to undergo the pain of remorse as a means of
more and more effectually eradicating its cause. In this way religion
is intrinsically distinguished from superstition, which latter rears in
the mind, not reverence for the sublime, but dread and apprehension
of the all-powerful Being to whose will terror-stricken man sees
himself subjected, yet without according Him due honour. From
this nothing can arise but grace-begging and vain adulation, instead
of a religion consisting in a good life.

Sublimity, therefore, does not reside in any of the things of nature,
but only in our own mind, in so far as we may become conscious
of our superiority over nature within, and thus also over nature
without us (as exerting influence upon us). Everything that provokes
this feeling in us, including the *might* of nature which challenges
our strength, is then, though improperly, called sublime, and it is
only under presupposition of this idea within us, and in relation to
it, that we are capable of attaining to the idea of the sublimity of
that Being which inspires deep respect in us, not by the mere display
of its might in nature, but more by the faculty which is planted in
us of estimating that might without fear, and of regarding our estate
as exalted above it.

## § 29

### MODALITY OF THE JUDGEMENT ON THE SUBLIME IN NATURE

Beautiful nature contains countless things as to which we at once
take every one as in their judgement concurring with our own, and
as to which we may further expect this concurrence without facts
finding us far astray. But in respect of our judgement upon the
sublime in nature we cannot so easily vouch for ready acceptance
by others. For a far higher degree of culture, not merely of the
aesthetic judgement, but also of the faculties of cognition which lie
at its basis, seems to be requisite to enable us to lay down a judgement upon this high distinction of natural objects.

The proper mental mood for a feeling of the sublime postulates
the mind's susceptibility for ideas, since it is precisely in the failure
of nature to attain to these—and consequently only under presup-

position of this susceptibility and of the straining of the imagination to use nature as a schema for ideas—that there is something forbidding to sensibility, but which, for all that, has an attraction for us, arising from the fact of its being a dominion which reason exercises over sensibility with a view to extending it to the requirements of its own realm (the practical) and letting it look out beyond itself into the infinite, which for it is an abyss. In fact, without the development of moral ideas, that which, thanks to preparatory culture, we call sublime, merely strikes the untutored man as terrifying. He will see in the evidences which the ravages of nature give of her dominion, and in the vast scale of her might, compared with which his own is diminished to insignificance, only the misery, peril, and distress that would compass the man who was thrown to its mercy. So the simple-minded, and, for the most part, intelligent, Savoyard peasant, (as Herr von Sassure relates,) unhesitatingly called all lovers of snow-mountains fools. And who can tell whether he would have been so wide of the mark, if that student of nature had taken the risk of the dangers to which he exposed himself merely, as most travellers do, for a fad, or so as some day to be able to give a thrilling account of his adventures? But the mind of Sassure was bent on the instruction of mankind, and soul-stirring sensations that excellent man indeed had, and the reader of his travels got them thrown into the bargain.

But the fact that culture is requisite for the judgement upon the sublime in nature (more than for that upon the beautiful) does not involve its being an original product of culture and something introduced in a more or less conventional way into society. Rather is it in human nature that its foundations are laid, and, in fact, in that which, at once with common understanding, we may expect every one to possess and may require of him, namely, a native capacity for the feeling for (practical) ideas, i.e. for moral feeling.

This, now, is the foundation of the necessity of that agreement between other men's judgements upon the sublime and our own, which we make our own imply. For just as we taunt a man who is quite inappreciative when forming an estimate of an object of nature in which we see beauty, with want *of taste*, so we say of a man who remains unaffected in the presence of what we consider sublime, that he has no *feeling*. But we demand both taste and feeling of every man, and, granted some degree of culture, we give him credit for both. Still, we do so with this difference: that, in the case of the former, since judgement there refers the imagination merely to the understanding, as the faculty of concepts, we make the requirement as a matter of course, whereas in the case of the latter, since here the judgement refers the imagination to reason, as a faculty of ideas, we do so only under a subjective presupposition, (which, however, we believe we are warranted in making,) namely, that of the moral feeling in man. And, on this assumption, we attribute necessity to the latter aesthetic judgement also.

In this modality of aesthetic judgements, namely their assumed necessity, lies what is for the Critique of Judgement a moment of capital importance. For this is exactly what makes an *a priori* principle apparent in their case, and lifts them out of the sphere of empirical psychology, in which otherwise they would remain buried amid the feelings of gratification and pain (only with the senseless epithet of *finer* feeling), so as to place them, and, thanks to them, to place the faculty of judgement itself, in the class of judgements of which the basis of an *a priori* principle is the distinguishing feature, and, thus distinguished, to introduce them into transcendental philosophy.

# On Genius

FINE ART IS THE ART OF GENIUS

*G*enius is the talent (natural endowment) which gives the rule to art. Since talent, as an innate productive faculty of the artist, belongs itself to nature, we may put it this way: *Genius* is the innate mental aptitude *(ingenium) through which* nature gives the rule to art.

Whatever may be the merits of this definition, and whether it is merely arbitrary, or whether it is adequate or not to the concept usually associated with the word *genius* (a point which the following sections have to clear up), it may still be shown at the outset that, according to this acceptation of the word, fine arts must necessarily be regarded as arts of *genius*.

For every art presupposes rules which are laid down as the foundation which first enables a product, if it is to be called one of art, to be represented as possible. The concept of fine art, however, does not permit of the judgement upon the beauty of its product being derived from any rule that has a *concept* for its determining ground, and that depends, consequently, on a concept of the way in which the product is possible. Consequently fine art cannot of its own self excogitate the rule according to which it is to effectuate its product. But since, for all that, a product can never be called art unless there is a preceding rule, it follows that nature in the individual (and by virtue of the harmony of his faculties) must give the rule to art, i.e. fine art is only possible as a product of genius.

From this it may be seen that genius (1) is a *talent* for producing that for which no definite rule can be given: and not an aptitude in the way of cleverness for what can be learned according to some rule; and that consequently *originality* must be its primary property. (2) Since there may also be original nonsense, its products must at the same time be models, i.e. be *exemplary;* and, consequently, though not themselves derived from imitation, they must serve that purpose for others, i.e. as a standard or rule of estimating. (3) It cannot indicate scientifically how it brings about its product, but rather gives the rule as *nature.* Hence, where an author owes a product to his genius, he does not himself know how the *ideas* for it have entered into his head, nor has he it in his power to invent the like at pleasure, or methodically, and communicate the same to others in such precepts as would put them in a position to produce similar products. (Hence, presumably, our word *Genie* is derived from *genius,* as the peculiar guardian and guiding spirit given to a man at his birth, by the inspiration of which those original ideas were obtained.) (4) Nature prescribes the rule through genius not to science but to art, and this also only in so far as it is to be fine art.

## § 47

### ELUCIDATION AND CONFIRMATION
### OF THE ABOVE EXPLANATION OF GENIUS

Every one is agreed on the point of the complete opposition between genius and the *spirit of imitation.* Now since learning is nothing but imitation, the greatest ability, or aptness as a pupil (capacity), is still, as such, not equivalent to genius. Even though a man weaves his own thoughts or fancies, instead of merely taking in what others have thought, and even though he go so far as to bring fresh gains to art and science, this does not afford a valid reason for calling such a man of *brains,* and often great brains, a *genius,* in contradistinction to one who goes by the name of *shallow-pate,* because he can never do more than merely learn and follow a lead. For what is accomplished in this way is something that *could* have been learned. Hence it all lies in the natural path of investigation and reflection according to rules, and so is not specifically distinguishable from what may be acquired as the result of industry backed up by imitation. So all that *Newton* has set forth in his immortal work on the Principles of Natural Philosophy may well be learned, however great a mind it took to find it all out, but we cannot learn to write in a true poetic vein, no matter how complete all the precepts of the poetic art may be, or however excellent its models. The reason is that all the steps that Newton had to take from the first elements of geometry to his greatest and most profound discoveries were such as he could make intuitively evident and plain to follow, not only for himself but for every one else. On the other hand no *Homer* or *Wieland* can show how his ideas, so rich at once in fancy and in thought, enter and assemble themselves in his brain, for the good reason that he does not himself know, and so cannot teach others. In matters of science, therefore, the greatest inventor differs only in degree from the most laborious imitator and apprentice, whereas he differs specifically from one endowed by nature for fine art. No disparagement, however, of those great men, to whom the human race is so deeply indebted, is involved in this comparison of them with those who on the score of their talent for fine art are the elect of nature. The talent for science is formed for the continued advances of greater perfection in knowledge, with all its dependent practical advantages, as also for imparting the same to others. Hence scientists can boast a ground of considerable superiority over those who merit the honour of being called geniuses, since genius reaches a point at which art must make a halt, as there is a limit imposed upon it which it cannot transcend. This limit has in all probability been long since attained. In addition, such skill cannot be communicated, but requires to be bestowed directly from the hand of nature upon each individual, and so with him it dies, awaiting the day when nature once again endows another in the same way—one who needs no more than an example to set the talent of which he is conscious at work on similar lines.

Seeing, then, that the natural endowment of art (as fine art) must furnish the rule, what kind of rule must this be? It cannot be one set down in a formula and serving as a precept—for then the judgement upon the beautiful would be determinable according to concepts. Rather must the rule be gathered from the performance, i.e. from the product, which others may use to put their own talent to the test, so as to let it serve as a model, not for *imitation*, but for *following.* The possibility of this is difficult to explain. The artist's ideas arouse like ideas on the part of his pupil, presuming nature to have visited him with a like proportion of the mental powers. For this reason the models of fine art are the only means of handing down this art to posterity. This is something which cannot be done by mere descriptions (especially not in the line of the arts of speech), and in these arts, furthermore, only those models can become classical of which the ancient, dead languages, preserved as learned, are the medium.

Despite the marked difference that distinguishes mechanical art, as an art merely depending upon industry and learning, from fine art, as that of genius, there is still no fine art in which something mechanical, capable of being at once comprehended and followed in obedience to rules, and consequently something *academic* does not constitute the essential condition of the art. For the thought of something as end must be present, or else its product would not be ascribed to an art at all, but would be a mere product of chance. But the effectuation of an end necessitates determinate rules which we cannot venture to dispense with. Now, seeing that originality of talent is one (though not the sole) essential factor that goes to make up the character of genius, shallow minds fancy that the best evidence they can give of their being full-blown geniuses is by emancipating themselves from all academic constraint of rules, in the belief that one cuts a finer figure on the back of an ill-tempered than of a trained horse. Genius can do no more than furnish rich *material* for products of fine art; its elaboration and its *form* require a talent academically trained, so that it may be employed in such a way as to stand the test of judgement. But, for a person to hold forth and pass sentence like a genius in matters that fall to the province of the most patient rational investigation, is ridiculous in the extreme. One is at a loss to know whether to laugh more at the impostor who envelops himself in such a cloud—in which we are given fuller scope to our imagination at the expense of all use of our critical faculty,—or at the simple-minded public which imagines that its inability clearly to cognize and comprehend this masterpiece of penetration is due to its being invaded by new truths *en masse,* in comparison with which, detail, due to carefully weighed exposition and an academic examination of root-principles, seems to it only the work of a tyro.

## § 48
### THE RELATION OF GENIUS TO TASTE

For *estimating* beautiful objects, as such, what is required is *taste;* but for fine art, i.e. the *production* of such objects, one needs *genius*.

If we consider genius as the talent for fine art (which the proper signification of the word imports), and if we would analyse it from this point of view into the faculties which must concur to constitute such a talent, it is imperative at the outset accurately to determine the difference between beauty of nature, which it only requires taste to estimate, and beauty of art, which requires genius for its possibility (a possibility to which regard must also be paid in estimating such an object).

A beauty of nature is a *beautiful thing;* beauty of art is a *beautiful representation* of a thing.

To enable me to estimate a beauty of nature, as such, I do not need to be previously possessed of a concept of what sort of a thing the object is intended to be, i.e. I am not obliged to know its material finality (the end), but, rather, in forming an estimate of it apart from any knowledge of the end, the mere form pleases on its own account. If, however, the object is presented as a product of art, and is as such to be declared beautiful, then, seeing that art always presupposes an end in the cause (and its causality), a concept of what the thing is intended to be must first of all be laid at its basis. And, since the agreement of the manifold in a thing with an inner character belonging to it as its end constitutes the perfection of the thing, it follows that in estimating beauty of art the perfection of the thing must be also taken into account—a matter which in estimating a beauty of nature, as beautiful, is quite irrelevant.—It is true that in forming an estimate, especially of animate objects of nature, e.g. of a man or a horse, objective finality is also commonly taken into account with a view to judgement upon their beauty; but then the judgement also ceases to be purely aesthetic, i.e. a mere judgement of taste. Nature is no longer estimated as it appears like art, but rather in so far as it actually *is* art, though superhuman art; and the teleological judgement serves as basis and condition of the aesthetic, and one which the latter must regard. In such a case, where one says, for example, 'that is a beautiful woman,' what one in fact thinks is only this, that in her form nature excellently portrays the ends present in the female figure. For one has to extend one's view beyond the mere form to a concept, to enable the object to be thought in such manner by means of an aesthetic judgement logically conditioned.

Where fine art evidences its superiority is in the beautiful descriptions it gives of things that in nature would be ugly or displeasing. The Furies, diseases, devastations of war, and the like, can (as evils) be very beautifully described, nay even represented in pictures. One kind of ugliness alone is incapable of being represented conformably to nature without destroying all aesthetic delight, and consequently artistic beauty, namely, that which excites *disgust*. For, as in this strange sensation, which depends purely on the imagination, the object is represented as insisting, as it were, upon our enjoying it, while we still set our face against it, the artificial representation of the object is no longer distinguishable from the nature of the object itself in our sensation, and so it cannot possibly be regarded as beautiful. The art of sculpture, again, since in its products art is almost confused with nature, has excluded from its creations the direct representation of ugly objects, and, instead, only sanctions, for example, the representation of death (in a beautiful genius), or of the warlike spirit (in Mars), by means of an allegory, or attributes which wear a pleasant guise, and so only indirectly, through an interpretation on the part of reason, and not for the pure aesthetic judgement.

So much for the beautiful representation of an object, which is properly only the form of the presentation of a concept, and the means by which the latter is universally communicated. To give this form, however, to the product of fine art, taste merely is required. By this the artist, having practised and corrected his taste by a variety of examples from nature or art, controls his work and, after many, and often laborious, attempts to satisfy taste, finds the form which commends itself to him. Hence this form is not, as it were, a matter of inspiration, or of a free swing of the mental powers, but rather of a slow and even painful process of improvement, directed to making the form adequate to his thought without prejudice to the freedom in the play of those powers.

Taste is, however, merely a critical, not a productive faculty; and what conforms to it is not, merely on that account, a work of fine art. It may belong to useful and mechanical art, or even to science, as a product following definite rules which are capable of being learned and which must be closely followed. But the pleasing form imparted to the work is only the vehicle of communication and a mode, as it were, of execution, in respect of which one remains to a certain extent free, notwithstanding being otherwise tied down to a definite end. So we demand that table appointments, or even a moral dissertation, and, indeed, a sermon, must bear this form of fine art, yet without its appearing *studied*. But one would not call them on this account works of fine art. A poem, a musical composition, a picture-gallery, and so forth, would, however, be placed under this head; and so in a would-be work of fine art we may frequently recognize genius without taste, and in another taste without genius.

## § 49

### THE FACULTIES OF THE MIND WHICH CONSTITUTE GENIUS

Of certain products which are expected, partly at least, to stand on the footing of fine art, we say they are *soul*less; and this, although we find nothing to censure in them as far as taste goes. A poem may be very pretty and elegant, but is soulless. A narrative has precision and method, but is soulless. A speech on some festive occasion may be good in substance and ornate withal, but may be soulless. Conversation frequently is not devoid of entertainment, but yet soulless. Even of a woman we may well say, she is pretty, affable, and refined, but soulless. Now what do we here mean by 'soul'?

'*Soul*' (*Geist*) in an aesthetical sense, signifies the animating principle in the mind. But that whereby this principle animates the psychic substance (*Seele*)—the material which it employs for that purpose—is that which sets the mental powers into a swing that is final, i.e. into a play which is self-maintaining and which strengthens those powers for such activity.

Now my proposition is that this principle is nothing else than the faculty of presenting *aesthetic ideas*. But, by an aesthetic idea I mean that representation of the imagination which induces much thought, yet without the possibility of any definte thought whatever, i.e. *concept*, being adequate to it, and which language, consequently, can never get quite on level terms with or render completely intelligible.—It is easily seen, that an aesthetic idea is the counterpart (pendant) of a *rational idea,* which, conversely, is a concept, to which no *intuition* (representation of the imagination) can be adequate.

The imagination (as a productive faculty of cognition) is a powerful agent for creating, as it were, a second nature out of the material supplied to it by actual nature. It affords us entertainment where experience proves too commonplace; and we even use it to remodel experience, always following, no doubt, laws that are based on analogy, but still also following principles which have a higher seat in reason (and which are every whit as natural to us as those followed by the understanding in laying hold of empirical nature). By this means we get a sense of our freedom from the law of association (which attaches to the empirical employment of the imagination), with the result that the material can be borrowed by us from nature in accordance with that law, but be worked up by us into something else—namely, what surpasses nature.

Such representations of the imagination may be termed *ideas.* This is partly because they at least strain after something lying out beyond the confines of experience, and so seek to approximate to a presentation of rational concepts (i.e. intellectual ideas), thus giving to these concepts the semblance of an objective reality. But, on the other hand, there is this most important reason, that no concept can be wholly adequate to them as internal intuitions. The poet essays the task of interpreting to sense the rational ideas of invisible beings, the kingdom of the blessed, hell, eternity, creation, etc. Or, again, as to things of which examples occur in experience, e.g. death, envy, and all vices, as also love, fame, and the like, transgressing the limits of experience he attempts with the aid of an imagination which emulates the display of reason in its attainment of a maximum, to body them forth to sense with a completeness of which nature affords no parallel; and it is in fact precisely in the poetic art that the faculty of aesthetic ideas can show itself to full advantage. This faculty, however, regarded solely on its own account, is properly no more than a talent (of the imagination).

If, now, we attach to a concept a representation of the imagination belonging to its presentation, but inducing solely on its own account such a wealth of thought as would never admit of comprehension in a definite concept, and, as a consequence, giving aesthetically an unbounded expansion to the concept itself, then the imagination here displays a creative activity, and it puts the faculty of intellectual ideas (reason) into motion—a motion, at the instance of a representation, towards an extension of thought, that, while germane, no doubt, to the concept of the object, exceeds what can be laid hold of in that representation or clearly expressed.

Those forms which do not constitute the presentation of a given concept itself, but which, as secondary representations of the imagination, express the derivatives connected with it, and its kinship with other concepts, are called (aesthetic) *attributes* of an object, the concept of which, as an idea of reason, cannot be adequately presented. In this way Jupiter's eagle, with the lightning in its claws, is an attribute of the mighty king of heaven, and the peacock of its stately queen. They do not, like *logical attributes,* represent what lies in our concepts of the sublimity and majesty of creation, but rather something else—something that gives the imagination an incentive to spread its flight over a whole host of kindred representations that provoke more thought than admits of expression in a concept determined by words. They furnish an *aesthetic idea,* which serves the above rational idea as a substiture for logical presentation, but with the proper function, however, of animating the mind by opening out for it a prospect into a field of kindred representations stretching beyond its ken. But it is not alone in the arts of painting or sculpture, where the name of attribute is customarily employed, that fine art acts in this way; poetry and rhetoric also derive the soul that animates their works wholly from the aesthetic attributes of the objects—attributes which go hand in hand with the logical, and give the imagination an impetus to bring more thought into play in the matter, though in an undeveloped manner, than allows of being brought within the embrace of a concept, or, therefore, of being definitely formulated in language.—For the sake of brevity I must confine myself to a few examples only. When the great king expresses himself in one of his poems by saying:

Oui, finissons sans trouble, et mourons sans regrets,
En laissant l'Univers comblé de nos bienfaits.
Ainsi l'Astre du jour, au bout de sa carrière,
Répand sur l'horizon une douce lumière,

Et les derniers rayons qu'il darde dans les airs
Sont les derniers soupirs qu'il donne à l'Univers;

he kindles in this way his rational idea of a cosmopolitan sentiment even at the close of life, with the help of an attribute which the imagination (in remembering all the pleasures of a fair summer's day that is over and gone—a memory of which pleasures is suggested by a serene evening) annexes to that representation, and which stirs up a crowd of sensations and secondary representations for which no expression can be found. On the other hand, even an intellectual concept may serve, conversely, as attribute for a representation of sense, and so animate the latter with the idea of the supersensible; but only by the aesthetic factor subjectively attaching to the consciousness of the supersensible being employed for the purpose. So, for example, a certain poet says in his description of a beautiful morning: 'The sun arose, as out of virtue rises peace.' The consciousness of virtue, even where we put oursleves only in thought in the position of a virtuous man, diffuses in the mind a multitude of sublime and tranquillizing feelings, and gives a boundless outlook into a happy future, such as no expression within the compass of a definite concept completely attains.[1]

In a word, the aesthetic idea is a representation of the imagination, annexed to a given concept, with which, in the free employment of imagination, such a multiplicity of partial representations are bound up, that no expression indicating a definite concept can be found for it—one which on that account allows a concept to be supplemented in thought by much that is indefinable in words, and the feeling of which quickens the cognitive faculties, and with language, as a mere thing of the letter, binds up the spirit (soul) also.

The mental powers whose union in a certain relation constitutes *genius* are imagination and understanding. Now, since the imagination, in its employment on behalf of cognition, is subjected to the constraint of the understanding and the restriction of having to

1. Perhaps there has never been a more sublime utterance, or a thought more sublimely expressed, than the well-known inscription upon the Temple of Isis (Mother Nature): 'I am all that is, and that was, and that shall be, and no mortal hath raised the veil from before my face.' *Segner* made use of this idea in a suggestive vignette on the frontispiece of his Natural Philosophy, in order to inspire his pupil at the threshold of that temple into which he was about to lead him, with such a holy awe as would dispose his mind to serious attention.

be conformable to the concept belonging thereto, whereas aesthetically it is free to furnish of its own accord, over and above that agreement with the concept, a wealth of undeveloped material for the understanding, to which the latter paid no regard in its concept, but which it can make use of, not so much objectively for cognition, as subjectively for quickening the cognitive faculties, and hence also indirectly for cognitions, it may be seen that genius properly consists in the happy relation, which science cannot teach nor industry learn, enabling one to find out ideas for a given concept, and, besides, to hit upon the *expression* for them—the expression by means of which the subjective mental condition induced by the ideas as the concomitant of a concept may be communicated to others. This latter talent is properly that which is termed soul. For to get an expression for what is indefinable in the mental state accompanying a particular representation and to make it universally communicable—be the expression in language or painting or statuary—is a thing requiring a faculty for laying hold of the rapid and transient play of the imagination, and for unifying it in a concept (which for that very reason is original, and reveals a new rule which could not have been inferred from any preceding principles or examples) that admits of communication without any constraint of rules.

If, after this analysis, we cast a glance back upon the above definition of what is called *genius,* we find: *First,* that it is a talent for art—not one for science, in which clearly known rules must take the lead and determine the procedure. *Secondly,* being a talent in the line of art, it presupposes a definite concept of the product—as its end. Hence it presupposes understanding, but, in addition, a representation, indefinite though it be, of the material, i.e. of the intuition, required for the presentation of that concept, and so a relation of the imagination to the understanding. *Thirdly,* it displays itself, not so much in the working out of the projected end in the presentation of a definite *concept,* as rather in the portrayal, or expression of *aesthetic ideas* containing a wealth of material for effecting that intention. Consequently the imagination is represented by it in its freedom from all guidance of rules, but still as final for the presentation of the given concept. *Fourthly,* and lastly, the unsought and undesigned subjective finality in the free harmonizing of the imagination with the understanding's conformity to law presupposes a proportion and accord between these faculties such as cannot be brought about by any observance of rules, whether of science or mechanical imitation, but can only be produced by the nature of the individual.

Genius, according to these presuppositions, is the exemplary originality of the natural endowments of an individuual in the *free* employment of his cognitive faculties. On this showing, the product of a genius (in respect of so much in this product as is attributable to genius, and not to possible learning or academic instruction,) is an example, not for imitation (for that would mean the loss of the element of genius, and just the very soul of the work), but to be followed by another genius—one whom it arouses to a sense of his own originality in putting freedom from the constraint of rules so into force in his art, that for art itself a new rule is won—which is what shows a talent to be exemplary. Yet, since the genius is one of nature's elect—a type that must be regarded as but a rare phenomenon—for other clever minds his example gives rise to a school, that is to say a methodical instruction according to rules, collected, so far as the circumstances admit, from such products of genius and their peculiarities. And, to that extent, fine art is for such persons a matter of imitation, for which nature, through the medium of a genius, gave the rule.

But this imitation becomes *aping* when the pupil *copies* everything down to the deformities which the genius only of necessity suffered to remain, because they could hardly be removed without loss of force to the idea. This courage has merit only in the case of a genius. A certain *boldness* of expression, and, in general, many a deviation from the common rule becomes him well, but in no sense is it a thing worthy of imitation. On the contrary it remains all through intrinsically a blemish, which one is bound to try to remove, but for which the genius is, as it were, allowed to plead a privilege, on the ground that a scrupulous carefulness would spoil what is inimitable in the impetuous ardour of his soul. *Mannerism* is another kind of aping—an aping of *peculiarity* (originality) in general, for the sake of removing oneself as far as possible from imitators, while the talent requisite to enable one to be at the same time *exemplary* is absent.—There are, in fact, two modes (*modi*) in general of arranging one's thoughts for utterance. The one is called a *manner (modus aestheticus),* the other a *method (modus logicus).* The distinction between them is this: the former possesses no standard other than the *feeling* of unity in the presentation, whereas the latter here follows definite *principles.* As a consequence the former is alone admissible for fine art. It is only, however, where the manner of carrying the idea into execution in a product of art is *aimed* at singularity instead of being made appropriate to the idea, that *mannerism* is properly ascribed to such a product. The ostentatious (*précieux*), forced, and affected styles, intended to mark one out from the common herd (though soul is wanting), resemble the behaviour of a man who, as we say, hears himself talk, or who stands and moves about as if he were on a stage to be gaped at—action which invariably betrays a tyro.

## § 50

### THE COMBINATION OF TASTE AND GENIUS
### IN PRODUCTS OF FINE ART

To ask whether more stress should be laid in matters of fine art upon the presence of genius or upon that of taste, is equivalent to asking whether more turns upon imagination or upon judgement. Now, imagination rather entitles an art to be called an *inspired* (*geistreiche*) than a *fine* art. It is only in respect of judgement that the name of fine art is deserved. Hence it follows that judgement, being the indispensable condition (*conditio sine qua non*), is at least what one must look to as of capital importance in forming an estimate of art as fine art. So far as beauty is concerned, to be fertile and original in ideas is not such an imperative requirement as it is that the imagination in its freedom should be in accordance with the understanding's conformity to law. For in lawless freedom imagination, with all its wealth, produces nothing but nonsense; the power of judgement, on the other hand, is the faculty that makes it consonant with understanding.

Taste, like judgement in general, is the discipline (or corrective) of genius. It severely clips its wings, and makes it orderly or polished; but at the same time it gives it guidance, directing and controlling its flight, so that it may preserve its character of finality. It introduces a clearness and order into the plenitude of thought, and in so doing gives stability to the ideas, and qualifies them at once for permanent and universal approval, for being followed by others, and for a continually progressive culture. And so, where the interests of both these qualities clash in a product, and there has to be a sacrifice of something, then it should rather be on the side of genius; and judgement, which in matters of fine art bases its decision on its own proper principles, will more readily endure an abatement of the freedom and wealth of the imagination, than that the understanding should be compromised.

The requisites for fine art are, therefore, *imagination, understanding, soul,* and *taste.*[2]

---

2. The first three faculties are first *brought into union* by means of the fourth. *Hume,* in his history, informs the English that although they are second in their works to no other people in the world in respect of the evidences they afford of the three first qualities *separately* considered, still in what unites them they must yield to their neighbours, the French.

# Dialectic of Aesthetic Judgement

## § 55

For a power of judgement to be dialectical it must first of all be rationalizing; that is to say, its judgements must lay claim to universality,[1] and do so *a priori,* for it is in the antithesis of such judgements that dialectic consists. Hence there is nothing dialectical in the irreconcilability of aesthetic judgements of sense (upon the agreeable and disagreeable). And in so far as each person appeals merely to his own private taste, even the conflict of judgements of taste does not form a dialectic of taste—for no one is proposing to make his own judgement into a universal rule. Hence the only concept left to us of a dialectic affecting taste is one of a dialectic of the *Critique* of taste (not of taste itself) in respect of its *principles*: for, on the question of the ground of the possibility of judgements of taste in general, mutually conflicting concepts naturally and un-avoidably make their appearance. The transcendental Critique of taste will, therefore, only include a part capable of bearing the name of a dialectic of the aesthetic judgement if we find an antinomy of the principles of this faculty which throws doubt upon its conform-ity to law, and hence also upon its inner possibility.

1. Any judgement which sets up to be universal may be termed a rationalizing judgement *(indicium ratiocinans);* for so far as universal it may serve as the major premise of a syllogism. On the other hand, only a judgement which is thought as the conclusion of a syllogism, and, therefore, as having an *a priori* foundation, can be called rational *(iudicium ratiocinatum).*

## § 56
### REPRESENTATION OF THE ANTINOMY OF TASTE

The first commonplace of taste is contained in the proposition under cover of which every one devoid of taste thinks to shelter himself from reproach: *every one has his own taste*. This is only another way of saying that the determining ground of this judgement is merely subjective (gratification or pain), and that the judgement has no right to the necessary agreement of others.

Its second commonplace, to which even those resort who concede the right of the judgement of taste to pronounce with validity for every one, is: *there is no disputing about taste*. This amounts to saying that even though the determining ground of a judgement of taste be objective, it is not reducible to definite concepts, so that in respect of the judgement itself no *decision* can be reached by proofs, although it is quite open to us to *contend* upon the matter, and to contend with right. For though *contention* and *dispute* have this point in common, that they aim at bringing judgements into accordance out of and by means of their mutual opposition; yet they differ in the latter hoping to effect this from definite concepts, as grounds of proof, and, consequently, adopting *objective concepts* as grounds of the judgement. But where this is considered impracticable, dispute is regarded as alike out of the question.

Between these two commonplaces an intermediate proposition is readily seen to be missing. It is one which has certainly not become proverbial, but yet it is at the back of every one's mind. It is that *there may be contention about taste* (although not a dispute). This proposition, however, involves the contrary of the first one. For in a matter in which contention is to be allowed, there must be a hope of coming to terms. Hence one must be able to reckon on grounds of judgement that possess more than private validity and are thus not merely subjective. And yet the above principle, *every one has his own taste*, is directly opposed to this.

The principle of taste, therefore, exhibits the following antinomy:

1. *Thesis*. The judgement of taste is not based upon concepts; for, if it were, it would be open to dispute (decision by means of proofs).

2. *Antithesis*. The judgement of taste is based on concepts; for otherwise, despite diversity of judgement, there could be no room

even for contention in the matter (a claim to the necessary agreement of others with this judgement).

## § 57
### SOLUTION OF THE ANTINOMY OF TASTE

There is no possibility of removing the conflict of the above principles, which underlie every judgement of taste (and which are only the two peculiarities of the judgement of taste previously set out in the Analytic) except by showing that the concept to which the Object is made to refer in a judgement of this kind is not taken in the same sense in both maxims of the aesthetic judgement; that this double sense, or point of view, in our estimate, is necessary for our power of transcendental judgement; and that nevertheless the false appearance arising from the confusion of one with the other is a natural illusion, and so unavoidable.

The judgement of taste must have reference to some concept or other, as otherwise it would be absolutely impossible for it to lay claim to necessary validity for every one. Yet it need not on that account be provable from a concept. For a concept may be either determinable, or else at once intrinsically undetermined and indeterminable. A concept of the understanding, which is determinable by means of predicates borrowed from sensible intuition and capable of corresponding to it, is of the first kind. But of the second kind is the transcendental rational concept of the supersensible, which lies at the basis of all that sensible intuition and is, therefore, incapable of being further determined theoretically.

Now the judgement of taste applies to objects of sense, but not so as to determine a *concept* of them for the understanding; for it is not a cognitive judgement. Hence it is a singular representation of intuition referable to the feeling of pleasure, and, as such, only a private judgement. And to that extent it would be limited in its validity to the individual judging: the object is *for me* an object of delight, for others it may be otherwise:—every one to his taste.

For all that, the judgement of taste contains beyond doubt an enlarged reference on the part of the representation of the Object (and at the same time on the part of the Subject also), which lays the foundation of an extension of judgements of this kind to necessity for every one. This must of necessity be founded upon some concept or other, but such a concept as does not admit of being determined by intuition, and affords no knowledge of anything. Hence, too, it is a concept *which does not afford any proof* of the judgement of taste. But the mere pure rational concept of the supersensible lying at the basis of the object (and of the judging Subject for that matter) as Object of sense, and thus as phenomenon, is just such a concept. For unless such a point of view were adopted there would be no means of saving the claim of the judgement of taste to universal validity. And if the concept forming the required basis were a concept of understanding, though a mere confused one, as, let us say, of perfection, answering to which the sensible intuition of the beautiful might be adduced, then it would be at least intrinsically possible to found the judgement of taste upon proofs, which contradicts the thesis.

All contradiction disappears, however, if I say: The judgement of taste does depend upon a concept (of a general ground of the subjective finality of nature for the power of judgement), but one from which nothing can be cognized in respect of the Object, and nothing proved, because it is in itself indeterminable and useless for knowledge. Yet by means of this very concept it acquires at the same time validity for every one (but with each individual, no doubt, as a singular judgement immediately accompanying his intuition): because its determining ground lies, perhaps, in the concept of what may be regarded as the supersensible substrate of humanity.

The solution of an antinomy turns solely on the possibility of two apparently conflicting propositions not being in fact contradictory, but rather being capable of consisting together, although the explanation of the possibility of their concept transcends our faculties of cognition. That this illusion is also natural and for human reason unavoidable, as well as why it is so, and remains so, although upon the solution of the apparent contradiction it no longer misleads us, may be made intelligible from the above considerations.

For the concept, which the universal validity of a judgement must have for its basis, is taken in the same sense in both the conflicting judgements, yet two opposite predicates are asserted of it. The thesis should therefore read: The judgement of taste is not based on *determinate* concepts; but the antithesis: The judgement of taste does rest upon a concept, although an *indeterminate* one, (that, namely, of the supersensible substrate of phenomena); and then there would be no conflict between them.

Beyond removing this conflict between the claims and counter-claims of taste we can do nothing. To supply a determinate objective principle of taste in accordance with which its judgements might be derived, tested, and proved, is an absolute impossiblity, for then it would not be a judgement of taste. The subjective principle—that is to say, the inderterminate idea of the supersensible within us—can only be indicated as the unique key to the riddle of this faculty, itself concealed from us in its sources; and there is no means of making it any more intelligible.

The antinomy here exhibited and resolved rests upon the proper concept of taste as a merely reflective aesthetic judgement, and the two seemingly conflicting principles are reconciled on the ground that *they may be true,* and this is sufficient. If, on the other hand, owing to the fact that the representation lying at the basis of the judgement of taste is singular, the determining ground of taste is taken, as by some it is, to be *agreeableness,* or, as others, looking to its universal validity, would have it, the principle of *perfection,* and if the definition of taste is framed accordingly, the result is an antinomy which is absolutely irresolvable unless we show *the falsity of both propositions* as contraries (not as simple contradictories). This would force the conclusion that the concept upon which each is founded is self-contradictory. Thus it is evident that the removal of the antinomy of the aesthetic judgement pursues a course similar to that followed by the Critique in the solution of the antinomies of pure theoretical reason; and that the antinomies, both here and in the Critique of Practical Reason, compel us, whether we like it or not, to look beyond the horizon of the sensible, and to seek in the supersensible the point of union of all our faculties *a priori:* for we are left with no other expedient to bring reason into harmony with itself.

## § 59
### BEAUTY AS THE SYMBOL OF MORALITY

Intuitions are always required to verify the reality of our concepts. If the concepts are empirical the intuitions are called *examples:* if they are pure concepts of the understanding the intuitions go by the name of *schemata*. But to call for a verification of the objective reality of rational concepts, i.e. of ideas, and, what is more, on behalf of the theoretical cognition of such a reality, is to demand an impossibility, because absolutely no intuition adequate to them can be given.

All *hypotyposis* (presentation, *subjectio sub adspectum*), as a rendering in terms of sense, is twofold. Either it is *schematic,* as where the intuition corresponding to a concept comprehended by the understanding is given a *priori,* or else it is *symbolic,* as where the concept is one which only reason can think, and to which no sensible intuition can be adequate. In the latter case the concept is supplied with an intuition such that the procedure of judgement in dealing with it is merely analogous to that which it observes in schematism. In other words, what agrees with the concept is merely the rule of this procedure, and not the intuition itself. Hence the agreement is merely in the form of reflection, and not in the content.

Notwithstanding the adoption of the word *symbolic* by modern logicians in a sense opposed to an *intuitive* mode of representation, it is a wrong use of the word and subversive of its true meaning; for the symbolic is only a *mode* of the intuitive. The intuitive mode of representation is, in fact, divisible into the *schematic* and the *symbolic.* Both are hypotyposes, i.e. presentations *(exhibitiones),* not mere *marks.* Marks are merely designations of concepts by the aid of accompanying sensible signs devoid of any intrinsic connexion with the intuition of the Object. Their sole function is to afford a means of reinvoking the concepts according to the imagination's law of association—a purely subjective rôle. Such marks are either words or visible (algebraic or even mimetic) signs, simply as *expressions* for concepts.[2]

All intuitions by which a *priori* concepts are given a foothold are, therefore, either *schemata* or *symbols.* Schemata contain direct, symbols indirect, presentations of the concept. Schemata effect this presentation demonstratively, symbols by the aid of an analogy (for which recourse is had even to empirical intuitions), in which analogy judgement performs a double function: first in applying the concept to the object of a sensible intuition, and then, secondly, in applying

2. The intuitive mode of knowledge must be contrasted with the discursive mode (not with the symbolic). The former is either *schematic,* by means of *demonstration,* or *symbolic,* as a representation following a mere *analogy.*

the mere rule of its reflection upon that intuition to quite another object, of which the former is but the symbol. In this way a monarchical state is represented as a living body when it is governed by constitutional laws, but as a mere machine (like a hand-mill) when it is governed by an individual absolute will; but in both cases the representation is merely *symbolic*. For there is certainly no likeness between a despotic state and a hand-mill, whereas there surely is between the rules of reflection upon both and their causality. Hitherto this function has been but little analysed, worthy as it is of a deeper study. Still this is not the place to dwell upon it. In language we have many such indirect presentations modelled upon an analogy enabling the expression in question to contain, not the proper schema for the concept, but merely a symbol for reflection. Thus the words *ground* (support, basis), *to depend* (to be held up from above), to *flow* from (instead of to follow), *substance* (as Locke puts it: the support of accidents), and numberless others, are not schematic, but rather symbolic hypotyposes, and express concepts without employing a direct intuition for the purpose, but only drawing upon an analogy with one, i.e. transferring the reflection upon an object of intuition to quite a new concept, and one with which perhaps no intuition could ever directly correspond. Supposing the name of knowledge may be given to what only amounts to a mere mode of representation (which is quite permissible where this is not a principle of the theoretical determination of the object in respect of what it is in itself, but of the practical determination of what the idea of it ought to be for us and for its final employment), then all our knowledge of God is merely symbolic; and one who takes it, with the properties of understanding, will, and so forth, which only evidence their objective reality in beings of this world, to be schematic, falls into anthropomorphism, just as, if he abandons every intuitive element, he falls into Deism which furnishes no knowledge whatsoever—not even from a practical point of view.

Now, I say, the beautiful is the symbol of the morally good, and only in this light (a point of view natural to every one, and one which every one exacts from others as a duty) does it give us pleasure with an attendant claim to the agreement of every one else, whereupon the mind becomes conscious of a certain ennoblement and elevation above mere sensibility to pleasure from impressions of sense, and also appraises the worth of others on the score of a like maxim of their judgement. This is that *intelligible* to which taste, as noticed in the preceding paragraph, extends its view. It is, that is to say, what brings even our higher cognitive faculties into common accord, and is that apart from which sheer contradiction would arise between their nature and the claims put forward by taste. In this faculty judgement does not find itself subjected to a heteronomy of laws of experience as it does in the empirical estimate of things— in respect of the objects of such a pure delight it gives the law to itself, just as reason does in respect of the faculty of desire. Here, too, both on account of this inner possibility in the Subject, and on account of the external possibility of a nature harmonizing therewith, it finds a reference in itself to something in the Subject itself and outside it, and which is not nature, nor yet freedom, but still is connected with the ground of the latter, i.e. the supersensible— a something in which the theoretical faculty gets bound up into unity with the practical in an intimate and obscure manner. We shall bring out a few points of this analogy, while taking care, at the same time, not to let the points of difference escape us.

(1) The beautiful pleases *immediately* (but only in reflective intuition, not, like morality, in its concept). (2) It pleases *apart from all interest* (pleasure in the morally good is no doubt necessarily bound up with an interest, but not with one of the kind that are antecedent to the judgement upon the delight, but with one that judgement itself for the first time calls into existence). (3) *The freedom* of the imagination (consequently of our faculty in respect of its sensibility) is, in estimating the beautiful, represented as in accord with the understanding's conformity to law (in moral judgements the freedom of the will is thought as the harmony of the latter with itself according to universal laws of Reason). (4) The subjective principle of the estimate of the beautiful is represented as *universal,* i.e. valid for every man, but as incognizable by means of any universal concept (the objective principle of morality is set forth as also universal, i.e. for all individuals, and, at the same time, for all actions of the same individual, and, besides, as cognizable by means of a universal concept). For this reason the moral judgement not alone admits of definite constitutive principles, but is *only* possible by adopting these principles and their universality as the ground of its maxims.

Even common understanding is wont to pay regard to this analogy; and we frequently apply to beautiful objects of nature or of art names that seem to rely upon the basis of a moral estimate. We call buildings or trees majestic and stately, or plains laughing and gay; even colours are called innocent, modest, soft, because they excite sensations containing something analogous to the consciousness of the state of mind produced by moral judgements. Taste makes, as it were, the transition from the charm of sense to habitual moral interest possible without too violent a leap, for it represents the imagination, even in its freedom, as amenable to a final determination for understanding, and teaches us to find, even in sensuous objects, a free delight apart from any charm of sense.

# ON
# HISTORY

# Idea for a Universal History from a Cosmopolitan Point of View[1]

Whatever concept one may hold, from a metaphysical point of view, concerning the freedom of the will, certainly its appearances, which are human actions, like every other natural event are determined by universal laws. However obscure their causes, history, which is concerned with narrating these appearances, permits us to hope that if we attend to the play of freedom of the human will in the large, we may be able to discern a regular movement in it, and that what seems complex and chaotic in the single individual may be seen from the standpoint of the human race as a whole to be a steady and progressive though slow evolution of its original endowment. Since the free will of man has obvious influence upon marriages, births, and deaths, they seem to be subject to no rule by which the number of them could be reckoned in

1. A statement in the "Short Notices' or the twelfth number of *Gothaische Gelehrte Zeitung* of this year [1784], which no doubt was based on my conversation with a scholar who was traveling through, occasions this essay, without which that statement could not be understood.

[The notice said: "A favorite idea of Professor Kant's is that the ultimate purpose of the human race is to achieve the most perfect civic constitution, and he wishes that a philosophical historian might undertake to give us a history of humanity from this point of view, and to show to what extent humanity in various ages has approached or drawn away from this final purpose and what remains to be done in order to reach it."]

advance. Yet the annual tables of them in the major countries prove that they occur according to laws as stable as [those of] the unstable weather, which we likewise cannot determine in advance, but which, in the large, maintain the growth of plants, the flow of rivers, and other natural events in an unbroken, uniform course. Individuals and even whole peoples think little on this. Each, according to his own inclination, follows his own purpose, often in opposition to others; yet each individual and people, as if following some guiding thread, go toward a natural but to each of them unknown goal; all work toward furthering it, even if they would set little store by it if they did know it.

Since men in their endeavors behave, on the whole, not just instinctively, like the brutes, nor yet like rational citizens of the world according to some agreed-on plan, no history of man conceived according to a plan seems to be possible, as it might be possible to have such a history of bees or beavers. One cannot suppress a certain indignation when one sees men's actions on the great world-stage and finds, beside the wisdom that appears here and there among individuals, everything in the large woven together from folly, childish vanity, even from childish malice and destructiveness. In the end, one does not know what to think of the human race, so conceited in its gifts. Since the philosopher cannot presuppose any [conscious] individual purpose among men in their great drama, there is no other expedient for him except to try to see if he can discover a natural purpose in this idiotic course of things human. In keeping with this purpose, it might be possible to have a history with a definite natural plan for creatures who have no plan of their own.

We wish to see if we can succeed in finding a clue to such a history; we leave it to Nature to produce the man capable of composing it. Thus Nature produced Kepler, who subjected, in an unexpected way, the eccentric paths of the planets to definite laws; and she produced Newton, who explained these laws by a universal natural cause.

# FIRST THESIS

*All natural capacities of a creature are destined to evolve completely to their natural end.*

Observation of both the outward form and inward structure of all animals confirms this of them. An organ that is of no use, an arrangement that does not achieve its purpose, are contradictions in the teleological theory of nature. If we give up this fundamental principle, we no longer have a lawful but an aimless course of nature, and blind chance takes the place of the guiding thread of reason.

# SECOND THESIS

*In man* (as the only rational creature on earth) *those natural capacities which are directed to the use of his reason are to be fully developed only in the race, not in the individual.*

Reason in a creature is a faculty of widening the rules and purposes of the use of all its powers far beyond natural instinct; it acknowledges no limits to its projects. Reason itself does not work instinctively, but requires trial, practice, and instruction in order gradually to progress from one level of insight to another. Therefore a single man would have to live excessively long in order to learn to make full use of all his natural capacities. Since Nature has set only a short period for his life, she needs a perhaps unreckonable series of generations, each of which passes its own enlightenment to its successor in order finally to bring the seeds of enlightenment to that degree of development in our race which is completely suitable to Nature's purpose. This point of time must be, at least as an ideal, the goal of man's efforts, for otherwise his natural capacities would have to be counted as for the most part vain and aimless. This would destroy all practical principles, and Nature, whose wisdom must serve as the fundamental principle in judging all her other offspring, would thereby make man alone a contemptible plaything.

# THIRD THESIS

*Nature has willed that man should, by himself, produce everything that goes beyond the mechanical ordering of his animal existence, and that he should partake of no other happiness or perfection than that which he himself, independently of instinct, has created by his own reason.*

Nature does nothing in vain, and in the use of means to her goals she is not prodigal. Her giving to man reason and the freedom of the will which depends upon it is clear indication of her purpose.

Man accordingly was not to be guided by instinct, not nurtured and instructed with ready-made knowledge; rather, he should bring forth everything out of his own resources. Securing his own food, shelter, safety and defense (for which Nature gave him neither the horns of the bull, nor the claws of the lion, nor the fangs of the dog, but hands only), all amusement which can make life pleasant, insight and intelligence, finally even goodness of heart—all this should be wholly his own work. In this, Nature seems to have moved with the strictest parsimony, and to have measured her animal gifts precisely to the most stringent needs of a beginning existence, just as if she had willed that, if man ever did advance from the lowest barbarity to the highest skill and mental perfection and thereby worked himself up to happiness (so far as it is possible on earth), he alone should have the credit and should have only himself to thank—exactly as if she aimed more at his rational self-esteem than at his well-being. For along this march of human affairs, there was a host of troubles awaiting him. But it seems not to have concerned Nature that he should live well, but only that he should work himself upward so as to make himself, through his own actions, worthy of life and of well-being.

It remains strange that the earlier generations appear to carry through their toilsome labor only for the sake of the later, to prepare for them a foundation on which the later generations could erect the higher edifice which was Nature's goal, and yet that only the latest of the generations should have the good fortune to inhabit the building on which a long line of their ancestors had (unintentionally) labored without being permitted to partake of the fortune they had prepared. However puzzling this may be, it is necessary if one assumes that a species of animals should have reason, and, as a class of rational beings each of whom dies while the species is immortal, should develop their capacities to perfection.

# FOURTH THESIS

*The means employed by Nature to bring about the development of all the capacities of men is their antagonism in society, so far as this is, in the end, the cause of a lawful order among men.*

By "antagonism" I mean the unsocial sociability of men, i.e., their propensity to enter into society, bound together with a mutual opposition which constantly threatens to break up the society. Man has an inclination to associate with others, because in society he feels himself to be more than man, i.e., as more than the developed form of his natural capacities. But he also has a strong propensity to isolate himself from others, because he finds in himself at the same time the unsocial characteristic of wishing to have everything go according to his own wish. Thus he expects opposition on all sides because, in knowing himself, he knows that he, on his own part, is inclined to oppose others. This opposition it is which awakens all his powers, brings him to conquer his inclination to laziness and, propelled by vainglory, lust for power, and avarice, to achieve a rank among his fellows whom he cannot tolerate but from whom he cannot withdraw. Thus are taken the first true steps from barbarism to culture, which consists in the social worth of man; thence gradually develop all talents, and taste is refined; through continued enlightenment the beginnings are laid for a way of thought which can in time convert the coarse, natural disposition for moral discrimination into definite practical principles, and thereby change a society of men driven together by their natural feelings into a moral whole. Without those in themselves unamiable characteristics of unsociability from whence opposition springs—characteristics each man must find in his own selfish pretensions—all talents would remain hidden, unborn in an Arcadian shepherd's life, with all its concord, contentment, and mutual affection. Men, good-natured as the sheep they herd, would hardly reach a higher worth than their beasts; they would not fill the empty place in creation by achieving their end, which is rational nature. Thanks be to Nature, then, for the incompatibility, for heartless competitive vanity, for the insatiable desire to possess and to rule! Without them, all the excellent natural capacities of humanity would forever sleep, undeveloped. Man wishes concord; but Nature knows better what is good for the race; she wills discord. He wishes to live comfortably and pleasantly; Nature wills that he should be plunged from sloth and passive contentment into labor and trouble, in order that he may find means of extricating himself from them. The natural urges to this, the sources of unsociableness and mutual opposition from which so many evils arise, drive men to new exertions of their forces and thus to the manifold development of their capacities. They thereby perhaps show the ordering of a wise Creator and not the hand of an evil spirit, who bungled in his great work or spoiled it out of envy.

# FIFTH THESIS

*The greatest problem for the human race, to the solution of which Nature drives man, is the achievement of a universal civic society which administers law among men.*

The highest purpose of Nature, which is the development of all the capacities which can be achieved by mankind, is attainable only in society, and more specifically in the society with the greatest freedom. Such a society is one in which there is mutual opposition among the members, together with the most exact definition of freedom and fixing of its limits so that it may be consistent with the freedom of others. Nature demands that humankind should itself achieve this goal like all its other destined goals. Thus a society in which freedom under external laws is associated in the highest degree with irresistible power, i.e., a perfectly just civic constitution, is the highest problem Nature assigns to the human race; for Nature can achieve her other purposes for mankind only upon the solution and completion of this assignment. Need forces men, so enamored otherwise of their boundless freedom, into this state of constraint. They are forced to it by the greatest of all needs, a need they themselves occasion inasmuch as their passions keep them from living long together in wild freedom. Once in such a preserve as a civic union, these same passions subsequently do the most good. It is just the same with trees in a forest: each needs the others, since each in seeking to take the air and sunlight from others must strive upward, and thereby each realizes a beautiful, straight stature, while those that live in isoated freedom put out branches at random and grow stunted, crooked, and twisted. All culture, art which adorns mankind, and the finest social order are fruits of unsociableness, which forces itself to discipline itself and so, by a contrived art, to develop the natural seeds to perfection.

# SIXTH THESIS

*This problem is the most difficult and the last to be solved by mankind.*

The difficulty which the mere thought of this problem puts before our eyes is this. Man is an animal which, if it lives among others of its kind, requires a master. For he certainly abuses his freedom with respect to other men, and although as a reasonable being he wishes to have a law which limits the freedom of all, his selfish animal impulses tempt him, where possible, to exempt himself from them. He thus requires a master, who will break his will and force him to obey a will that is universally valid, under which each can be free. But whence does he get this master? Only from the human race. But then the master is himself an animal, and needs a master. Let him begin it as he will, it is not to be seen how he can procure a magistracy which can maintain public justice and which is itself just, whether it be a single person or a group of several elected persons. For each of them will always abuse his freedom if he has none above him to exercise force in accord with the laws. The highest master should be just in himself, and yet a man. This task is therefore the hardest of all; indeed, its complete solution is impossible, for from such crooked wood as a man is made of, nothing perfectly straight can be built.[2] That it is the last problem to be solved follows also from this: it requires that there be a correct conception of a possible constitution, great experience gained in many paths of life, and—far beyond these—a good will ready to accept such a constitution. Three such things are very hard, and if they are ever to be found together, it will be very late and after many vain attempts.

# SEVENTH THESIS

*The problem of establishing a perfect civic constitution is dependent upon the problem of a lawful external relation among states and cannot be solved without a solution of the latter problem.*

What is the use of working toward a lawful civic constitution among individuals, i.e., toward the creation of a commonwealth? The same unsociability which drives man to this causes any single commonwealth to stand in unrestricted freedom in relation to oth-

2. The role of man is very artificial. How it may be with the dwellers on other planets and their nature we do not know. If, however, we carry out well the mandate given us by Nature, we can perhaps flatter ourselves that we may claim among our neighbors in the cosmos no mean rank. Maybe among them each individual can perfectly attain his destiny in his own life. Among us, it is different; only the race can hope to attain it.

ers; consequently, each of them must expect from another precisely the evil which oppressed the individuals and forced them to enter into a lawful civic state. The friction among men, the inevitable antagonism, which is a mark of even the largest societies and political bodies, is used by Nature as a means to establish a condition of quiet and security. Through war, through the taxing and never-ending accumulation of armament, through the want which any state, even in peacetime, must suffer internally, Nature forces them to make at first inadequate and tentative attempts; finally, after devastations, revolutions, and even complete exhaustion, she brings them to that which reason could have told them at the beginning and with far less sad experience, to wit, to step from the lawless condition of savages into a league of nations. In a league of nations, even the smallest state could expect security and justice, not from its own power and by its own decrees, but only from this great league of nations (*Foedus Amphictyonum*), from a united power acting according to decisions reached under the laws of their united will. However fantastical this idea may seem—and it was laughed at as fantastical by the Abbé de St. Pierre and by Rousseau, perhaps because they believed it was too near to realization—the necessary outcome of the destitution to which each man is brought by his fellows is to force the states to the same decision (hard though it be for them) that savage man also was reluctantly forced to take, namely, to give up their brutish freedom and to seek quiet and security under a lawful constitution.

All wars are accordingly so many attempts (not in the intention of man, but in the intention of Nature) to establish new relations among states, and through the destruction or at least the dismemberment of all of them to create new political bodies, which, again, either internally or externally, cannot maintain themselves and which must thus suffer like revolutions; until finally, through the best possible civic constitution and common agreement and legislation in external affairs, a state is created which, like a civic commonwealth, can maintain itself automatically.

[There are three questions here, which really come to one.] Would it be expected from an Epicurean concourse of efficient causes that states, like minute particles of matter in their chance contacts, should form all sorts of unions which in their turn are destroyed by new impacts, until once, finally, by chance a structure should arise which could maintain its existence—a fortunate accident that could hardly occur? Or are we not rather to suppose that Nature here follows a lawful course in gradually lifting our race from the lower levels of animality to the highest level of humanity, doing this by her own secret art, and developing in accord with her law all the original gifts of man in this apparently chaotic disorder? Or perhaps we should prefer to conclude that, from all these actions and counteractions of men in the large, absolutely nothing, at least nothing wise, is to issue? That everything should remain as it always was, that we cannot therefore tell but that discord, natural to our race, may not prepare for us a hell of evils, however civilized we may now be, by annihilating civilization and all cultural progress through barbarous devastation? (This is the fate we may well have to suffer under the rule of blind chance—which is in fact identical with lawless freedom—if there is no secret wise guidance in Nature.) These three questions, I say, mean about the same as this: Is it reasonable to assume a purposiveness in all the parts of nature and to deny it to the whole?

Purposeless savagery held back the development of the capacities of our race; but finally, through the evil into which it plunged mankind, it forced our race to renounce this condition and to enter into a civic order in which those capacities could be developed. The same is done by the barbaric freedom of established states. Through wasting the powers of the commonwealths in armaments to be used against each other, through devastation brought on by war, and even more by the necessity of holding themselves in constant readiness for war, they stunt the full development of human nature. But because of the evils which thus arise, our race is forced to find, above the (in itself healthy) opposition of states which is a consequence of their freedom, a law of equilibrium and a united power to give it effect. Thus it is forced to institute a cosmopolitan condition to secure the external safety of each state.

Such a condition is not unattended by the danger that the vitality of mankind may fall asleep; but it is at least not without a principle of balance among men's actions and counteractions, without which they might be altogether destroyed. Until this last step to a union of states is taken, which is the halfway mark in the development of mankind, human nature must suffer the cruelest hardships under the guise of external well-being; and Rousseau was not far wrong in preferring the state of savages, so long, that is, as the last stage to which the human race must climb is not attained.

To a high degree we are, through art and science, *cultured*. We are *civilized*—perhaps too much for our own good—in all sorts of social grace and decorum. But to consider ourselves as having reached *morality*—for that, much is lacking. The ideal of morality belongs to culture; its use for some simulacrum of morality in the love of honor and outward decorum constitutes mere civilization. So long as states waste their forces in vain and violent self-expansion, and thereby constantly thwart the slow efforts to improve the minds of their citizens by even withdrawing all support from them, nothing in the way of a moral order is to be expected. For such an end, a long internal working of each political body toward the education of its citizens is required. Everything good that is not based on a morally good disposition, however, is nothing but pretense and glittering misery. In such a condition the human species will no doubt remain until, in the way I have described, it works its way out of the chaotic conditions of its international relations.

# EIGHTH THESIS

*The history of mankind can be seen, in the large, as the realization of Nature's secret plan to bring forth a perfectly constituted state as the only condition in which the capacities of mankind can be fully developed, and also bring forth that external relation among states which is perfectly adequate to this end.*

This is a corollary to the preceding. Everyone can see that philosophy can have her belief in a millennium, but her millenarianism is not Utopian, since the Idea can help, though only from afar, to bring the millennium to pass. The only question is: Does Nature reveal anything of a path to this end? And I say: She reveals something, but very little. This great revolution seems to require so long for its completion that the short period during which humanity has been following this course permits us to determine its path and the relation of the parts to the whole with as little certainty as we can determine, from all previous astronomical observation, the path of the sun and his host of satellites among the fixed stars. Yet, on the fundamental premise of the systematic structure of the cosmos and from the little that has been observed, we can confidently infer the reality of such a revolution.

Moreover, human nature is so constituted that we cannot be indifferent to the most remote epoch our race may come to, if only we may expect it with certainty. Such indifference is even less possible for us, since it seems that our own intelligent action may hasten this happy time for our posterity. For that reason, even faint indications of approach to it are very important to us. At present, states are in such an artificial relation to each other that none of them can neglect its internal cultural development without losing power and influence among the others. Therefore the preservation of this natural end [culture], if not progress in it, is fairly well assured by the ambitions of states. Furthermore, civic freedom can hardly be infringed without the evil consequences being felt in all walks of life, especially in commerce, where the effect is loss of power of the state in its foreign relations. But this freedom spreads by degrees. When the citizen is hindered in seeking his own welfare in his own way, so long as it is consistent with the freedom of others, the vitality of the entire enterprise is sapped, and therewith the powers of the whole are diminished. Therefore limitations on personal actions are step by step removed, and general religious freedom is permitted. Enlightenment comes gradually, with intermittent folly and caprice, as a great good which must finally save men from the selfish aggrandizement of their masters, always assuming that the latter know their own interest. This enlightenment, and with it a certain commitment of heart which the enlightened man cannot fail to make to the good he clearly understands, must step by step ascend the throne and influence the principles of government.

Although, for instance, our world rulers at present have no money left over for public education and for anything that concerns what is best in the world, since all they have is already committed to future wars, they will still find it to their own interest at least not to hinder the weak and slow, independent efforts of their peoples in this work. In the end, war itself will be seen as not only so artificial, in outcome so uncertain for both sides, in aftereffects so painful in the form of an ever-growing war debt (a new invention) that cannot be met, that it will be regarded as a most dubious undertaking. The impact of any revolution on all states on our continent, so closely knit together through commerce, will be so obvious that the other states, driven by their own danger but without any legal basis, will offer themselves as arbiters, and thus they will prepare the way for a distant international government for which there is no precedent in world history. Although this government at present exists only as a rough outline, nevertheless in all the members there is rising a feeling which each has for the preservation of the whole. This gives hope finally that after many reformative revolutions, a universal cosmopolitan condition, which Nature has as her ultimate purpose, will come into being as the womb wherein all the original capacities of the human race can develop.

# NINTH THESIS

*A philosophical attempt to work out a universal history according to a natural plan directed to achieving the civic union of the human race must be regarded as possible and, indeed, as contributing to this end of Nature.*

It is strange and apparently silly to wish to write a history in accordance with an Idea of how the course of the world must be if it is to lead to certain rational ends. It seems that with such an Idea only a romance could be written. Nevertheless, if one may assume that Nature, even in the play of human freedom, works not without plan or purpose, this Idea could still be of use. Even if we are too blind to see the secret mechanism of its workings, this Idea may still serve as a guiding thread for presenting as a system, at least in broad outlines, what would otherwise be a planless conglomeration of human actions. For if one starts with Greek history, through which every older or contemporaneous history has been handed down or at least certified;[3] if one follows the influence of Greek history on the construction and misconstruction of the Roman state which swallowed up the Greek, then the Roman influence on

3. Only a learned public, which has lasted from its beginning to our own day, can certify ancient history. Outside it, everything else is *terra incognita;* and the history of peoples outside it can only be begun when they come into contact with it. This happened with the Jews in the time of the Ptolemies through the translation of the Bible into Greek, without which we would give little credence to their isolated narratives. From this point, when once properly fixed, we can retrace their history. And so with all other peoples. The first page of Thucydides, says Hume, is the only beginning of all real history.

the barbarians who in turn destroyed it, and so on down to our times; if one adds episodes from the national histories of other peoples insofar as they are known from the history of the enlightened nations, one will discover a regular progress in the constitution of states on our continent (which will probably give law, eventually, to all the others). If, further, one concentrates on the civic constitutions and their laws and on the relations among states, insofar as through the good they contained they served over long periods of time to elevate and adorn nations and their arts and sciences, while through the evil they contained they destroyed them, if only a germ of enlightenment was left to be further developed by this overthrow and a higher level was thus prepared—if, I say, one carries through this study, a guiding thread will be revealed. It can serve not only for clarifying the confused play of things human, and not only for the art of prophesying later political changes (a use which has already been made of history even when seen as the disconnected effect of lawless freedom), but for giving a consoling view of the future (which could not be reasonably hoped for without the presupposition of a natural plan) in which there will be exhibited in the distance how the human race finally achieves the condition in which all the seeds planted in it by Nature can fully develop and in which the destiny of the race can be fulfilled here on earth.

Such a justification of Nature—or, better, of Providence—is no unimportant reason for choosing a standpoint toward world history. For what is the good of esteeming the majesty and wisdom of Creation in the realm of brute nature and of recommending that we contemplate it, if that part of the great stage of supreme wisdom which contains the purpose of all the others—the history of mankind—must remain an unceasing reproach to it? If we are forced to turn our eyes from it in disgust, doubting that we can ever find a perfectly rational purpose in it and hoping for that only in another world?

That I would want to displace the work of practicing empirical historians with this Idea of world history, which is to some extent based upon an a priori principle, would be a misinterpretation of my intention. It is only a suggestion of what a philosophical mind (which would have to be well versed in history) could essay from another point of view. Otherwise the notorious complexity of a history of our time must naturally lead to serious doubt as to how our descendants will begin to grasp the burden of the history we shall leave to them after a few centuries. They will naturally value the history of earlier times, from which the documents may long since have disappeared, only from the point of view of what interests them, i.e., in answer to the question of what the various nations and governments have contributed to the goal of world citizenship, and what they have done to damage it. To consider this, so as to direct the ambitions of sovereigns and their agents to the only means by which their fame can be spread to later ages: this can be a minor motive for attempting such a philosophical history.

# What Is Enlightenment?

Enlightenment is man's release from his self-incurred tutelage. Tutelage is man's inability to make use of his understanding without direction from another. Self-incurred is this tutelage when its cause lies not in lack of reason but in lack of resolution and courage to use it without direction from another. *Sapere aude!* "Have courage to use your own reason!" —that is the motto of enlightenment.

Laziness and cowardice are the reasons why so great a portion of mankind, after nature has long since discharged them from external direction *(naturaliter maiorennes),* nevertheless remains under lifelong tutelage, and why it is so easy for others to set themselves up as their guardians. It is so easy not to be of age. If I have a book which understands for me, a pastor who has a conscience for me, a physician who decides my diet, and so forth, I need not trouble myself. I need not think, if I can only pay—others will readily undertake the irksome work for me.

That the step to competence is held to be very dangerous by the far greater portion of mankind (and by the entire fair sex) —quite apart from its being arduous—is seen to by those guardians who have so kindly assumed superintendence over them. After the guardians have first made their domestic cattle dumb and have made sure that these placid creatures will not dare take a single step without the harness of the cart to which they are tethered, the guardians then show them the danger which threatens if they try to go alone. Actually, however, this danger is not so great, for by falling a few times they would finally learn to walk alone. But an example of this failure makes them timid and ordinarily frightens them away from all further trials.

For any single individual to work himself out of the life under tutelage which has become almost his nature is very difficult. He has come to be fond of this state, and he is for the present really incapable of making use of his reason, for no one has ever let him try it out. Statutes and formulas, those mechanical tools of the rational employment or rather misemployment of his natural gifts, are the fetters of an everlasting tutelage. Whoever throws them off makes only an uncertain leap over the narrowest ditch because he is not accustomed to that kind of free motion. Therefore, there are few who have succeeded by their own exercise of mind both in freeing themselves from incompetence and in achieving a steady pace.

But that the public should enlighten itself is more possible; indeed, if only freedom is granted, enlightenment is almost sure to follow. For there will always be some independent thinkers, even among the established guardians of the great masses, who, after throwing off the yoke of tutelage from their own shoulders, will disseminate the spirit of the rational appreciation of both their own worth and every man's vocation for thinking for himself. But be it noted that the public, which has first been brought under this yoke by their guardians, forces the guardians themselves to remain bound when it is incited to do so by some of the guardians who are themselves capable of some enlightenment—so harmful is it to implant prejudices, for they later take vengeance on their cultivators or on their descendants. Thus the public can only slowly attain enlightenment. Perhaps a fall of personal despotism or of avaricious or tyrannical oppression may be accomplished by revolution, but never a true reform in ways of thinking. Rather, new prejudices will serve as well as old ones to harness the great unthinking masses.

For this enlightenment, however, nothing is required but freedom, and indeed the most harmless among all the things to which this term can properly be applied. It is the freedom to make public use of one's reason at every point. But I hear on all sides, "Do not argue!" The officer says: "Do not argue but drill!" The tax collector: "Do not argue but pay!" The cleric: "Do not argue but believe!" Only one prince in the world says, "Argue as much as you will, and about what you will, but obey!" Everywhere there is restriction on freedom.

Which restriction is an obstacle to enlightenment, and which is not an obstacle but a promoter of it? I answer: The public use of one's reason must always be free, and it alone can bring about enlightenment among men. The private use of reason, on the other hand, may often be very narrowly restricted without particularly hindering the progress of enlightenment. By the public use of one's reason I understand the use which a person makes of it as a scholar before the reading public. Private use I call that which one may make of it in a particular civil post or office which is entrusted to him. Many affairs which are conducted in the interest of the community require a certain mechanism through which some members of the community must passively conduct themselves with an artificial unanimity, so that the government may direct them to public ends, or at least prevent them from destroying those ends. Here argument is certainly not allowed—one must obey. But so far as a part of the mechanism regards himself at the same time as a member of the whole community or of a society of world citizens, and thus in the role of a scholar who addresses the public (in the proper sense of the word) through his writings, he certainly can argue without hurting the affairs for which he is in part responsible as a passive member. Thus it would be ruinous for an officer in service to debate about the suitability or utility of a command given to him by his superior; he must obey. But the right to make remarks on errors in the military service and to lay them before the public for judgment cannot equitably be refused him as a scholar. The citizen cannot refuse to pay the taxes imposed on him; indeed, an impudent complaint at those levied on him can be punished as a scandal (as it could occasion general refractoriness). But the same person nevertheless does not act contrary to his duty as a citizen when, as a scholar, he publicly expresses his thoughts on the inappropriateness or even the injustice of these levies. Similarly a clergyman is obligated to make his sermon to his pupils in catechism and his congregation conform to the symbol of the church which he serves, for he has been accepted on his condition. But as a scholar he has complete freedom, even the calling, to communicate to the public all his carefully tested and well-meaning thoughts on that which is erroneous in the symbol and to make suggestions for the better organization of the religious body and church. In doing this there is nothing that could be laid as a burden on his conscience. For what he teaches as a consequence of his office as a representative of the church, this he considers something about which he has no freedom to teach according to his own lights; it is something which he is appointed to propound at the dictation of and in the name of another. He will say, "Our church teaches this or that; those are the proofs which it adduces." He thus extracts all practical uses for his congregation from statutes to which he himself would not subscribe with full conviction but to the enunciation of which he can very well pledge himself because it is not impossible that truth lies hidden in them, and, in any case, there is at least nothing in them contradictory to inner religion. For if he believed he had found such in them, he could not conscientiously discharge the duties of his office; he would have to give it up. The use, therefore, which an appointed teacher makes of his reason before his congregation is merely private, because this congregation is only a domestic one (even if it be a large gathering); with respect to it, as a priest, he is not free, nor can he be free, because he carries out the orders of another. But as a scholar, whose writings speak to his public, the world, the clergyman in the public use of his reason enjoys an unlimited freedom to use his own reason and to speak in his own person. That the guardians of the people (in spiritual things) should themselves be incompetent is an absurdity which amounts to the eternalization of absurdities.

But would not a society of clergymen, perhaps a church conference or a venerable classis (as they call themselves among the Dutch), be justified in obligating itself by oath to a certain unchangeable symbol in order to enjoy an unceasing guardianship over each of its members and thereby over the people as a whole, and even to make it eternal? I answer that this is altogether impossible. Such a contract, made to shut off all further enlightenment from the human race, is absolutely null and void even if confirmed by the supreme power, by parliaments, and by the most ceremonious of peace treaties. An age cannot bind itself and ordain to put the succeeding one into such a condition that it cannot extend its (at best very occasonal) knowledge, purify itself of errors, and progress in general enlightenment. That would be a crime against human nature, the proper destination of which lies precisely in this progress; and the descendants would be fully justified in rejecting those decrees as having been made in an unwarranted and malicious manner.

The touchstone of everything that can be concluded as a law for a people lies in the question whether the people could have imposed such a law on itself. Now such a religious compact might be possible for a short and definitely limited time, as it were, in expectation of a better. One might let every citizen, and especially the clergyman, in the role of scholar, make his comments freely and publicly, i.e., through writing, on the erroneous aspects of the present institution. The newly introduced order might last until insight into the nature of these things had become so general and widely approved that through uniting their voices (even if not unanimously) they could bring a proposal to the throne to take those congregations under protection which had united into a changed religious organization according to their better ideas, without, however, hindering others who wish to remain in the order. But to unite in a permanent religious institution which is not to be subject to doubt before the public even in the lifetime of one man, and thereby to make a period of time fruitless in the progress of mankind toward improvement, thus working to the disadvantage of posterity—that is absolutely forbidden. For himself (and only for a short time) a man may postpone enlightenment in what he ought to know, but to renounce it for himself and even more to renounce it for posterity is to injure and trample on the rights of mankind.

And what a people may not decree for itself can even less be decreed for them by a monarch, for his law-giving authority rests on his uniting the general public will in his own. If he only sees to it that all true or alleged improvement stands together with civil order, he can leave it to his subjects to do what they find necessary for their spiritual welfare. This is not his concern, though it is incumbent on him to prevent one of them from violently hindering another in determining and promoting this welfare to the best of his ability. To meddle in these matters lowers his own majesty, since by the writings in which his subjects seek to present their views he may evaluate his own governance. He can do this when, with deepest understanding, he lays upon himself the reproach, "Caesar non est supra grammaticos." Far more does he injure his own majesty when he degrades his supreme power by supporting the ecclesiastical despotism of some tyrants in his state over his other subjects.

If we are asked, "Do we now live in an *enlightened age?*" the answer is, "No," but we do live in an *age of enlightenment*. As things now stand, much is lacking which prevents men from being, or easily becoming, capable of correctly using their own reason in religious matters with assurance and free from outside direction. But, on the other hand, we have clear indications that the field has now been opened wherein men may freely deal with these things and that the obstacles to general enlightenment or the release from self-imposed tutelage are gradually being reduced. In this respect, this is the age of enlightenment, or the century of Frederick.

A prince who does not find it unworthy of himself to say that he holds it to be his duty to prescribe nothing to men in religious matters but to give them complete freedom while renouncing the haughty name of *tolerance,* is himself enlightened and deserves to be esteemed by the grateful world and posterity as the first, at least from the side of government, who divested the human race of its tutelage and left each man free to make use of his reason in matters of conscience. Under him venerable ecclesiastics are allowed, in the role of scholars, and without infringing on their official duties, freely to submit for public testing their judgments and views which here and there diverge from the established symbol. And an even greater freedom is enjoyed by those who are restricted by no official duties. This spirit of freedom spreads beyond this land, even to those in which it must struggle with external obstacles erected by a government which misunderstands its own interest. For an example gives evidence to such a government that in freedom there is not the least cause for concern about public peace and the stability of the community. Men work themselves gradually out of barbarity if only intentional artifices are not made to hold them in it.

I have placed the main point of enlightenment—the escape of men from their self-incurred tutelage—chiefly in matters of religion because our rulers have no interest in playing the guardian with respect to the arts and sciences and also because religious incompetence is not only the most harmful but also the most degrading of all. But the manner of thinking of the head of a state who favors religious enlightenment goes further, and he sees that there is no danger to his law-giving in allowing his subjects to make public use of their reason and to publish their thoughts on a better formulation of his legislation and even their open-minded criticisms of the laws already made. Of this we have a shining example wherein no monarch is superior to him whom we honor.

But only one who is himself enlightened is not afraid of shadows, and who has a numerous and well-disciplined army to assure public peace, can say: "Argue as much as you will, and about what you will, only obey!" A republic could not dare say such a thing. Here is shown a strange and unexpected trend in human affairs in which almost everything, looked at in the large, is paradoxical. A greater degree of civil freedom appears advantageous to the freedom of mind of the people, and yet it places inescapable limitations upon it; a lower degree of civil freedom, on the contrary, provides the mind with room for each man to extend himself to his full capacity. As nature has uncovered from under this hard shell the seed for which she most tenderly cares—the propensity and vocation to free thinking—this gradually works back upon the character of the people, who thereby gradually become capable of managing freedom; finally, it affects the principles of government, which finds it to its advantage to treat men, who are now more than machines, in accordance with their dignity.[1]

1. Today I read in the *Büschingsche Wöchentliche Nachrichten* for September 13 an announcement of the *Berlinische Monatsschrift* for this month, which cites the answer to the same question by Mr. Mendelssohn. But this issue has not yet come to me; if it had, I would have held back the present essay, which is now put forth only in order to see how much agreement in thought can be brought about by chance.

# Perpetual Peace

Whether this satirical inscription on a Dutch innkeeper's sign upon which a burial ground was painted had for its object mankind in general, or the rules of states in particular, who are insatiable of war, or merely the philosophers who dream this sweet dream, it is not for us to decide. But one condition the author of this essay wishes to lay down. The practical politician assumes the attitude of looking down with great self-satisfaction on the political theorist as a pedant whose empty ideas in no way threaten the security of the state, inasmuch as the state must proceed on empirical principles; so the theorist is allowed to play his game without interference from the worldly-wise statesman. Such being his attitude, the practical politician—and this is the condition I make—should at least act consistently in the case of a conflict and not suspect some danger to the state in the political theorist's opinions which are ventured and publicly expressed without any ulterior purpose. By this *clausula salvatoria* the author desires formally and emphatically to deprecate herewith any malevolent interpretation which might be placed on his words.

# Section I
# Containing the Preliminary Articles
# for Perpetual Peace among States

1. *"No treaty of peace shall be held valid in which there is tacitly reserved matter for a future war"*

Otherwise a treaty would be only a truce, a suspension of hostilities but not peace, which means the end of all hostilities—so much so that even to attach the word "perpetual" to it is a dubious pleonasm. The causes for making future wars (which are perhaps unknown to the contracting parties) are without exception annihilated by the treaty of peace, even if they should be dug out of dusty documents by acute sleuthing. When one or both parties to a treaty of peace, being too exhausted to continue warring with each other, make a tacit reservation *(reservatio mentalis)* in regard to old claims to be elaborated only at some more favorable opportunity in the future, the treaty is made in bad faith, and we have an artifice worthy of the casuistry of a Jesuit. Considered by itself, it is beneath the dignity of a sovereign, just as the readiness to indulge in this kind of reasoning is unworthy of the dignity of his minister.

But if, in consequence of enlightened concepts of statecraft, the glory of the state is placed in its continual aggrandizement by whatever means, my conclusion will appear merely academic and pedantic.

2. *"No independent states, large or small, shall come under the dominion of another state by inheritance, exchange, purchase, or donation"*

A state is not, like the ground which it occupies, a piece of property *(patrimonium)*. It is a society of men whom no one else has any right to command or to dispose except the state itself. It is a trunk with its own roots. But to incorporate it into another state, like a graft, is to destroy its existence as a moral person, reducing it to a thing; such incorporation thus contradicts the idea of the original contract without which no right over a people can be conceived.[1] Everyone knows to what dangers Europe, the only part of the world where this manner of acquisition is known, has been brought, even down to the most recent times, by the presumption that states could espouse one another; it is in part a new kind of industry for gaining ascendancy by means of family alliances and without expenditure of forces, and in part a way of extending one's domain. Also the hiring-out of troops by one state to another, so that they can be used against an enemy not common to both, is to be counted under this principle; for in this manner the subjects, as though they were things to be manipulated at pleasure, are used and also used up.

### 3. "Standing armies (miles perpetuus) *shall in time be totally abolished*"

For they incessantly menace other states by their readiness to appear at all times prepared for war; they incite them to compete with each other in the number of armed men, and there is no limit to this. For this reason, the cost of peace finally becomes more oppressive than that of a short war, and consequently a standing army is itself a cause of offensive war waged in order to relieve the state of this burden. Add to this that to pay men to kill or to be killed seems to entail using them as mere machines and tools in the hand of another (the state), and this is hardly compatible with the rights of mankind in our own person. But the periodic and voluntary military exercises of citizens who thereby secure themselves and their country against foreign aggression are entirely different.

The accumulation of treasure would have the same effect, for, of the three powers—the power of armies, of alliances, and of money—the third is perhaps the most dependable weapon. Such accumulation of treasure is regarded by other states as a threat of war, and if it were not for the difficulties in learning the amount, it would force the other state to make an early attack.

---

1. A hereditary kingdom is not a state which can be inherited by another state, but the right to govern it can be inherited by another physical person. The state thereby acquires a ruler, but he, as a ruler (i.e., as one already possessing another realm), does not acquire the state.

### 4. *"National debts shall not be contracted with a view to the external friction of states"*

This expedient of seeking aid within or without the state is above suspicion when the purpose is domestic economy (e.g., the improvement of roads, new settlements, establishment of stores against unfruitful years, etc.). But as an opposing machine in the antagonism of powers, a credit system whih grows beyond sight and which is yet a safe debt for the present requirements—because all the creditors do not require payment at one time—constitutes a dangerous money power. This ingenious invention of a commercial people [England] in this century is dangerous because it is a war treasure which exceeds the treasures of all other states; it cannot be exhausted except by default of taxes (which is inevitable), though it can be long delayed by the stimulus to trade which occurs through the reaction of credit on industry and commerce. This facility in making war, together with the inclination which seems inborn in human nature—is thus a great hindrance to perpetual peace. Therefore, to forbid this credit system must be a preliminary article of perpetual peace all the more because it must eventually entangle many innocent states in the inevitable bankruptcy and openly harm them. They are therefore justified in allying themselves against such a state and its measures.

### 5. *"No state shall by force interfere with the constitution or government of another state"*

For what is there to authorize it to do so? The offense, perhaps, which a state gives to the subjects of another state? Rather the example of the evil into which a state has fallen because of its lawlessness should serve as a warning. Moreover, the bad example which one free person affords another as a *scandalum acceptum* is not an infringement of his rights. But it would be quite different if a state, by internal rebellion, should fall into two parts, each of which pretended to be a separate state making claim to the whole. To lend assistance to one of these cannot be considered an interference in the constitution of the other state (for it is then in a state of anarchy). But so long as the internal dissension has not come to this critical point, such interference by foreign powers would infringe on the rights of an independent people struggling with its internal disease; hence it would itself be an offense and would render the autonomy of all states insecure.

6. *"No state shall, during war, permit such acts of hostility which would make mutual confidence in the subsequent peace impossible: Such are the employment of assassins* (percussores), poisoners (venefici), *breach of capitulation, and incitement to treason* (perduellio) *in the opposing state"*

These are dishonorable stratagems. For some confidence in the character of the enemy must remain even in the midst of war, as otherwise no peace could be concluded and the hostilities would degenerate into a war of extermination *(bellum internecinum)*. War, however, is only the sad recourse in the state of nature (where there is no tribunal which could judge with the force of law) by which each state asserts its right by violence and in which neither party can be adjudged unjust (for that would presuppose a juridical decision); in lieu of such a decision, the issue of the conflict (as if given by a so-called "judgment of God") decides on which side justice lies. But between states no punitive war *(bellum punitivum)* is conceivable, because there is no relation between them of master and servant.

It follows that a war of extermination, in which the destruction of both parties and of all justice can result, would permit perpetual peace only in the vast burial ground of the human race. Therefore, such a war and the use of all means leading to it must be absolutely forbidden. But that the means cited do inevitably lead to it is clear from the fact that these infernal arts, vile in themselves, when once used would not long be confined to the sphere of war. Take, for instance, the use of spies *(uti exploratoribus)*. In this, one employs the infamy of others (which can never be entirely eradicated) only to encourage its persistence even into the state of peace, to the undoing of the very spirit of peace.

Although the laws stated are objectively, i.e., in so far as they express the intention of rulers, mere prohibitions *(leges prohibiti-*

*vae),* some of them are of that strict kind which hold regardless of circumstances *(leges strictae)* and which demand prompt execution. Such are Nos. 1, 5, and 6. Others, like Nos. 2, 3, and 4, while not exceptions from the rule of law, nevertheless are subjectively broader *(leges latae)* in respect to their observation, containing permission to delay their execution without, however, losing sight of the end. This permission does not authorize, under No. 2, for example, delaying until doomsday (or, as Augustus used to say, *ad calendas Graecas)* the re-establishment of the freedom of states which have been deprived of it—i.e., it does not permit us to fail to do it, but it allows a delay to prevent precipitation which might injure the goal striven for. For the prohibition concerns only the manner of acquisition which is no longer permitted, but not the possession, which, though not bearing a requisite title of right, has nevertheless been held lawful in all states by the public opinion of the time (the time of the putative acquisition).[2]

2. It has not without cause hitherto been doubted whether besides the commands *(leges praeceptivae)* and prohibitions *(leges prohibitivae)* there could also be permissive laws *(leges permissivae)* of pure reason. For laws as such contain a principle of objective practical necessity, while permission implies a principle of the practical contingency of certain actions. Hence a law of permission would imply constraint to an action to do that to which no one can be constrained. If the object of the law has the same meaning in both cases, this is a contradiction. But in permissive law, which is in question here, the prohibition refers only to the future mode of acquisition of a right (e.g., by succession), while the permission annuls this prohibition only with reference to the present possession. This possession, though only putative, may be held to be just *(possessio putativa)* in the transition from the state of nature to a civil state, by virtue of a permissive law included under natural law, even though it is [strictly] illegal. But, as soon as it is recognized as illegal in the state of nature, a similar mode of acquisition in the subsequent civil state (after this transition has occurred) is forbidden, and this right to continuing possession would not hold if such a presumptive acquisition had taken place in the civil state. For in this case it would be an infringement which would have to cease as soon as its illegality was discovered.

I have wished only to call the attention of the teachers of natural law to the concept of a *lex permissiva,* which systematic reason affords, particularly since in civil (statute) law use is often made of it. But in the ordinary use of it, there is this difference: prohibitive law stands alone, while permission is not introduced into it as a limiting condition (as it should be) but counted among the exceptions to it. Then it is said, "This or that is forbidden, except Nos. 1, 2, 3," and so on indefinitely. These exceptions are added to the law only as an afterthought required by our groping around among cases as they arise, and not by any principle. Otherwise the conditions would have had to be introduced into the formula of the prohibition, and in this way it would itself have become a permissive law. It is, therefore,

# Section II
# Containing the definitive articles for perpetual peace among states

The state of peace among men living side by side is not the natural state *(status naturalis);* the natural state is one of war. This does not always mean open hostilities, but at least an unceasing threat of war. A state of peace, therefore, must be *established,* for in order to be secured against hostility it is not sufficient that hostilities simply be not committed; and, unless this security is pledged to each by his neighbor (a thing that can occur only in a civil state), each may treat his neighbor, from whom he demands this security, as an enemy.[1]

---

unfortunate that the subtle question proposed by the wise and acute Count von Windischgrätz was never answered and soon consigned to oblivion, because it insisted on the point here discussed. For the possibility of a formula similar to those of mathematics is the only legitimate criterion of a consistent legislation, and without it the so-called *ius certum* must always remain a pious wish. Otherwise we shall have merely general laws (which apply to a great number of cases), but no universal laws (which apply to all cases) as the concept of a law seems to require.

1. We ordinarily assume that no one may act inimically toward another except when he has been actively injured by the other. This is quite correct if both are under civil law, for, by entering into such a state, they afford each other the requisite security through the sovereign which has power over both. Man (or the people) in the state of nature deprives me of this security and injures me, if he is near me, by this mere status of his, even though he does not injure me actively *(facto);* he does so by the lawlessness of his condition *(statu iniusto)* which constantly threatens me. Therefore, I can compel him either to enter with me into a state of civil law or to remove himself from my neighborhood. The postulate which is basic to all the following articles is: All men who can reciprocally influence each other must stand under some civil constitution.

Every juridical constitution which concerns the person who stands under it is one of the following:

(1) The constitution conforming to the civil law of men in a nation *(ius civitatis).*

(2) The constitution conforming to the law of nations in their relation to one another *(ius gentium).*

(3) The constitution conforming to the law of world citizenship, so far as men and states are considered as citizens of a universal state of men, in their external mutual relationships *(ius cosmopoliticum).*

This division is not arbitrary, being necessary in relation to the idea of perpetual peace. For if only one state were related to another by physical influence and were yet in a state of nature, war would necessarily follow, and our purpose here is precisely to free ourselves of war.

## First Definitive Article for Perpetual Peace

### *"The civil constitution of every state should be republican"*

The only constitution which derives from the idea of the original compact, and on which all juridical legislation of a people must be based, is the republican.[2] This constitution is established, firstly, by principles of the freedom of the members of a society (as men); secondly, by principles of dependence of all upon a single common legislation (as subjects); and, thirdly, by the law of their equality (as citizens). The republican constitution, therefore, is, with respect to law, the one which is the original basis of every form of civil

---

2. Juridical (and hence) external freedom cannot be defined, as is usual, by the privilege of doing anything one wills so long as he does not injure another. For what is a privilege? It is the possibility of an action so far as one does not injure anyone by it. Then the definition would read: Freedom is the possibility of those actions by which one does no one an injury. One does another no injury (he may do as he pleases) only if he does another no injury—an empty tautology. Rather, my external (juridical) freedom is to be defined as follows: It is the privilege to lend obedience to no external laws except those to which I could have given consent. Similarly, external (juridical) equality in a state is that relationship among the citizens in which no one can lawfully bind another without at the same time subjecting himself to the law by which he also can be bound. No definition of juridical dependence is needed, as this already lies in the concept of a state's constitution as such.

The validity of these inborn rights, which are inalienable and belong necessarily to humanity, is raised to an even higher level by the principle of the juridical relation of man to higher beings, for, if he believes in them, he regards himself by the same principles as a citizen of a supersensuous world. For in what concerns my freedom, I have no obligation with respect to divine law, which can be acknowledged by my reason alone, except in so far as I could have given my consent to it. Indeed, it is only through the law of freedom of my own reason that I frame a concept of the divine will. With regard to the most sublime reason in the world that I can think of, with the exception of God—say, the great Aeon—when I do my duty in my post as he does in his, there is no reason under the law of equality why obedience to duty should fall only to me and the right to command only to him. The reason why this principle of equality does not pertain to our relation to God (as the principle of freedom does) is that this Being is the only one to which the concept of duty does not apply.

But with respect to the right of equality of all citizens as subjects, the question of whether a hereditary nobility may be tolerated turns upon the answer to the question as to whether the pre-eminent rank granted by the state to one citizen over another ought to precede merit or follow it. Now it is obvious that, if rank is associated with birth, it is uncertain whether merit (political skill and integrity) will also follow; hence it would be as if a favorite without any merit were given command. The general will of the people would never agree to this in the original contract,

constitution. The only question now is: Is it also the one which can lead to perpetual peace?

The republican constitution, besides the purity of its origin (having sprung from the pure source of the concept of law), also gives a favorable prospect for the desired consequence, i.e., perpetual peace. The reason is this: if the consent of the citizens is required in order to decide that war should be declared (and in this constitution it cannot but be the case), nothing is more natural than that they would be very cautious in commencing such a poor game, decreeing for themselves all the calamities of war. Among the latter would be: having to fight, having to pay the costs of war from their own resources, having painfully to repair the devastation war leaves behind, and, to fill up the measure of evils, load themselves with a heavy national debt that would embitter peace itself and that can never be liquidated on account of constant wars in the future. But, on the other hand, in a constitution which is not republican, and under which the subjects are not citizens, a declaration of war is the easiest thing in the world to decide upon, because war does not require of the ruler, who is the proprietor and not a member of the state, the least sacrifice of the pleasures of his table, the chase, his country houses, his court functions, and the like. He may, therefore, resolve on war as on a pleasure party for the most trivial reasons, and with perfect indifference leave the justification which decency requires to the diplomatic corps who are ever ready to provide it.

In order not to confuse the republican constitution with the democratic (as is commonly done), the following should be noted. The forms of a state *(civitas)* can be divided either according to the persons who possess the sovereign power or according to the mode of administration exercised over the people by the chief, whoever he may be. The first is properly called the form of sovereignty *(forma imperii)*, and there are only three possible forms of it: autocracy, in which one, aristocracy, in which some associated together, or

---

which is the principle of all law, for a nobleman is not necessarily a noble man. With regard to the nobility of office (as we might call the rank of the higher magistracy) which one must earn by merit, this rank does not belong to the person as his property; it belongs to his post, and equality is not thereby infringed, because when a man quits his office he renounces the rank it confers and re-enters into the class of his fellows.

democracy, in which all those who constitute society, possess sovereign power. They may be characterized, repectively, as the power of a monarch, of the nobility, or of the people. The second division is that by the form of government *(forma regiminis)* and is based on the way in which the state makes use of its power; this way is based on the constitution, which is the act of the general will through which the many persons become one nation. In this respect government is either republican or despotic. Republicanism is the political principle of the separation of the executive power (the administration) from the legislative; despotism is that of the autonomous execution by the state of laws which it has itself decreed. Thus in a despotism the public will is administered by the ruler as his own will. Of the three forms of the state, that of democracy is, properly speaking, necessarily a despotism, because it establishes an executive power in which "all" decide for or even against one who does not agree; that is, "all," who are not quite all, decide, and this is a contradiction of the general will with itself and with freedom.

Every form of government which is not representative is, properly speaking, without form. The legislator can unite in one and the same person his function as legislative and as executor of his will just as little as the universal of the major premise in a syllogism can also be the subsumption of the particular under the universal in the minor. And even though the other two constitutions are always defective to the extent that they do leave room for this mode of administration, it is at least possible for them to assume a mode of government conforming to the spirit of a representative system (as when Frederick II at least *said* he was merely the first servant of the state).[3] On the other hand, the democratic mode of government makes this impossible, since everyone wishes to be master. Therefore, we can say: the smaller the personnel of the government

3. The lofty epithets of "the Lord's anointed," "the executor of the divine will on earth," and "the vicar of God," which have been lavished on sovereigns, have been frequently censured as crude and intoxicating flatteries. But this seems to me without good reason. Far from inspiring a monarch with pride, they should rather render him humble, providing he possesses some intelligence (which we must assume). They should make him reflect that he has taken an office too great for man, an office which is the holiest God has ordained on earth, to be the trustee of the rights of men, and that he must always stand in dread of having in some way injured this "apple of God's eye."

280 · Immanuel Kant

(the smaller the number of rulers), the greater is their representation and the more nearly the constitution approaches to the possibility of republicanism; thus the constitution may be expected by gradual reform finally to raise itself to republicanism. For these reasons it is more difficult for an aristocracy than for a monarchy to achieve the one completely juridical constitution, and it is impossible for a democracy to do so except by violent revolution.

The mode of government,[4] however, is incomparably more important to the people than the form of sovereignty, although much depends on the greater or lesser suitability of the latter to the end of [good] government. To conform to the concept of law, however, government must have a representative form, and in this system only a republican mode of government is possible; without it, government is despotic and arbitrary, whatever the constitution may be. None of the ancient so-called "republics" knew this system, and they all finally and inevitably degenerated into despotism under the sovereignty of one, which is the most bearable of all forms of despotism.

## Second Definitive Article for a Perpetual Peace

### "The law of nations shall be founded on a federation of free states"

Peoples, as states, like individuals, may be judged to injure one another merely by their coexistence in the state of nature (i.e., while independent of external laws). Each of them may and should for the sake of its own security demand that the others enter with it into a constitution similar to the civil constitution, for under such

---

4. Mallet du Pan, in his pompous but empty and hollow language, pretends to have become convinced, after long experience, of the truth of Pope's well-known saying: "For forms of government let fools contest: What'er is best administered, is best." If that means that the best-administered state is the state that is best administered, he has, to make use of Swift's expression, "cracked a nut to come at a maggot." But if it means that the best-administered state also has the best mode of government, i.e., the best constitution, then it is thoroughly wrong, for examples of good governments prove nothing about the form of government. Whoever reigned better than a Titus and a Marcus Aurelius? Yet one was succeeded by a Domitian and the other by a Commodus. This could never have happened under a good constitution, for their unworthiness for this post was known early enough and also the power of the ruler was sufficient to have excluded them.

a constitution each can be secure in his right. This would be a league of nations, but it would not have to be a state consisting of nations. That would be contradictory, since a state implies the relation of a superior (legislating) to an inferior (obeying), i.e., the people, and many nations in one state would then constitute only one nation. This contradicts the presupposition, for here we have to weigh the rights of nations against each other so far as they are distinct states and not amalgamated into one.

When we see the attachment of savages to their lawless freedom, preferring ceaseless combat to subjection to a lawful constraint which they might establish, and thus preferring senseless freedom to rational freedom, we regard it with deep contempt as barbarity, rudeness, and a brutish degradation of humanity. Accordingly, one would think that civilized people (each united in a state) would hasten all the more to escape, the sooner the better, from such a depraved condition. But, instead, each state places its majesty (for it is absurd to speak of the majesty of the people) in being subject to no external juridical restraint, and the splendor of its sovereign consists in the fact that many thousands stand at its command to sacrifice themselves for something that does not concern them and without his needing to place himself in the least danger.[5] The chief difference between European and American savages lies in the fact that many tribes of the latter have been eaten by their enemies, while the former know how to make better use of their conquered enemies than to dine off them; they know better how to use them to increase the number of their subjects and thus the quantity of instruments for even more extensive wars.

When we consider the perverseness of human nature which is nakedly revealed in the uncontrolled relations between nations (this perverseness being veiled in the state of civil law by the constraint exercised by government), we may well be astonished that the word "law" has not yet been banished from war politics as pedantic, and that no state has yet been bold enough to advocate this point of view. Up to the present, Hugo Grotius, Pufendorf, Vattel, and many other irritating comforters have been cited in justification of war, though their code, philosophically or diplomatically formulated,

---

5. A Bulgarian prince gave the following answer to the Greek emperor who good-naturedly suggested that they settle their difference by a duel: "A smith who has tongs won't pluck the glowing iron from the fire with his bare hands."

282 · Immanuel Kant

has not and cannot have the least legal force, because states as such do not stand under a common external power. There is no instance on record that a state has ever been moved to desist from its purpose because of arguments backed up by the testimony of such great men. But the homage which each state pays (at least in words) to the concept of law proves that there is slumbering in man an even greater moral disposition to become master of evil principle in himself (which he cannot disclaim) and to hope for the same from others. Otherwise the word "law" would never be pronounced by states which wish to war upon one another; it would be used only ironically, as a Gallic prince interpreted it when he said, "It is the prerogative which nature has given the stronger that the weaker should obey him."

States do not plead their case before a tribunal; war alone is their way of bringing suit. But by war and its favorable issue in victory, right is not decided, and though by a treaty of peace this particular war is brought to an end, the state of war, of always finding a new pretext to hostilities, is not terminated. Nor can this be declared wrong, considering the fact that in this state each is the judge of his own case. Notwithstanding, the obligation which men in a lawless condition have under the natural law, and which requires them to abandon the state of nature, does not quite apply to states under the law of nations, for as states they already have an internal juridical constitution and have thus outgrown compulsion from others to submit to a more extended lawful constitution according to their ideas of right. This is true in spite of the fact that reason, from its throne of supreme moral legislating authority, absolutely condemns war as a legal recourse and makes a state of peace a direct duty, even though peace cannot be established or secured except by a compact among nations.

For these reasons there must be a league of a particular kind, which can be called a league of peace *(foedus pacificum),* and which would be distinguished from a treaty of peace *(pactum pacis)* by the fact that the latter terminates only one war, while the former seeks to make an end of all wars forever. This league does not tend to any dominion over the power of the state but only to the maintenance and security of the freedom of the state itself and of other states in league with it, without there being any need for them to submit to civil laws and their compulsion, as men in a state of nature must submit.

The practicability (objective reality) of this idea of federation, which should gradually spread to all states and thus lead to perpetual peace, can be proved. For if fortune directs that a powerful and enlightened people can make itself a republic, which by its nature must be inclined to perpetual peace, this gives a fulcrum to the federation with other states so that they may adhere to it and thus secure freedom under the idea of the law of nations. By more and more such associations, the federation may be gradually extended.

We may readily conceive that a people should say, "There ought to be no war among us, for we want to make ourselves into a state; that is, we want to establish a supreme legislative, executive, and judiciary power which will reconcile our differences peaceably." But when this state says, "There ought to be no war between myself and other states, even though I acknowledge no supreme legislative power by which our rights are mutually guaranteed," it is not at all clear on what I can base my confidence in my own rights unless it is the free federation, the surrogate of the civil social order, which reason necessarily associates with the concept of the law of nations—assuming that something is really meant by the latter.

The concept of a law of nations as a right to make war does not really mean anything, because it is then a law of deciding what is right by unilateral maxims through force and not by universally valid public laws which restrict the freedom of each one. The only conceivable meaning of such a law of nations might be that it serves men right who are so inclined that they should destroy each other and thus find perpetual peace in the vast grave that swallows both the atrocities and their perpetrators. For states in their relation to each other, there cannot be any reasonable way out of the lawless condition which entails only war except that they, like individual men, should give up their savage (lawless) freedom, adjust themselves to the constraints of public law, and thus establish a continuously growing state consisting of various nations (*civitas gentium*), which will ultimately include all the nations of the world. But under the idea of the law of nations they do not wish this, and reject in practice what is correct in theory. If all is not to be lost, there can be, in place of the positive idea of a world republic, only the negative surrogate of an alliance which averts war, endures, spreads, and holds back the stream of those hostile passions which fear the law, though such an alliance is in constant peril of their breaking loose again.[6] *Furor impius intus . . . fremit horridus ore cruento* (Virgil).


## Third Definitive Article for a Perpetual Peace

*"The law of world citizenship shall be limited to conditions of universal hospitality"*

Here, as in the preceding articles, it is not a question of philanthropy but of right. Hospitality means the right of a stranger not to be treated as an enemy when he arrives in the land of another. One may refuse to receive him when this can be done without causing his destruction; but, so long as he peacefully occupies his place, one may not treat him with hostility. It is not the right to be a permanent visitor that one may demand. A special beneficent agreement would be needed in order to give an outsider a right to become a fellow inhabitant for a certain length of time. It is only a right of temporary sojourn, a right to associate, which all men have. They have it by virtue of their common possession of the surface of all the earth, where, as a globe, they cannot infinitely disperse and hence must finally tolerate the presence of each other. Originally, no one had more right than another to a particular part of the earth.

Uninhabitable parts of the earth—the sea and the deserts—divide this community of all men, but the ship and the camel (the desert ship) enable them to approach each other across these unruled regions and to establish communication by using the common right

6. It would not ill become a people that has just terminated a war to decree, besides a day of thanksgiving, a day of fasting in order to ask heaven, in the name of the state, for forgiveness for the great iniquity which the human race still goes on to perpetuate in refusing to submit to a lawful constitution in their relation to other peoples, preferring, from pride in their independence, to make use of the barbarous means of war even though they are not able to attain what is sought, namely, the rights of a single state. The thanksgiving for victory won during the war, the hymns which are sung to the God of Hosts (in good Israelitic manner), stand in equally sharp contrast to the moral idea of the Father of Men. For they not only show a sad enough indifference to the way in which nations seek their rights, but in addition express a joy in having annihilated a multitude of men or their happiness.

to the face of the earth, which belongs to human beings generally. The inhospitality of the inhabitants of coasts (for instance, of the Barbary Coast) in robbing ships in neighboring seas or enslaving stranded travelers, or the inhospitality of the inhabitants of the deserts (for instance, the Bedouin Arabs) who view contact with nomadic tribes as conferring the right to plunder them, is thus opposed to natural law, even though it extends the right of hospitality, i.e., the privilege of foreign arrivals, no further than to conditions of the possibility of seeking to communicate with the prior inhabitants. In this way distant parts of the world can come into peaceable relations with each other, and these are finally publicly established by law. Thus the human race can gradually be brought closer and closer to a constitution establishing world citizenship.

But to this perfection compare the inhospitable actions of the civilized and especially of the commercial states of our part of the world. The injustice which they show to lands and peoples they visit (which is equivalent to conquering them) is carried by them to terrifying lengths. America, the lands inhabited by the Negro, the Spice Islands, the Cape, etc., were at the time of their discovery considered by these civilized intruders as lands without owners, for they counted the inhabitants as nothing. In East India (Hindustan), under the pretense of establishing economic undertakings, they brought in foreign soldiers and used them to oppress the natives, excited widespread wars among the various states, spread famine, rebellion, perfidy, and the whole litany of evils which afflict mankind.

China[7] and Japan (Nippon), who have had experience with such guests, have wisely refused them entry, the former permitting their approach to their shores but not their entry, while the latter permit

7. To call this great empire by the name it gives itself, namely "China" and not "Sina" or anything like that, we have only to refer to [A.] Georgi, *Alphabetum Tibetanum*, pp. 651–54, especially note b. According to the note of Professor [Johann Eberhard] Fischer of Petersburg, there is no definite word used in that country as its name; the most usual word is "Kin," i.e., gold (which the Tibetans call "Ser"). Accordingly, the emperor is called "the king of gold," that is, king of the most splendid country in the world. In the empire itself, this word may be pronounced *Chin*, while because of the guttural sound the Italian missionaries may have called it *Kin*.—It is clear that what the Romans called the "Land of Seres" was China; the silk, however, was sent to Europe across Greater Tibet (through Lesser Tibet, Bukhara, Persia, and then on).

this approach to only one European people, the Dutch, but treat them like prisoners, not allowing them any communication with the inhabitants. The worst of this (or, to speak with the moralist, the best) is that all these outrages profit them nothing, since all these commercial ventures stand on the verge of collapse, and the Sugar Islands, that place of the most refined and cruel slavery, produces no real revenue except indirectly, only serving a not very praiseworthy purpose of furnishing sailors for war fleets and thus for the conduct of war in Europe. This service is rendered to powers which make a great show of their piety, and, while they drink injustice like water, they regard themselves as the elect in point of orthodoxy.

Since the narrower or wider community of the peoples of the earth has developed so far that a violation of rights in one place is felt throughout the world, the idea of a law of world citizenship is no high-flown or exaggerated notion. It is a supplement to the unwritten code of the civil and international law, indispensable for the maintenance of the public human rights and hence also of perpetual peace. One cannot flatter oneself into believing one can approach this peace except under the condition outlined here.

---

This suggests many reflections concerning the antiquity of this wonderful state, in comparison with that of Hindustan at the time of its union with Tibet and thence with Japan. We see, on the contrary, that the name "Sina" or "Tshina," said to have been used by the neighbors of the country, suggests nothing.

Perhaps we can also explain the very ancient but never well-known intercourse of Europe with Tibet by considering the shout, *"Konx Ompax"*, of the hierophants in the Elusinian mysteries, as we learn from Hysichius (cf. *Travels of the Young Anacharsis*, Part V, p. 447 ff.). For, according to Georgi, *op. cit.*, the word *Concoia* means God, which has a striking resemblance to *Konx. Pah-cio (ibid., 520)*, which the Greeks may well have pronounced *pax*, means the *promulgator legis*, divinity pervading the whole of nature (also called *Cencresi*, p. 177). *Om*, however, which La Croze translates as *benedictus* ("blessed"), when applied to divinity perhaps means "the beatified" (p. 507). P. Franz Orazio often asked the Lamas of Tibet what they understood by "God" *(Concoia)* and always got the answer, "It is the assembly of saints" (i.e., the assembly of the blessed ones who, according to the doctrine of rebirth, finally, after many wanderings through bodies of all kinds, have returned to God, or *Burchane;* that is to say, they are transmigrated souls, beings to be worshipped, p. 223). That mysterious *Konx Ompax* may well mean "the holy" *(Konx)*, the blessed *(Om)*, the wise *(Pax)*, the supreme being pervading the world (nature personified). Its use in the Greek mysteries may indicate monotheism among the epopts in contrast to the polytheism of the people (though Orazio scented atheism there). How that mysterious word came to the Greeks via Tibet can perhaps be explained in this way; and the early traffic of Europe with China, also through Tibet, and perhaps earlier than communication with Hindustan, is made probable.

# First Supplement
# of the Guarantee for Perpetual Peace

The guarantee of perpetual peace is nothing less than that great artist, nature *(natura daedala rerum)*. In her mechanical course we see that her aim is to produce a harmony among men, against their will and indeed through their discord. As a necessity working according to laws we do not know, we call it destiny. But, considering its design in world history, we call it "providence," inasmuch as we discern in it the profound wisdom of a higher cause which predetermines the course of nature and directs it to the objective final end of the human race.[1] We do not observe or infer this providence in the cunning contrivances of nature, but, as in questions of the relation of the form of things to ends in general, we

---

1. In the mechanism of nature, to which man belongs as a sensuous being, a form is exhibited which is basic to its existence; we can conceive of this form only as dependent upon the end to which the Author of the world has previously destined it. This predetermination we call "divine providence" generally, and so far as it is exercised at the beginning of the world we call it "founding providence" *(Providentia conditrix; semel iussit, semper parent,* Augustine). As maintaining nature in its course by universal laws of design, it is called "ruling providence" *(providentia gubernatrix);* as directing nature to ends not foreseen by man and only conjectured from the actual result, it is called "guiding providence" *(providentia directrix).*With respect to single events as divine ends, it is no longer called "providence" but "dispensation" *(directio extraordinaria).* But since "divine dispensation" indicates miracles, even if the events themselves are not called such, it is a foolish pretension of man to wish to interpret them as such, since it is absurd to infer from a single event to a particular principle of the efficient cause, namely, that this event is an end and not merely a mechanical corollary of another end wholly unknown to us. However pious and humble such talk may be, it is full of self-conceit. The division of providence, considered not formally but materially, i.e., with respect to objects in the world to which it is directed, into either general or particular providence, is false and self-contradictory. (This division appears, for instance, in the statement that providence cares for the preservation of the species but leaves individuals to chance.) It is contradictory because it is called universal in its purpose, and therefore no single thing can be excluded from it. Presumably, therefore, a formal distinction is intended, according to the way in which providence seeks its ends. This is the distinction between the ordinary and the special ways of providence. (Under the former we may cite the annual dying-out and rebirth of nature with the changes of the season; under the latter, the transport of wood by ocean currents to arctic lands where it cannot grow, yet where it is needed by the inhabitants who could not live without it.) Although we can very well explain the physico-mechanical cause of these extraordinary cases (e.g., by reference to the wooded banks of rivers in temperate lands, the falling of trees into the rivers, and then their being carried along by the Gulf Stream), we must not overlook the teleological cause, which intimates the foresight of a wisdom commanding over nature.

can and must supply it from our own minds in order to conceive of its possibility by analogy to actions of human art. The Idea of the relationship and harmony beween these actions and the end which reason directly assigns to us is transcendent from a theoretical point of view; from a practical standpoint, with respect, for example, to the ideal of perpetual peace, the concept is dogmatic and its reality is well established, and thus the mechanism of nature may be employed to that end. The use of the word "nature" is more fitting to the limits of human reason and more modest than an expression indicating a providence unknown to us. This is especially true when we are dealing with questions of theory and not of religion, as at present, for human reason in questions of the relation of effects to their causes must remain within the limits of possible experience. On the other hand, the use of the word "providence" here intimates the possession of wings like those of Icarus, conducting us toward the secret of its unfathomable purpose.

Before we more narrowly define the guarantee which nature gives, it is necessary to examine the situation in which she has placed her actors on her vast stage, a situation which finally assures peace among them. Then we shall see how she accomplishes the latter. Her preparatory arrangements are:

---

The concept of intervention or concurrence *(concursus)* in producing an effect in the world of sense must be given up, though it is quite usual in the schools. For to try to pair the disparate *(gryphes iungere equis)*, and to let that which is itself the perfect cause of events in the world supplement its own predetermining providence in the course of the world (which would therefore have to have been inadequate), is self-contradictory. We fall into this self-contradiction, for example, when we say that next to God it was the physician who cured the ill, as if God had been his helper. For *causa solitaria non iuvat;* God is the author of the physician and all his medicines, and if we insist on ascending to the highest but theoretically inconceivable first cause, the effect must be ascribed entirely to Him. Or we can ascribe it entirely to the physician, so far as we consider the occurrence as explicable in a chain of causes under the order of nature.

But, besides being self-contradictory, such a mode of thought brings an end to all definite principles in judging an effect. In a morally practical point of view, however, which is directed exclusively to the supersensuous, the concept of the divine *concursus* is quite suitable and even necessary. We find this, for instance, in the belief that God will compensate for our own lack of justice, provided our intention was genuine; that He will do so by means that are inconceivable to us, and that therefore we should not relent in our endeavor after the good. But it is self-evident that no one should try to explain a good action (as an event in the world) as a result of this *concursus,* for this would be a vain theoretical knowledge of the supersensuous and therefore absurd.

1. In every region of the world she has made it possible for men to live.

2. By war she has driven them even into the most inhospitable regions in order to populate them.

3. By the same means, she has forced them into more or less lawful relations with each other.

That in the cold wastes by the Arctic Ocean the moss grows which the reindeer digs from the snow in order to make itself the prey or the conveyance of the Ostyak or Samoyed; or that the saline sandy deserts are inhabited by the camel which appears created as it were in order that they might not go unused—that is already wonderful. Still clearer is the end when we see how besides the furry animals of the Arctic there are also the seal, the walrus, and the whale which afford the inhabitants food from their flesh and warmth from their blubber. But the care of nature excites the greatest wonder when we see how she brings wood (though the inhabitants do not know whence it comes) to these barren climates, without which they would have neither canoes, weapons, nor huts, and when we see how these natives are so occupied with their war against the animals that they live in peace with each other—but what drove them there was presumably nothing else than war.

The first instrument of war among the animals which man learned to tame and to domesticate was the horse (for the elephant belongs to later times, to the luxury of already established states). The art of cultivating certain types of plants (grain) whose original characteristics we do not know, and the increase and improvement of fruits by transplantation and grafting (in Europe perhaps only the crab apple and the wild pear), could arise only under conditions prevailing in already established states where property was secure. Before this could take place, it was necessary that men who had first subsisted in anarchic freedom by hunting,[2] fishing, and sheep-

---

2. Among all modes of life there is undoubtedly none more opposed to a civilized constitution than that of hunting, because families which must dwell separately soon become strangers and, scattered in extensive forests, also enemies, since each needs a great deal of space for obtaining food and clothing. The Noachic ban on blood (Genesis 9:4–6) (which was imposed by the baptized Jews as a condition on the later Christians who were converted from heathenism, though in a different connection—see The Acts 15:20; 21:25) seems to have been originally nothing more than a prohibition against the hunting life, because here raw flesh must often have been eaten; when the latter was forbidden, so also was the former.

herding should have been forced into an agricultural life. Then salt and iron were discovered. These were perhaps the first articles of commerce for the various peoples and were sought far and wide; in this way a peaceful traffic among nations was established, and thus understanding, conventions, and peaceable relations were established among the most distant peoples.

As nature saw to it that men *could* live everywhere in the world, she also despotically willed that they *should* do so, even against their inclination and without this *ought* being based on a concept of duty to which they were bound by a moral law. She chose war as the means to this end. So we see peoples whose common language shows that they have a common origin. For instance, the Samoyeds on the Arctic Ocean and a people with a similar language a thousand miles away in the Altaian Mountains are separated by a Mongolian people adept at horsemanship and hence at war; the latter drove the former into the most inhospitable Arctic regions where they certainly would not have spread of their own accord.[3] Again, it is the same with the Finns who in the most northerly part of Europe are called Lapps; Goths and Sarmatians have separated them from the Hungarians to whom they are related in language. What can have driven the Eskimos, a race entirely distinct from all others in America and perhaps descended from primeval European adventurers, so far into the North, or the Pescherais as far south as Tierra del Fuego, if it were not war which nature uses to populate the whole earth? War itself requires no special motive but appears to be engrafted on human nature; it passes even for something noble, to which the love of glory impels men quite apart from any selfish urges. Thus among the American savages, just as much as among those of Europe during the age of chivalry, military valor is held to be of great worth in itself, not only during war (which is natural) but in order that there should be war. Often war is waged only in

3. One could ask: If nature willed that these icy coasts should not remain uninhabited, what would become of the inhabitants if nature ever failed (as might be expected) to bring driftwood to them? For it is reasonable to believe that, in the progress of civilization, the occupants of the temperate zone would make better use of the wood along rivers than simply to let it fall into the water and be carried to the sea. I answer: If nature compels them to peace, the dwellers along the Ob, the Yenisei, or the Lena will bring it to them, exchanging it for animal products in which the sea around the Arctic coasts abounds.

order to show valor; thus an inner dignity is ascribed to v
and even some philosophers have praised it as an ennoblen....
humanity, forgetting the pronouncement of the Greek who said,
"War is an evil inasmuch as it produces more wicked men than it
takes away." So much for the measures nature takes to lead the
human race, considered as a class of animals, to her own end.

Now we come to the question concerning that which is most
essential in the design of perpetual peace: What has nature done
with regard to this end which man's own reason makes his duty?
That is, what has nature done to favor man's moral purpose, and
how has she guaranteed (by compulsion but without prejudice to
his freedom) that he shall do that which he ought to but does not
do under the laws of freedom? This question refers to all three
phases of public law, namely, civil law, the law of nations, and the
law of world citizenship. If I say of nature that she wills that this
or that occur, I do not mean that she imposes a duty on us to do
it, for this can be done only by free practical reason; rather I mean
that she herself does it, whether we will or not *(fata volentem
ducunt, nolentem trahunt).*

1. Even if a people were not forced by internal discord to submit
to public laws, war would compel them to do so, for we have already
seen that nature has placed each people near another which presses
upon it, and against this it must form itself into a state in order to
defend itself. Now the republican constitution is the only one entirely fitting to the rights of man. But it is the most difficult to
establish and even harder to preserve, so that many say a republic
would have to be a nation of angels, because men with their selfish
inclinations are not capable of a constitution of such sublime form.
But precisely with these inclinations nature comes to the aid of the
general will established on reason, which is revered even though
impotent in practice. Thus it is only a question of a good organization of the state (which does lie in man's power), whereby the
powers of each selfish inclination are so arranged in opposition that
one moderates or destroys the ruinous effect of the other. The
consequence for reason is the same as if none of them existed,
and man is forced to be a good citizen even if not a morally good
person.

The problem of organizing a state, however hard it may seem, can be solved even for a race of devils, if only they are intelligent. The problem is: "Given a multitude of rational beings requiring universal laws for their preservation, but each of whom is secretly inclined to exempt himself from them, to establish a constitution in such a way that, although their private intentions conflict, they check each other, with the result that their public conduct is the same as if they had no such intentions."

A problem like this must be capable of solution; it does not require that we know how to attain the moral improvement of men but only that we should know the mechanism of nature in order to use it on men, organizing the conflict of the hostile intentions present in a people in such a way that they must compel themselves to submit to coercive laws. Thus a state of peace is established in which laws have force. We can see, even in actual states, which are far from perfectly organized, that in their foreign relations they approach that which the idea of right prescribes. This is so in spite of the fact that the intrinsic element of morality is certainly not the cause of it. (A good constitution is not to be expected from morality, but, conversely, a good moral condition of a people is to be expected only under a good constitution.) Instead of genuine morality, the mechanism of nature brings it to pass through selfish inclinations, which naturally conflict outwardly but which can be used by reason as a means for its own end, the sovereignty of law, and, as concerns the state, for promoting and securing internal and external peace.

This, then, is the truth of the matter: Nature inexorably wills that the right should finally triumph. What we neglect to do comes about by itself, though with great inconveniences to us. "If you bend the reed too much, you break it; and he who attempts too much attempts nothing" (Bouterwek).

2. The idea of international law presupposes the separate existence of many independent but neighboring states. Although this condition is itself a state of war (unless a federative union prevents the outbreak of hostilities), this is rationally preferable to the amalgamation of states under one superior power, as this would end in one universal monarchy, and laws always lose in vigor what government gains in extent; hence a soulless despotism falls into anarchy after stifling the seeds of the good. Nevertheless, every state, or its ruler, desires to establish lasting peace in this way, aspiring if possible to rule the whole world. But nature wills otherwise. She

employs two means to separate peoples and to prevent them from mixing: differences of language and of religion.[4] These differences involve a tendency to mutual hatred and pretexts for war, but the progress of civilization and men's gradual approach to greater harmony in their principles finally leads to peaceful agreement. This is not like that peace which despotism (in the burial ground of freedom) produces through a weakening of all powers; it is, on the contrary, produced and maintained by their equilibrium in liveliest competition.

3. Just as nature wisely separates nations, which the will of every state, sanctioned by the principles of international law, would gladly unite by artifice or force, nations which could not have secured themselves against violence and war by means of the law of world citizenship unite because of mutual interest. The spirit of commerce, which is incompatible with war, sooner or later gains the upper hand in every state. As the power of money is perhaps the most dependable of all the powers (means) included under the state power, states see themselves forced, without any moral urge, to promote honorable peace and by mediation to prevent war wherever it threatens to break out. They do so exactly as if they stood in perpetual alliances, for great offensive alliances are in the nature of the case rare and even less often successful.

In this manner nature guarantees perpetual peace by the mechanism of human passions. Certainly she does not do so with sufficient certainty for us to predict the future in any theoretical sense, but adequately from a practical point of view, making it our duty to work toward this end, which is not just a chimerical one.

4. Difference of religion—a singular expression! It is precisely as if one spoke of different moralities. There may very well be different kinds of historical faiths attached to different means employed in the promotion of religion, and they belong merely in the field of learned investigation. Similarly there may be different religious texts (Zendavesta, the Veda, the Koran, etc.), but such differences do not exist in religion, there being only one religion valid for all men and in all ages. These can, therefore, be nothing else than accidental vehicles of religion, thus changing with times and places.

# Second Supplement
## Secret Article for Perpetual Peace

A secret article in contracts under public law is objectively, i.e., from the standpoint of its content, a contradiction. Subjectively, however, a secret clause can be present in them, because the persons who dictate it might find it compromising to their dignity to declare openly that they are its authors.

The only article of this kind is contained in the statement: "The opinions of philosophers on the conditions of the possibility of public peace shall be consulted by those states armed for war."

But it appears humiliating to the legislative authority of a state, to whom we must naturally attribute the utmost wisdom, to seek instruction from subjects (the philosophers) on principles of conduct toward other states. It is nevertheless very advisable to do so. Therefore, the state tacitly and secretly invites them to give their opinions, that is, the state will let them publicly and freely talk about the general maxims of warfare and of the establishment of peace (for they will do that of themselves, provided they are not forbidden to do so). It does not require a particular convention among states to see that this is done, since their agreement on this point lies in an obligation already established by universal human reason which is morally legislative.

I do not mean that the state should give the principles of philosophers any preference over the decisions of lawyers (the representatives of the state power); I only ask that they be given a hearing. The lawyer, who has made not only the scales of right but also the sword of justice his symbol, generally uses the latter not merely to keep back all foreign influences from the former, but, if the scale does not sink the way he wishes he also throws the sword into it *(vae victis)*, a practice to which he often has the greatest temptation because he is not also a philosopher, even in morality. His office is only to apply positive laws, not to inquire whether they might not need improvement. The administrative function, which is the lower one in his faculty, he counts as the higher because it is invested with power (as is the case also with the other faculties [of medicine and theology]). The philosophical faculty occupies a very low rank against this allied power. Thus it is said of philosophy, for example, that she is the handmaiden to theology, and the other faculties claim as much. But one does not see distinctly whether she precedes her mistress with a flambeau or follows bearing her train.

That kings should philosophize or philosophers become kings is not to be expected. Nor is it to be wished, since the possession of power inevitably corrupts the untrammeled judgment of reason. But kings or kinglike peoples which rule themselves under laws of equality should not suffer the class of philosphers to disappear or to be silent, but should let them speak openly. This is indispensable to the enlightenment of the business of government, and, since the class of philosophers is by nature incapable of plotting and lobbying, it is above suspicion of being made up of propagandists.

# Appendix I
## On the Opposition Between Morality and Politics with Respect to Perpetual Peace

Taken objectively, morality is in itself practical, being the totality of unconditionally mandatory laws according to which we ought to act. It would obviously be absurd, after granting authority to the concept of duty, to pretend that we cannot do our duty, for in that case this concept would itself drop out of morality (*ultra posse nemo obligatur*). Consequently, there can be no conflict of politics, as a practical doctrine of right, with ethics, as a theoretical doctrine of right. That is to say, there is no conflict of practice with theory, unless by ethics we mean a general doctrine of prudence, which would be the same as a theory of the maxims for choosing the most fitting means to accomplish the purposes of self-interest. But to give this meaning to ethics is equivalent to denying that there is any such thing at all.

Politics says, "Be ye wise as serpents"; morality adds, as a limiting condition, "and guileless as doves." If these two injunctions are incompatible in a single command, then politics and morality are really in conflict; but if these two qualities ought always to be united, the thought of contrariety is absurd, and the question as to how the conflict between morals and politics is to be resolved cannot even be posed as a problem. Although the proposition, "Honesty is the best policy," implies a theory which practice unfortunately often refutes, the equally theoretical "Honesty is better than any policy" is beyond refutation and is indeed the indispensable condition of policy.

The tutelary divinity of morality yields not to Jupiter, for this tutelary divinity of force still is subject to destiny. That is, reason is not yet sufficiently enlightened to survey the entire series of pre-determining causes, and such vision would be necesary for one to be able to foresee with certainty the happy or unhappy effects which follow human actions by the mechanism of nature (though we know enough to have hope that they will accord with our wishes). But what we have to do in order to remain in the path of duty (according to rules of wisdom) reason instructs us by her rules, and her teaching suffices for attaining the ultimate end.

Now the practical man, to whom morality is mere theory even though he concedes that it can and should be followed, ruthlessly renounces our fond hope [that it will be followed]. He does so because he pretends to have seen in advance that man, by his nature, will never will what is required for realizing the goal of perpetual peace. Certainly the will of each individual to live under a juridical constitution according to principles of freedom (i.e., the distributive unity of the will of all) is not sufficient to this end. That all together should will this condition (i.e., the collective unity of the united will)—the solution to this troublous problem—is also required. Thus a whole of civil society is formed. But since a uniting cause must supervene upon the variety of particular volitions in order to produce a common will from them, establishing this whole is something no one individual in the group can perform; hence in the practical execution of this idea we can count on nothing but force to establish the juridical condition, on the compulsion of which public law will later be established. We can scarcely hope to find in the legislator a moral intention sufficient to induce him to commit to the general will the establishment of a legal constitution after he has formed the nation from a horde of savages; therefore, we cannot but expect (in practice) to find in execution wide deviations from this idea (in theory).

It will then be said that he who once has power in his hands will not allow the people to prescribe laws for him; a state which once is able to stand under no external laws will not submit to the decision of other states how it should seek its rights against them; and one continent, which feels itself superior to another, even though the other does not interfere with it, will not neglect to increase its power by robbery or even conquest. Thus all theoretical plans of civil and international laws and laws of world citizenship vanish into empty and impractical ideas, while practice based on empirical principles of human nature, not blushing to draw its maxims from the usages of the world, can alone hope to find a sure ground for its political edifice.

If there is no freedom and no morality based on freedom, and everything which occurs or can occur happens by the mere mechanism of nature, certainly politics (which is the art of using this mechanism for ruling men) is the whole of practical wisdom, and the concept of right is an empty thought. But if we find it necessary to connect the latter with politics, and even to raise it to a limiting condition thereon, the possibility of their being united must be conceded. I can easily conceive of a moral politician, i.e., one who so chooses political principles that they are consistent with those of morality; but I cannot conceive of a political moralist, one who forges a morality in such a way that it conforms to the statesman's advantage.

When a remediable defect is found in the constitution of the state or in its relations to others, the principle of the moral politician will be that it is a duty, especially of the rulers of the state, to inquire how it can be remedied as soon as possible in a way conforming to natural law as a model presented by reason; this he will do even if it costs self-sacrifice. But it would be absurd to demand that every defect be immediately and impetuously changed, since the disruption of the bonds of a civil society or a union of world citizens before a better constitution is ready to take its place is against all politics agreeing with morality. But it can be demanded that at least the maxim of the necessity of such a change should be taken to heart by those in power, so that they may continuously approach the goal of the constitution that is best under laws of right. A state may exercise a republican rule, even though by its present constitution it has a despotic sovereignty, until gradually the people becomes susceptible to the influence simply of the idea of the authority of law (as if it possessed physical power) and thus is found fit to be its own legislator (as its own legislation is originally established on law). If a violent revolution engendered by a bad constitution, introduces by illegal means a more legal constitution, to lead the people back to the earlier constitution would not be permitted; but, while the revolution lasted, each person who openly or covertly shared in it would have justly incurred the punishment due to those who rebel. As to the external relations of states, a state cannot be expected to renounce its constitution even though it is a despotic one (which has the advantage of being stronger in relation to foreign enemies) so long as it is exposed to the danger of being swallowed up by other states. Thus even in the case of the intention to improve the constitution, postponement to a more propitious time may be permitted.[1]

It may be that despotizing moralists, in practice blundering, often violate rules of political prudence through measures they adopt or propose too precipitately; but experience will gradually retrieve them from their infringement of nature and lead them on to a better course. But the moralizing politician, by glossing over principles of politics which are opposed to the right with the pretext that human nature is not capable of the good as reason prescribes it, only makes reform impossible and perpetuates the violation of law.

Instead of possessing the *practical science* they boast of, these politicans have only *practices;* they flatter the power which is then ruling so as not to be remiss in their private advantage, and they sacrifice the nation and, possibly, the whole world. This is the way of all professional lawyers (not legislators) when they go into politics. Their task is not to reason too nicely about the legislation but to execute the momentary commands on the statute books; consequently, the legal constitution in force at any time is to them the best, but when it is amended from above, this amendment always seems best, too. Thus everything is preserved in its accustomed mechanical order. Their adroitness in fitting into all circumstances gives them the illusion of being able to judge constitutional principles according to concepts of right (not empirically, but a priori). They make a great show of understanding *men* (which is certainly something to be expected of them, since they have to deal with so

1. These are permissive laws of reason. Public law laden with injustice must be allowed to stand, either until everything is of itself ripe for complete reform or until this maturity has been brought about by peaceable means; for a legal constitution, even though it be right to only a low degree, is better than none at all, the anarchic condition which would result from precipitate reform. Political wisdom, therefore, will make it a duty to introduce reforms which accord with the ideal of public law. But even when nature herself produces revolutions, political wisdom will not employ them to legitimize still greater oppression. On the contrary, it will use them as a call of nature for fundamental reforms to produce a lawful constitution founded upon principles of freedom, for only such a constitution is durable.

many) without understanding *man* and what can be made of him, for they lack the higher point of view of anthropological observation which is needed for this. If with these ideas they go into civil and international law, as reason prescribes it, they take this step in a spirit of chicanery, for they still follow their accustomed mechanical routine of despotically imposed coercive laws in a field where only concepts of reason can establish a legal compulsion according to the principles of freedom, under which alone a just and durable constitution is possible. In this field the pretended practical man thinks he can solve the problem of establishing such a constitution without the rational Idea but solely from the experience he has had with what was previously the most lasting constitution—a constitution which in many cases was opposed to the right.

The maxims which he makes use of (though he does not divulge them) are, roughly speaking, the following sophisms:

1. *Fac et excusa.* Seize every favorable opportunity for usurping the right of the state over its own people or over a neighboring people; the justification will be easier and more elegant *ex post facto,* and the power can be more easily glossed over, especially when the supreme power in the state is also the legislative authority which must be obeyed without argument. It is much more difficult to do the violence when one has first to wait upon the consideration of convincing arguments and to meet them with counterarguments. Boldness itself gives the appearance of inner conviction of the legitimacy of the deed, and the god of success is afterward the best advocate.

2. *Si fecisti, nega.* What you have committed, deny that it was your fault—for instance, that you have brought your people to despair and hence to rebellion. Rather assert that it was due to the obstinacy of your subjects; or, if you have conquered a neighboring nation, say that the fault lies in the nature of man, who, if not met by force, can be counted on to make use of it to conquer you.

3. *Divide et impera.* That is, if there are certain privileged persons in your nation who have chosen you as their chief *(primus inter pares),* set them at variance with one another and embroil them with the people. Show the latter visions of greater freedom, and all will soon depend on your untrammeled will. Or if it is foreign states that concern you, it is a pretty safe means to sow discord among them so that, by seeming to protect the weaker, you can conquer them one after another.

Certainly no one is now the dupe of these political maxims, for they are already universally known. Nor are they blushed at, as if their injustice were too glaring, for great powers blush only at the judgment of other great powers but not at that of the common masses. It is not that they are ashamed of revealing such principles (for all of them are in the same boat with respect to the morality of their maxims); they are ashamed only when these maxims fail, for they still have political honor which cannot be disputed—and this honor is the aggrandizement of their power by whatever means.[2]

All these twistings and turnings of an immoral doctrine of prudence in leading men from their natural state of war to a state of peace prove at least that men in both their private and their public relationships cannot reject the concept of right or trust themselves openly to establish politics merely on the artifices of prudence. Thus they do not refuse obedience to the concept of public law, which is especially manifest in international law; on the contrary, they give all the due honor to it, even when they are inventing a hundred pretenses and subterfuges to escape from it in practice, imputing its authority, as the source and union of all laws, to crafty force.

Let us put an end to this sophism, if not to the injustice it protects, and force the false representatives of power to confess that they do not plead in favor of the right but in favor of might. This is revealed

2. Even if we doubt a certain wickedness in the nature of men who live together in a state, and instead plausibly cite lack of civilization, which is not yet sufficiently advanced, i.e., regard barbarism as the cause of those antilawful manifestations of their character, this viciousness is clearly and incontestably shown in the foreign relations of states. Within each state it is veiled by the compulsion of civil laws, because the inclination to violence between the citizens is fettered by the stronger power of the government. This relationship not only gives a moral veneer *(causae non causae)* to the whole but actually facilitates the development of the moral disposition to a direct respect for the law by placing a barrier against the outbreak of unlawful inclinations. Each person believes that he himself would hold the concept of law sacred and faithfully follow it provided he were sure that he could expect the same from others, and the government does in part assure him of this. Thereby a great step (though not yet a moral step) is taken toward morality, which is attachment to this concept of duty for its own sake and without regard to hope of a similar response from others. But since each one with his own good opinion of himself presupposes a malicious disposition on the part of all the others, they all pronounce the judgment that they in fact are all worth very little. We shall not discuss how this comes about, though it cannot be blamed on the nature of man as a free being. But since even respect for the concept of right (which man cannot absolutely refuse to respect) solemnly sanctions the theory that he has the capacity of conforming to it, everyone sees that he, for his part, must act according to it, however others may act.

in the imperious tone they assume as if they themselves could command the right. Let us remove the delusion by which they and others are duped, and discover the supreme principle from which the intention to perpetual peace stems. Let us show that everything evil which stands in its way derives from the fact that the political moralist begins where the moral politician would correctly leave off, and that, since he thus subordinates principles to the end (putting the cart before the horse), he vitiates his own purpose of bringing politics into agreement with morality.

To make practical philosophy self-consistent, it is necessary, first to decide the question: In problems of practical reason, must we begin from its material principles, i.e., the end as the object of choice? Or should we begin from the formal principles of pure reason, i.e., from the principle which is concerned solely with freedom in outer relations and which reads, "So act that you can will that your maxim could become a universal law, regardless of the end"?

Without doubt it is the latter which has precedence, for as a principle of law it has unconditional necessity. On the other hand, the former is obligatory only if we presuppose the empirical conditions of the proposed end, i.e., its practicability. Thus if this end (in this case, perpetual peace) is a duty, it must be derived from the formal principle of the maxims of external actions. The first principle, that of the political moralist, pertaining to civil and international law and the law of world citizenship, is merely a problem of technique *(problema technicum);* the second, as the problem of the moral politician to whom it is an ethical problem *(problema morale),* is far removed from the other in its method of leading toward perpetual peace, which is wished not merely as a material good but also as a condition issuing from an acknowledgment of duty.

For the solution of the former, the problem of political prudence, much knowledge of nature is required so that its mechanism may be employed toward the desired end; yet all this is uncertain in its results for perpetual peace, with whatever sphere of public law we are concerned. It is uncertain, for example, whether the people are better kept in obedience and maintained in prosperity by severity or by the charm of distinctions which flatter their vanity, by the power of one or the union of various chiefs, or perhaps merely by a serving nobility or by the power of the people. History furnishes us with contradictory examples from all governments (with the exception of the truly republican, which can alone appeal to the mind of a moral politician). Still more uncertain is an international law allegedly erected on the statutes of ministries. It is, in fact, a word without meaning, resting as it does on compacts which, in the very act of being concluded, contain secret reservations for their violation.

On the other hand, the solution of the second problem, that of political wisdom, presses itself upon us, as it were; it is clear to everyone and puts to shame all affectation. It leads directly to the end, but, remembering discretion, it does not precipitately hasten to do so by force; rather, it continuously approaches it under the conditions offered by favorable circumstances.

Then it may be said, "Seek ye first the kingdom of pure practical reason and its righteousness, and your end (the blessing of perpetual peace) will necessarily follow." For it is the peculiarity of morals, especially with respect to its principles of public law and hence in relation to a politics known a priori, that the less it makes conduct depend on the proposed end, i.e., the intended material or moral advantage, the more it agrees with it in general. This is because it is the universal will given a priori (in a nation or in the relations among different nations) which determines the law among men, and if practice consistently follows it, this will can also, by the mechanism of nature, cause the desired result and make the concept of law effective. So, for instance, it is a principle of moral politics that a people should unite into a state according to juridical concepts of freedom and equality, and this principle is based not on prudence but on duty. Political moralists may argue as much as they wish about the natural mechanism of a mass of men forming a society, assuming a mechanism which would weaken those principles and vitiate their end; or they may seek to prove their assertions by examples of poorly organized constitutions of ancient and modern times (for instance, of democratics without representative systems). They deserve no hearing, particularly as such a pernicious theory may itself occasion the evil which it prophesies, throwing human beings into one class with all other living machines, differing from them only in their consciousness that they are not free, which makes them, in their own judgment, the most miserable of all beings in the world.

The true but somewhat boastful sentence which has become proverbial, *Fiat iustitia, pereat mundus* ("Let justice reign even if all the rascals in the world should perish from it"), is a stout principle of right which cuts asunder the whole tissue of artifice or force. But it should not be misunderstood as a permission to use one's own right with extreme rigor (which would conflict with ethical duty); it should be understood as the obligation of those in power not to limit or to extend anyone's right through sympathy or disfavor. This requires, first, an internal constitution of the state erected on pure principles of right, and, second, a convention of the state with other near or distant states (analogous to a universal state) for the legal settlement of their differences. This implies only that political maxims must not be derived from the welfare or happiness which a single state expects from obedience to them, and thus not from the end which one of them proposes for itself. That is, they must not be deduced from volition as the supreme yet empirical principle of political wisdom, but rather from the pure concept of the duty of right, from the *ought* whose principle is given a priori by pure reason, regardless of what the physical consequences may be. The world will by no means perish by a diminution in the number of evil men. Moral evil has the indiscerptible property of being opposed to and destructive of its own purposes (especially in the relationships between evil men); thus it gives place to the moral principle of the good, though only through a slow progress.

Thus objectively, or in theory, there is no conflict between morals and politics. Subjectively, however, in the selfish propensity of men (which should not be called "practice," as this would imply that it rested on rational maxims), this conflict will always remain. Indeed, it should remain, because it serves as a whetstone of virtue, whose true courage (by the principle, *tu ne cede malis, sed contra audentior ito*) in the present case does not so much consist in defying with strong resolve evils and sacrifices which must be undertaken along with the conflict, but rather in detecting and conquering the crafty and far more dangerously deceitful and treasonable principle of evil in ourselves, which puts forward the weakness of human nature as justification for every transgression.

In fact, the political moralist may say: The ruler and people, or nation and nation, do each other no injustice when by violence or fraud they make war on each other, although they do commit injustice in general in that they refuse to respect the concept of right, which alone could establish perpetual peace. For since the one does transgress his duty against the other, who is likewise lawlessly disposed toward him, each gets what he deserves when they destroy each other. But enough of the race still remains to let this game continue into the remotest ages in order that posterity, some day, might take these perpetrators as a warning example. Hence providence is justified in the history of the world, for the moral principle in man is never extinguished, while with advancing civilization reason grows pragmatically in its capacity to realize ideas of law. But at the same time the culpability for the transgressions also grows. If we assume that humanity never will or can be improved, the only thing which a theodicy seems unable to justify is creation itself, the act that a race of such corrupt beings ever was on earth. But the point of view necessary for such an assumption is far too high for us, and we cannot theoretically support our philosophical concepts of the supreme power which is inscrutable to us.

To such dubious consequences we are inevitably driven if we do not assume that pure principles of right have objective reality, i.e., that they may be applied, and that the people in a state and, further, states themselves in their mutual relations should act according to them, whatever objections empirical politics may raise. Thus true politics can never take a step without rendering homage to morality. Though politics by itself is a difficult art, its union with morality is no art at all, for this union cuts the knot which politics could not untie when they were in conflict. The rights of men must be held sacred, however much sacrifice it may cost the ruling power. One cannot compromise here and seek the middle course of a pragmatic conditional law between the morally right and the expedient. All politics must bend its knee before the right. But by this it can hope slowly to reach the stage where it will shine with an immortal glory.

# Appendix II
# Of the Harmony Which the
# Transcendental Concept of Public Right
# Establishes Between Morality and Politics

If, like the teacher of law, I abstract from all the material of public law (i.e., abstract from the various empirically given relationships of men in the state or of states to each other), there remains only the *form* of publicity, the possibility of which is implied by every legal claim, since without it there can be no justice (which can only be conceived as publicly known) and thus no right, since it can be conferred only in accordance with justice. Every legal claim must be capable of publicity. Since it is easy to judge whether it is so in a particular case, i.e., whether it can be compatible with the principles of the agent, this gives an easily applied criterion found a priori in reason, by which the falsity (opposition to law) of the pretended claim *(praetensio iuris)* can, as it were, be immediately known by an experiment of pure reason.

Having set aside everything empirical in the concept of civil or international law (such as the wickedness in human nature which necessitates coercion), we can call the following proposition the transcendental formula of public law: "All actions relating to the right of other men are unjust if their maxim is not consistent with publicity."

This principle is to be regarded not merely as ethical (as belonging to the doctrine of virtue) but also as juridical (concerning the right of man). A maxim which I cannot divulge without defeating my own purpose must be kept secret if it is to succeed; and, if I cannot publicly avow it without inevitably exciting universal opposition to my project, the necessary and universal opposition which can be foreseen a priori is due only to the injustice with which the maxim threatens everyone. This principle is, furthermore, only negative, i.e., it only serves for the recognition of what is not just to others. Like an axiom, it is indemonstrably certain and, as will be seen in the following examples of public law, easily applied.

1. In the law of the state *(ius civitatis)* or domestic law, there is a question which many hold to be difficult to answer, yet it is easily solved by the transcendental principle of publicity. The question is: "Is rebellion a legitimate means for a people to employ in throwing off the yoke of an alleged tyrant *(non titulo, sed exercitio talis)?*" The rights of the people are injured; no injustice befalls the tyrant when he is deposed. There can be no doubt on this point. Nevertheless, it is in the highest degree illegitimate for the subjects to seek their rights in this way. If they fail in the struggle and are then subjected to severest punishment, they cannot complain about injustice any more than the tyrant could if they had succeeded.

If one wishes to decide this question by a dogmatic deduction of legal grounds, there can be much arguing pro and con; only the transcendental principle of the publicity of public law can free us of this prolixity. According to this principle, a people would ask itself before the establishment of the civil contract whether it dare publish the maxim of its intention to revolt on occasion. It is clear that if, in the establishment of a constitution, the condition is made that the people may in certain cases employ force against its chief, the people would have to pretend to a legitimate power over him, and then he would not be the chief. Or if both are made the condition of the establishment of the state, no state would be possible, though to establish it was the purpose of the people. The illegitimacy of rebellion is thus clear from the fact that its maxim, if openly acknowledged, would make its own purpose impossible. Therefore, it would have to be kept secret.

This secrecy, however, is not incumbent upon the chief of the state. He can openly say that he will punish every rebellion with the death of the ringleaders, however much they may believe that he was the first to overstep the basic law; for when he knows he possesses irresistible power (which must be assumed to be the case in every civil constitution, because he who does not have enough power to protect the people against every other also does not have the right to command them), he need not fear vitiating his own purpose by publishing his maxims. If the revolt of the people succeeds, what has been said is still quite compatible with the fact that the chief, on retiring to the status of a subject, cannot begin a revolt for his restoration but need not fear being made to account for his earlier administration of the state.

2. We can speak of international law only under the presupposition of some law-governed condition, i.e., of the external condition under which right can really be awarded to man. For, being a public law, it contains in its very concept the public announcement of a general will which assigns to each his rights, and this *status iuridicus* must result from some compact which is not founded on laws of compulsion (as in the case of the compact from which a single state arises). Rather, it must be founded on a free and enduring association, like the previously mentioned federation of states. For without there being some juridical condition, which actively binds together the different physical or moral persons, there can be only private law; this is the situation met with in the state of nature. Now here there is a conflict of politics with morality (regarding the latter as a science of right), and the criterion of publicity again finds an easy application in resolving it, though only if the compact between the states has been made with the purpose of preserving peace between them and other states, and not for conquest. The following cases of the antinomy between politics and morality occur (and they are stated with their solution).

*a)* "If one of these states has promised something to the other, such as aid, cession of some province, subsidies, and the like, and a case arises where the salvation of the state depends upon its being relieved of its promise, can it then consider itself in two roles: first as a sovereign (as it is responsible to no one in the state), and second as merely the highest official (who must give an account to the state)? From this dual capacity it would follow that in its latter role the state can relieve itself of what it has obliged itself to do in its former role." But if a state (or its chief) publicizes this maxim, others would naturally avoid entering an alliance with it, or ally themselves with others so as to resist such pretensions. This proves that politics with all its cunning would defeat its purpose by candor; therefore, that maxim must be illegitimate.

*b)* "If a neighboring power becomes formidable by its acquisitions *(potentia tremenda)*, and thus causes anxiety, can one assume because it *can* oppress that it *will?* And does this give the lesser power, in union with others, a right to attack it without having first been injured by it?" A state which made known that such was its maxim would produce the feared evil even more certainly and quickly, for the greater power would steal a march on the smaller. And the alliance of the smaller powers would be only a feeble reed against one who knew how to apply the maxim *divide et impera.* This maxim of political expediency, if made public, would necessarily defeat its own purpose, and hence it is illegitimate.

*c)* "If a smaller state is so situated as to break up the territory of a larger one, and continuous territory is necessary to the preservation of the larger, is the latter not justified in subjugating the smaller and incorporating it?" We easily see that the greater power cannot afford to let this maxim become known; otherwise the smaller states would very early unite, or other powers would dispute the prey, and thus publicity would render this maxim impracticable. This is a sign that it is illegitimate. It may be unjust to a very high degree, for a small object of injustice does not prevent the injustice from being very great.

3. I say nothing about the law of world citizenship, for its analogy with international law makes it a very simple matter to state and evaluate its maxims.

Thus in the principle of incompatibility between the maxims of international law and publicity we have a good distinguishing mark for recognizing the nonconformity of politics to morality (as a science of right). Now we need to know the condition under which these maxims agree with the law of nations, for we cannot infer conversely that the maxims which bear publicity are therefore just, since no one who has decidedly superior power needs to conceal his plans. The condition of the possibility of international law in general is this: a juridical condition must first exist. For without this there is no public law, since all law which one may think of outside of this, in the state of nature, is merely private law. We have seen that a federation of states which has for its sole purpose the maintenance of peace is the only juridical condition compatible with the freedom of the several states. Therefore the harmony of politics with morals is possible only in a federative alliance, and the latter is necessary and given a priori by the principle of right. Furthermore, all politics has for its juridical basis the establishment of this harmony to its greatest possible extent, and without this end all its sophisms are but folly and veiled injustice. This false politics outdoes the best Jesuit school in casuistry. It has *reservatio mentalis,* wording public compacts with such expressions as can on occasion be interpreted to one's own advantage (for example, it makes the distinction between *status quo de fait* and *de droit*). It has *probabilism* attributing hostile intentions to others, or even making probabilities of their possible superior power into legal grounds for destroying other, peaceful states. Finally, it has the *peccatum philosophicum (peccatillum, bagatelle),* holding it to be only a trifle when a small state is swallowed up in order that a much larger one may thereby approach more nearly to an alleged greater good for the world as a whole.[1]

The duplicity of politics in respect to morality, in using first one branch of it and then the other for its purposes, furthers these sophistic maxims. These branches are philanthropy and respect for the rights of men; and both are duty. The former is a conditional duty, while the latter is an unconditional and absolutely mandatory duty. One who wishes to give himself up to the sweet feeling of benevolence must make sure that he has not transgressed this absolute duty. Politics readily agrees with morality in its first branch (as ethics) in order to surrender the rights of men to their superiors. But with morality in the second branch (as a science of right), to which it must bend its knee, politics finds it advisable not to have any dealings, and rather denies it all reality, preferring to reduce all duties to mere benevolence. This artifice of a secretive politics would soon be unmasked by philosophy through publication of its maxims, if they only dared to allow the philosopher to publish his maxims.

In this regard I propose another affirmative and transcendental principle of public law, the formula of which is:

1. The precedents for such maxims may be seen in Counselor Garve's treatise, *On the Union of Morality with Politics* (1788). This worthy scholar admits in the beginning that he is not able to solve the problem completely. But to approve of this union while admitting that one cannot meet all objections which may be raised against it seems to show more tolerance than is advisable toward those who are inclined to abuse it.

"All maxims which *stand in need* of publicity in order not to fail their end, agree with politics and right combined."

For if they can attain their end only through publicity, they must accord with the public's universal end, happiness; and the proper task of politics is to promote this, i.e., to make the public satisfied with its condition. If, however, this end is attainable only by means of publicity, i.e., by removing all distrust in the maxims of politics, the latter must conform to the rights of the public, for only in this is the union of the goals of all possible.

The further development and discussion of this principle I must postpone to another occasion. But that it is a transcendental formula is to be seen from the exclusion of all empirical conditions (of the doctrine of happiness) as material of the law, and from the reference it makes to the form of universal lawfulness.

If it is a duty to make real (even if only through approximation in endless progress) the state of public law, and if there is well-grounded hope that this can actually be done, then perpetual peace, as the condition that will follow what has erroneously been called "treaties of peace" (but which in reality are only armistices), is not an empty idea. As the times required for equal steps of progress become, we hope, shorter and shorter, perpetual peace is a problem which, gradually working out its own solution, steadily approaches its goal.

## ACKNOWLEDGMENTS

Every reasonable effort has been made to locate the parties who hold rights to previously published translations reprinted here. We gratefully acknowledge permission to reprint the following:

Selections from *The Critique of Judgement,* translated by James Creed Meredith (1952), reprinted by permission of Oxford University Press.

Selections from *Foundations of the Metaphysics of Morals,* translated by Lewis W. Beck, © 1959, Library of Liberal Arts, reprinted with permission of the publisher, The Bobbs-Merrill Company, Inc., Indianapolis.

"Idea for a Universal History from a Cosmopolitan Point of View," translated by Lewis W. Beck, © 1963, Library of Liberal Arts, reprinted with permission of the publisher, The Bobbs-Merrill Company, Inc., Indianapolis.

"Perpetual Peace," translated by Lewis W. Beck, © 1963, Library of Liberal Arts, reprinted with permission of the publisher, The Bobbs-Merrill Company, Inc., Indianapolis.

"What Is Enlightenment?" translated by Lewis White Beck, in *Fundamentals of the Metaphysics of Morals and What Is Enlightenment?,* © 1963, Library of Liberal Arts, reprinted with permission of the publisher, The Bobbs-Merrill Company, Inc., Indianapolis.

# THE GERMAN LIBRARY
## In 100 Volumes

Volume 4
*German Medieval Tales*
Edited by Francis G. Gentry
Foreword by Thomas Berger

Volume 6
*German Humanism and Reformation*
Edited by Reinhard P. Becker
Foreword by Roland Bainton

Volume 15
Friedrich Schiller
*Plays: Intrigue and Love and Don Carlos*
Edited by Walter Hinderer
Foreword by Gordon Craig

Volume 21
*German Romantic Criticism*
Edited by A. Leslie Willson
Foreword by Ernst Behler

Volume 25
Heinrich von Kleist
*Plays*
Edited by Walter Hinderer
Foreword by E. L. Doctorow

Volume 26
E.T.A. Hoffman
*Tales*
Edited by Victor Lange

Volume 29
J. and W. Grimm and Others

Volume 45
Wilhelm Raabe
*Novels*
Edited by Volkmar Sander
Foreword by Joel Agee

Volume 46
Theodore Fontane
*Short Novels and Other Writings*
Edited by Peter Demetz
Foreword by Peter Gay

Volume 50
Wilhelm Busch and Others
*German Satirical Writings*
Edited by Dieter P. Lotze and Volkmar Sander
Foreword by John Simon

Volume 51
*Writings of German Composers*
Edited by Jost Hermand and James Steakley

Volume 55
Arthur Schnitzler
*Plays and Stories*
Edited by Egon Schwarz
Foreword by Stanley Elkin

Volume 70
Rainer Maria Rilke
*Prose and Poetry*
Edited by Egon Schwarz
Foreword by Howard Nemerov

Volume 83
*Essays on German Theater*
Edited by Margaret Herzfeld-Sander
Foreword by Martin Esslin

Volume 89
Friedrich Dürrenmatt
*Plays and Essays*
Edited by Volkmar Sander
Foreword by Martin Esslin

Volume 98
Hans Magnus Enzensberger
*Critical Essays*
Edited by Reinhold Grimm and Bruce Armstrong
Foreword by John Simon